DEFINING ISRAEL
THE JEWISH STATE, DEMOCRACY, AND THE LAW

DEFINING ISRAEL

The Jewish State, Democracy, and the Law

EDITED BY SIMON RABINOVITCH

HEBREW UNION COLLEGE PRESS

HEBREW UNION COLLEGE PRESS
© 2018 Hebrew Union College Press
Set in ITC Legacy Serif by Raphael Freeman, Renana Typesetting
Cover design by Paul Neff Design LLC
Printed in the United States of America

Library of Congress Cataloging-in-Publication Data

Names: Rabinovitch, Simon, editor.
Title: Defining Israel: the Jewish state, democracy, and the law / edited by
   Simon Rabinovitch.
Description: Cincinnati: Hebrew Union College Press, 2018.
Identifiers: LCCN 2018018053 | ISBN 9780878201624
Subjects: LCSH: Jews--Legal status, laws, etc.--Israel. | Jewish
   nationalism--Israel. | Zionism--Israel. | Constitutional law--Israel. |
   Judaism and state--Israel. | Democracy--Religious aspects--Judaism
Classification: LCC KMK1730.D44 2018 | DDC 342.5694--dc23
LC record available at https://lccn.loc.gov/2018018053

For Zoe, Jonah, and Mia

Contents

LAW

PART II. REFLECTIONS

A NOTE ON TRANSLITERATIONS AND TRANSLATIONS

Hebrew transliterations follow the style of the Academy of the Hebrew Language 2006 guidelines (omitting diacritical marks). Commonly used words (such as "Hatikvah" and "Eretz") and names (such as "Tzipi") follow accepted English spelling. The draft bills have been translated as literally as possible, both because they are legal documents and in order to highlight differences where they exist between the bills. So, for example, "mishpat ha-'Ivri" has been rendered as "Hebrew law" rather than Jewish law to distinguish it from halakha. While there are different ways to translate the final law's title, I have used the most literal possibility, Basic Law: Israel – The Nation-State of the Jewish People. Where references are made to Israeli newspapers, the article's title in English indicates the publication's English edition, and in transliterated Hebrew its Hebrew edition.

Acknowledgments

This volume is the product of an enormous amount of collaboration from many quarters. It was only possible because of the vision of Timothy Michael Law, Charles Halton, and Angela Roskop Erisman to found a publication, *Marginalia*, devoted to the public debate of important ideas relating to religion. TML, Charles, and Angie not only gave me the freedom as an editor to produce the forum that led to this volume, but at the time the pieces first came out, they, along with the modern Jewish history editors Adam Mendelsohn and Daniel Schwartz, did much of the actual editing too. I am also indebted to Angie for making the connection to HUC Press, and to then HUC Press co-directors Jason Kalman and David Aaron for taking this project on and being at all times very supportive. I am very grateful to have worked closely with Sonja Rethy at HUC Press – Managing Editor does not come close to describing the many hours of her thoughtful and precise editing or the good cheer with which she undertook the unwieldy task of managing a manuscript with so many contributors.

Boston University's Elie Wiesel Center for Jewish Studies, through its Director, Michael Zank, and its Program Administrator, Theresa Cooney, financially and logistically supported several trips to Israel where I made the necessary professional connections to make this volume possible. While in Israel I worked on this project over several summers as a guest of the David Berg Institute for Law and History at Tel Aviv University and I am very thankful to its Director, David Schorr, and all of the staff at the Berg Institute, for always making my time there so pleasant and productive. I was fortunate enough to complete this project with support from the Henry Luce Foundation and the American Council for Learned Societies as a Luce/ACLS Fellow in Religion, Journalism and International Affairs. I have spent the past academic year in residence at the Northeastern

University Humanities Center, supported in my work (and buoyed in my spirits) by its Director, Lori Lefkovitz, and Associate Director, Sari Altschuler.

Since the very beginning of the project I benefitted from the patient and regular advice of Ruth Gavison. Yousef Jabareen and Benny Begin both kindly responded to my pestering emails about the workings of the Knesset. Tzipi Livni and Ruth Calderon kindly sat for interviews with me which were first published in *Marginalia* and which I am happy to include here. Pnina Lahav has been a constant mentor for me on all things related to Israel, constitutionalism, and the law. My colleagues and co-teachers in Boston University's Core Curriculum, Kimberly Arkin and Margaret Litvin, taught this material with me for the first time in our class on Religion and Secularism, and the opportunity to teach the material together helped convince me of its pedagogical value.

The heart of the forum and volume are the many provocative essays, and I appreciate all the contributions and the authors' patience and willingness to revisit and revise. The first five bills were initially translated for online publication by Ekaterina Anderson with help from Rivka Brot and editorial work by me and Gil Rubin. I translated all of the bills proposed since then, as well as the final law, and returned to edit all of the documents in the "Sources" section together to ensure that when exact phrasing is repeated it appears the same, but the many small changes in wording made from bill to bill are reflected, as best as possible, in English translation. I am very thankful to Gil Rubin and Yehudah Mirsky for providing second and third sets of eyes and for their helpful fine-tuning. My friend Moshe Shashar also responded to texts at all hours of day and night with questions about how one word or another is used in colloquial Hebrew today. Needless to say, all errors that remain are mine alone.

As always, I am thankful for the unending support of my family, especially my wife Jodi, and in this case I am also thankful for the support of the families of everyone I just mentioned, and those of all of the contributors whom I stole away, no doubt, at the least convenient moments.

Preface

Defining Israel focuses on recent attempts – ultimately successful – to anchor constitutionally Israel's Jewish character, as well as on the debate generated by the proposals and final nation-state law. In 2014, during the 19th Knesset, I watched with curiosity the debates over whether to pass a Basic Law – the Israeli equivalent of a law with constitutional authority – defining Israel as the nation-state of the Jewish people. In the English-language press, few commentators understood what was in the proposed laws (it seemed few had read them) or what they were about. In Israel, the concern for this issue seemed to be outsized among legislators compared to the general public, for most of whom, especially in the Jewish majority, the proposed laws seemed to do little to affect their lives one way or another. For this reason, when the governing coalition fell apart, ostensibly over Justice Minister Tzipi Livni and Finance Minister Yair Lapid's opposition to a draft nation-state law put forward by Prime Minister Netanyahu, most of the Israeli public assumed the disagreement over this issue merely masked the real reason for the government's dissolution – be it the difficulty of compromising over a budget or simple political expediency. In Israel, few in the public were willing to believe that the government would collapse over something most people viewed as fairly inconsequential. Nonetheless, the issue reemerged in negotiations during the 20th Knesset, reared its head repeatedly thereafter, and a final version was passed into law on July 19, 2018.

As an editor of *The Marginalia Review of Books*, an online journal that seeks to make scholarship on history, religion, and culture accessible to a knowledgeable reading public, I saw an opportunity during the Israeli election campaign to the 20th Knesset to fulfill a public service, by making available English translations of all documents relevant to the nation-state issue and providing space for commentary by key voices from across the political spectrum. Over the course of ten months in 2015, *Marginalia*'s "Defining Israel Forum" published Ruth Gavison's recommendations to the minister of justice, English translations of all the draft nation-state bills submitted to Knesset up to that point (and Netanyahu's framework discussed in Cabinet), commentary by a dozen leading politicians and scholars, and an interview I conducted with Tzipi Livni focused solely on the issue. It is that forum from which the current volume originates, now considerably expanded with new bills, new perspectives, and my introduction. I came to this project not as a scholar of Israeli history, politics, or law, but rather as an editor at a publication attempting to bridge the divide between the academy and the public on matters of religion. The nation-state law thus seemed a perfect example of the yawning gap between public and scholarly perception of a significant issue (or whether that issue is even significant at all). I also believed that *Marginalia* had an opportunity to serve as a resource for journalists seeking more complex interpretations of Israel's constitutional crisis than were available elsewhere, by providing primary resources from which journalists, educators, and the public could draw their own conclusions.

This resulting volume is the first book – in either Hebrew or English – devoted to explaining and debating the contemporary and historical significance of Israel's nation-state law. It is also the first book, at least that I know of, in which an online forum has been acknowledged by an academic press as valuable to expand, publish, preserve, and distribute. Academics who see a duty to serve also as public intellectuals do so at considerable professional risk (at some universities, though not at all), and I hope this volume, in addition to being a valuable resource, can serve as a positive example of the role publicly-minded academics and their publications can fill in bringing the academy to the world we live in, and vice versa.

My introduction to *Defining Israel* is intended to orient readers to the genealogy of the bills – their history and chronology – and, as much as possible, sticks to the context without delving into interpretation (the domain of the subsequent essays and interviews), though I do provide my own understanding of how the law's passage has been interpreted in different segments of Israeli society. The volume's

Part I, "Sources," includes an English translation of Ruth Gavison's report, "Constitutional Anchoring of Israel's Vision: Recommendations Submitted to the Minister of Justice," as well as all of the proposed Basic Laws attempting to legally clarify what it means for Israel to be a Jewish and democratic state, and a briefly annotated translation of the law that passed.

One challenge in putting this volume together was composing the table of contents for Part II, "Reflections." As readers will discover, many of these essays are difficult to categorize. This section includes essays both stridently for and against a bill, philosophical arguments and pragmatic ones, personal meditations, legal arguments, and explanations focusing on one particular issue. In the end I decided it would be impossible to divide the essays into groups, and have instead arranged them in a tossed-salad approach, or, to use a different metaphor, as a tour moving from one viewpoint to another so that wherever one began or ended reading within the volume one would be exposed to a variety of perspectives and styles. All told, the "Reflections" include fifteen essays, two interviews, and an epilogue by Ruth Gavison. While there is no doubt that this is still a selection rather than the sum total of possible viewpoints on Israel's nation-state law, my hope is nonetheless that readers will find the full complexity of opinion regarding this issue in these pages.

Providing English readers with the key documents at the center of this important debate, combined with sophisticated analyses from scholars and politicians with widely varying perspectives, *Defining Israel* is intended to be a resource for anyone seeking a better understanding of why Israeli society is still struggling to determine what it means for the state to be Jewish. With these tools readers can make their own judgments on the merits and detriments, and the necessity or danger, of the Jewish nation-state law.

Simon Rabinovitch

Introduction

JEWISH AND DEMOCRATIC ACCORDING TO THE LAW

Simon Rabinovitch

Israel's Declaration of Independence (also known as the Independence Scroll), signed May 14, 1948, declares Israel the "Jewish State" (*Medina Yehudit*) but provides no explanation of what it means for Israel to be Jewish, other than as the reclamation of Jewish sovereignty in the holy land. Since then, Israel's Jewishness has been interpreted in as many ways as there have been Israelis. Evidently, to understand that Israel is a Jewish state is not the same as to understand what it means for a state to be Jewish. In Israel today, people who self-identify as Jewish form a majority of the population, Hebrew is the dominant language, and the rhythms of life – from Sabbath to state holidays – correspond with the Jewish religious calendar. Nonetheless, the state has no single official religion (it has multiple recognized religions) and its laws governing, regulating, and subsidizing all religious groups and matters of personal religious status are built on layers of Ottoman and British legal precedent.[1]

In the preamble to Israel's Declaration of Independence, the Declaration's authors chose to describe the historical justification for Jewish self-determination and its realization in Israel's founding as a Jewish state, rather than to define the character of the new state or what it means for the state to be Jewish.[2] The Declaration also

---

1 See Iris Agmon, *Family & Court: Legal Culture and Modernity in Late Ottoman Palestine* (Syracuse, NY: Syracuse University Press, 2006); Gad Barzilai, *Communities and Law: Politics and Cultures of Legal Identities* (Ann Arbor: University of Michigan Press, 2003); Assaf Likhovski, *Law and Identity in Mandate Palestine* (Chapel Hill: University of North Carolina Press, 2006); Menachem Mautner, *Law and the Culture of Israel* (Oxford; New York: Oxford University Press, 2011).
2 "The Declaration of the Establishment of the State of Israel," The Knesset, http://

claimed that an elected Constituent Assembly would craft a constitution in less than five months. The divisions within Jewish society in Israel that needed to be reconciled, or at least bridged, for the new state to survive instead led the political groups present at its founding to put off the divisive task of constitutionally enshrining the character of the state (or writing a constitution at all) for the distant future, and, since that time, Israel's constitutional law has been enacted ad hoc in regular legislation and in a series of Basic Laws considered to have constitutional grounding.[3]

ISRAEL'S CONSTITUTIONAL REVOLUTION

In recent years a debate emerged among Israeli lawmakers and the public about whether to attempt to settle the unfinished constitutional business of defining Israel's legal character, or if such a resolution is even possible. Beginning in 2004, several laws were drafted and proposals made about how and whether to anchor Israel's vision constitutionally, or its status as the nation-state of the Jewish people, in a Basic Law. But the story began with the passage of an earlier Basic Law, when, on March 25, 1992, Prime Minister Yitzhak Shamir, President Chaim Herzog, and Knesset Speaker Dov Shilansky signed Israel's Basic Law: Human Dignity and Liberty.[4] The purpose of this law, according to its first line, "is to protect human dignity and liberty, in order to establish in a Basic Law the values of the State of Israel as a Jewish and democratic state." Despite the centrality of Israel's values as a Jewish and democratic state to this law's purpose, the law's stipulations dealt solely with various aspects of Israel's individual citizens' rights to protection of their "life, body and dignity." The subsequent Knesset, under Prime Minister Yitzhak Rabin,

---

www.knesset.gov.il/docs/eng/megilat_eng.htm.

3 On the constitutional debates in Israel's first years see Orit Rozin, "Forming a Collective Identity: The Debate over the Proposed Constitution, 1948–1950," *Journal of Israeli History* 26, no. 2 (2007): 251–71.

4 "Basic Law: Human Dignity and Liberty," The Knesset, http://www.knesset.gov.il/laws/special/eng/basic3_eng.htm.

amended this Basic Law in a way that dramatically shifted the locus of the state's values as expressed in the law. As of March 10, 1994, the Basic Law: Human Dignity and Liberty, now begins with Section 1:

> Fundamental human rights in Israel are founded upon recognition of the value of the human being, the sanctity of human life, and the principle that all persons are free; these rights shall be upheld in the spirit of the principles set forth in the Declaration of the Establishment of the State of Israel.

This new preamble emphasized the centrality of individual freedom to the values of the state. But, by invoking the spirit of Israel's founding Declaration, it also circled back to the fact that the state is the "Jewish state," a fact impossible to ignore as the Declaration repeatedly refers to the new state as such.[5] The government passed this amendment at the same time as it annulled the 1992 Basic Law: Freedom of Occupation, and replaced it with a new law.[6] The new version of the Freedom of Occupation law included the same preamble as that amended to the Basic Law: Human Dignity and Liberty, and therefore both Basic Laws thereafter made reference to "the values of the State of Israel as a Jewish and democratic state."

Aharon Barak, who was at that time president of Israel's Supreme Court, considered the new Basic Laws on Human Dignity and Liberty and Freedom of Occupation to be a "constitutional revolution." Barak argued in 1992, thus even before the amendments, that the new Basic Laws elevated the legal force of all eleven Basic Laws over all other laws, and that, in particular, due to the new laws, "human rights in Israel have become legal norms of preferred constitutional states much like the situation in the United States, Canada and many other countries."[7] Barak further argued that because the new Basic

---

5 "The Declaration of the Establishment of the State of Israel," The Knesset, https://www.knesset.gov.il/docs/eng/megilat_eng.htm.

6 "Basic Law: Freedom of Occupation (1992)," The Knesset, http://www.knesset.gov.il/laws/special/eng/basic5_eng.htm; "Basic Law: Freedom of Occupation (1994)," The Knesset, http://www.knesset.gov.il/laws/special/eng/basic4_eng.htm.

7 Aharon Barak, "A Constitutional Revolution: Israel's Basic Laws," Yale Law School Faculty Scholarship Series Paper 3697 (1993), http://digitalcommons.law.yale.edu/cgi

Laws claimed as their purpose to entrench the values of the State of Israel as a Jewish and democratic state, the Supreme Court would now have to ask "What is a Jewish state, and what is a democratic state?" when determining the validity or invalidity of Knesset laws.

Critics responded that in contrast to Barak's articulation of the state's democratic values, which were very detailed and potent, his understanding of Jewish values was so abstract as to be, in essence, equivalent to the contributions of Judaism to democracy. Nonetheless, the 1992-1994 Basic Laws, Barak's individual response, and the Supreme Court's interpretation of those laws in several cases, generated a number of attempts to enact a full constitution in Israel, including a preamble that would further anchor its character as both "Jewish and democratic" and clarify the legal relationship between the Knesset and the courts. The 16th Knesset's Constitution, Law, and Justice Committee's seventeen members met dozens of times between 2003 and 2006 and sought the advice of hundreds of advisors and public figures. The first iteration of a proposal to, rather than write a constitution, anchor Israel's identity in a Basic Law that would define the key symbolic and practical elements of what it meant for the state to be Jewish, came in a proposal submitted to this committee by Moshe Koppel for a Basic Law entitled "The State of Israel as the State of the Jewish People" (see document A in this volume).

In February 2006, the Constitution, Law, and Justice Committee presented the Knesset with a draft proposal for a constitution and thousands of pages of background material.[8] Along with proposals made by the Knesset's Committee in 2006, potential constitutions were drafted by think-tanks and non-governmental organizations such as the Israel Democracy Institute (2005), the Institute for Zion-

/viewcontent.cgi?article=4700&context=fss_papers. For responses to the "constitutional revolution," see Yossi [Joseph] David, ed., *The State of Israel: Between Judaism and Democracy* (Jerusalem: Israel Democracy Institute, 2003), and the recent critique by a former minister of justice, Daniel Friedmann, in *The Purse and the Sword: The Trials of Israel's Legal Revolution*, trans. Haim Watzman (Oxford: Oxford University Press, 2016).

8 See Hanna Lerner, "Constitutional Impasse, Democracy, and Religion in Israel," in *Constitution Writing, Religion, and Democracy*, ed. Asli Bâli and Hanna Lerner (Cambridge: Cambridge University Press, 2017), 167-288.

ist Strategies (2006), and Adalah: The Legal Center for Arab Minority Rights in Israel (2007). Nonetheless, all of these attempts to create a full constitution, reflecting different ideological attitudes to these questions, have failed.

THE NATION-STATE LAWS IN THE 18TH AND 19TH KNESSET

The philosophical roots of the various efforts in the 2000s to create an Israeli constitution stem from the questions left unanswered at the state's founding about its particularity as a Jewish state, or its universality as a state for all its citizens. The Declaration of Independence includes elements of both, but does not spell out whether legal parity between the state's national or civic elements is desirable, and if so how to mediate between civic and national ideals when they are in legal conflict. The practical and immediate cause of what came to be the nation-state law, however, was the belief among some lawmakers that the high court's judicial advocacy was leading it to rule against Jewish national or collective interests for the sake of principles of civil or democratic equality. Consequently, some lawmakers sought a Basic Law that would force the justices to take the state's Jewish character into greater consideration when making legal decisions.

One proposal, made in 2010 by Yariv Levin (Likud) and David Rotem (Yisrael Beiteinu), would have amended the Basic Laws that use the term "Jewish and democratic," replacing that phrase with the words "a Jewish state with a democratic form of government," and thereby create a new legal hierarchy. Against this background, some proposed to create a Basic Law that would focus on the Jewish component in Israel's vision. Efforts to pass a Basic Law defining the state's character thus began in the Knesset in 2011 with a proposal (substantively similar to the one submitted by Koppel to the Constitution, Law, and Justice Committee) by Avraham (Avi) Dichter of the Kadima party, which was ultimately signed by thirty-six other members of Knesset (see 2011, P/18/3541). But in fact, the impetus may have begun in 2006 when the National Committee for the Heads of the Arab Local Authorities in Israel published a working paper titled "The Future Vision of the Palestinian Arabs in Israel," which called for, among other things, Arab collective national rights, on the principle that civil equality between Jews and Arabs would not be achieved without recognition of Arab rights to cultural and political autonomy.[9] This began an engagement in Arab civil society on the question of what civil and national rights the Arab minority should demand from the state, as well as on the broader question of what the character of the State of Israel should be.

Dichter's first proposed nation-state law was the product of a long process of response to those initiatives, and was led chiefly by the Jerusalem-based Institute for Zionist Strategies. In its definition of Israel as a Jewish state, the proposed law explicitly and singularly limited the right of national self-determination in Israel to the Jewish people. In its second clause, which addressed Israel as a democratic state, the law stipulated that Israel's form of government, or "regime," is democratic, without further expansion on the meaning of democracy to the state or its values. Of the subsequent principles detailed in the law, those dealing with the status of Hebrew and Arabic and the role of Hebrew law in the Knesset and the courts proved to be the most controversial and most discussed. Another scrutinized clause took particular aim at a Supreme Court ruling from 2000 which forced a Jewish cooperative community to sell a plot of land to an Arab family, effectively barring closed communities.[10] The new Basic Law proposed by Dichter sought to overturn this decision, stipulating, "The state may allow a community that includes followers of a single religion or members of a single nation to establish a separate

---

9 "The Future Vision of the Palestinian Arabs in Israel," The National Committee for the Heads of the Arab Local Authorities in Israel, 2006, http://www.adalah.org /uploads/oldfiles/newsletter/eng/dec06/tasawor-mostaqbali.pdf. See also Haviv Rettig Gur, "In the Jewish Nation-State Kerfuffle, Much Ado over Very Little Substance," *Times of Israel,* Nov 24, 2014, http://www.timesofisrael.com/in-the-jewish -nation-state-kerfuffle-much-ado-over-very-little-substance/.

10 H.C. 6698/95, Aadel Ka'adan v. Israel Lands Administration, 5(1) P.D. 258 (2000), https://www.escr-net.org/node/365464.

communal settlement." Tzipi Livni, then chairperson of Dichter's party, pressured him to shelve the bill because of her concern that it threatened to cause divisions within Israeli society and upset the balance between the Jewish and democratic elements in the state's character.

Elections in January 2013 led to the formation of the 19th Knesset. In forming the government, the Likud-Beiteinu (a joint slate created for the 19th Knesset elections) and Bayit Yehudi (the Jewish Home party) included in their coalition agreement a commitment to advance a Jewish nation-state Basic Law. Two competing bills were put forward in July of that year. Three members of the governing coalition – Ayelet Shaked (Bayit Yehudi), Yariv Levin, and Robert Ilatov (Yisrael Beiteinu) – put forward a bill similar to Dichter's in 2011 (and with the same title) but without mention of the status of languages or the right of communities to live separately, and with a new definition of the law's purpose: "to define the identity of the State of Israel as the nation-state of the Jewish people in order to anchor these values in a Basic Law, in the spirit of the principles in the Declaration of the Establishment of the State of Israel." The so-called Shaked bill (see 2013, P/19/1550) also provided some explanation of what it means to be a democratic regime, by adding a further clause declaring that Israel's foundations should be based on "freedom, justice, and peace as envisioned by the prophets of Israel, and committed to the individual rights of all its citizens as detailed by all Basic Laws." It is worth noting that the term used in Hebrew for individual rights – *zkhuyoteyhem ha-ishiyut* – could also be translated as personal rights, and is not a commonly used term. By declaring that the state is committed to the rights of all citizens on a personal or individual level, the law would thereby relegate to the sub-constitutional level any obligation to recognize the collective rights of citizens who are not Jewish.

At the same time, Ruth Calderon (Yesh Atid) and eight other members of Knesset drafted an alternative bill, submitted on the same day (July 22, 2013), entitled Basic Law Proposal: The Declaration of Independence and the Jewish and Democratic State (see 2013, P/19/1539). Leaving out its clauses on stability and immutability, this law had only one item, its purpose: "This Basic Law aims to secure and protect the values of the State of Israel as a Jewish and democratic state by giving the force of law to the basic principles stated in the Declaration of Independence, which is annexed verbatim to this law." The proposed law thus assumed that the Declaration of Independence sufficiently articulates the essence of the state's democratic and Jewish values, and therefore sought to give legal standing to the Declaration, something debated in the past but not enacted in the Knesset. As explained by the law's authors in the Explanatory Notes (which do not have the force of law), the Declaration of Independence expresses "the will and intention to establish a country that has a Jewish character on the one hand and is committed to equality on the other." The law's authors also explicitly declared "that the notion of a Jewish state does not refer to Judaism as a religion, but rather to the cultural character of the nation-state as the home of the Jewish people."

Calderon, Levin, Shaked, and the philosopher Moshe Halbertal had worked for a number of months to create a compromise bill that would work for all factions of the coalition (in which Calderon's party, Yesh Atid, was a member), all of whom, at least in principle, supported the idea of a bill clarifying the identity of the state constitutionally. According to Calderon, Shaked was swayed by the idea of giving constitutional standing to the Declaration of Independence, but Levin was not. Levin opposed any use of the term "equality" in a nation-state bill, including in reference to the Declaration of Independence (where, to be precise, the term used is "on the basis of full and equal citizenship" – *al yesod ezrakhut mal'e ve-shav'e*). The reason, in Calderon's telling, is that Levin believed that the complete equality – which might be interpreted as including national and civic rights – that may have been possible in 1948 when the Declaration of Independence was written, was no longer possible because of Palestinian national aspirations.[11] Though a compromise bill had seemed possible, the two camps' perspectives on where emphasis

---

11 See in this volume, "On the Declaration of Independence as a Basic Law and the Meaning of a Jewish Nation-State: A Conversation with Ruth Calderon."

in the state's values should be – Jewish or democratic – made this fundamental disagreement about whether to include a commitment to equality in the text itself too difficult to surmount.[12]

Tzipi Livni, as minister of justice in the 19th Knesset, declined to move any of the tabled nation-state bills forward, citing again the risk of upsetting the delicate balance of the state's values and legal culture. Nonetheless, in August 2013, with the debates about Israel's character raging and initiatives to create a law defining Israel as the nation-state of the Jews being tabled, Livni commissioned Professor Ruth Gavison, a prominent scholar of constitutional law, to address the question of how the constitutional anchoring of the state's vision as both Jewish and democratic could be accomplished. The idea was to formulate a proposal for a constitutional provision that would balance and integrate both Jewish and democratic values in its definition of the state's character. In addition to being active in organizations such as the Israeli Association for Civil Rights in Israel, and Metzilah: The Center for Zionist, Jewish, Liberal and Humanist Thought, Gavison had written extensively about constitutional law in Israel and about Israel's character as a Jewish and democratic state. She had also, in 2003, written, with Rabbi Yaacov Medan, the Gavison-Medan Covenant, which argued for a new social compact to govern religion-state issues.[13] Livni expressed the challenge to Gavison in the following words:

> The State of Israel defines itself as a Jewish and democratic state, but there is no suitable constitutional articulation of these two terms. Hence, we are facing substantial social and legal controversies, in which each side seeks to entrench a different worldview.
>
> I believe the time has come for a constitutional arrangement dealing with Israel's identity, which entrenches its components

---

12 Lahav Harkov, "Making the Jewish State a Jewish State," *Commentary Magazine*, October 1, 2013, https://www.commentarymagazine.com/articles/making-the-jewish -state-a-jewish-state/.

13 Yoav Artsieli, *The Gavison-Medan Covenant: Main Points and Principles* (Jerusalem: The Israel Democracy Institute, 2004), https://en.idi.org.il/publications/6597.

in a way that combines and balances these values, the Jewish as well as the democratic.[14]

The Gavison process, however, came to a sudden halt. In May 2014, just before Independence Day and after the collapse of peace talks with the Palestinians, Prime Minister Benjamin Netanyahu declared his intention to advance legislation on a nation-state bill without waiting for the process initiated by Livni to run its course and be fully discussed by the government and the public. Soon after this, Ze'ev Elkin revived the bill he had drafted with Dichter and submitted it to the Knesset (P/19/2502, which is identical to P/18/3541). Then, in June, Miri Regev revived the Shaked bill and put it forward once again (P/19/2530, which is identical to P/19/1550, and was put forward again in the 20th Knesset as P/20/1320). The war in Gaza, which lasted through much of the summer of 2014, froze debates about such laws until that fall when Elkin, Shaked, and others renewed their push for a Basic Law declaring Israel the nation-state of the Jewish people.

The prime minister presented his own statement of principles for drafting a new law at a Cabinet meeting on November 23, 2014 (see document E), prompting an angry response from Livni and Finance Minister Yair Lapid (the chairperson of Yesh Atid), both of whom refused to give preliminary reading support to the bill. By fourteen votes to six the Cabinet agreed that the prime minister's fourteen principles would form the basis for a bill that would subsume – in other words replace – the previous bills presented by Shaked and Levin.[15] The idea was for a government-sponsored bill based on the compromise principles to be written under the supervision of Attorney General Yehudah Weinstein and brought to the Knesset for a preliminary reading at some point in December of 2014.

Alternatives again quickly emerged, although, as it became clear

---

14 Ruth Gavison, *Igun khukati la-khazon ha-medina?* (Jerusalem: Metzilah Center, 2015), 135. English translation from http://www.justice.gov.il/StateIdentity/Documents/GaryJacobsohn.pdf.

15 For a pointed critique of Netanyahu's proposal see Alexander Yakobson, "A Manual on How Not to Write a Constitution," *The Marginalia Review of Books*, February 16, 2015, https://marginalia.lareviewofbooks.org/manual-write-constitution/.

the government would collapse, these alternatives were filed in the Knesset to establish for the record where factions stood on the issue, rather than with the hope of passage. Livni and five members of her party quickly drafted and submitted their own law the next day, November 24, which, in addition to proclaiming Israel as the nation-state of the Jewish people, described the state's democratic principles as founded on "freedom, justice, and peace and providing equality to all its citizens, as stated in the Declaration of the Establishment of the State" (see 2014, P/19/2883; as the sitting justice minister, Livni's name was not on the bill). Member of Knesset Hilik Bar (Labor) also revived the idea of constitutionally anchoring the Declaration of Independence, but he proposed, comparable to Calderon, to repeatedly use the term "equality" in order to make clear the law's purpose was to ensure the protection of all of the state's citizens.[16]

As conflicts between the prime minister and his coalition partners over the bills and other matters involving the budget came to a head, Benjamin Netanyahu dismissed the justice and finance ministers from their posts, thus ushering in the elections for the 20th Knesset. On November 19, only days before the Knesset's governing coalition broke apart, Gavison had filed her report (See "Constitutional Anchoring of Israel's Vision: Recommendations Submitted to the Minister of Justice"). She declined to draft a law or proposal, but instead compiled a report about why the Knesset should avoid legislating a Basic Law on either Israel's identity or vision. Her original intention had been to fulfill the minister of justice's request and to submit a proposal regarding the constitutional entrenchment of the state's vision. Gavison was planning a process that would, following public and parliamentary debate, lead to a "constitutional moment" when this issue would be clarified. Such a moment might have occurred had there been a real breakthrough in the negotiations with the Palestinians. But after a long consultative process with scholars and leading civil society figures in Israel and the Jewish Diaspora, Gavison concluded that the cost to civic cohesion in drafting the law,

16 Haviv Rettig Gur, "Labor MK Seeks to Make Declaration of Independence Part of 'Constitution,'" *Times of Israel*, December 1, 2014, http://www.timesofisrael.com/labor-mk-seeks-to-make-declaration-of-independence-part-of-constitution/.

and the effects on the legal system in enacting it, would outweigh benefits that were difficult to determine. (Her report does still make several suggestions should the Knesset deem legislation necessary.)

In the end, Gavison proved reticent to have the question of the state's character determined by the Knesset. In her words: "Legislation transforms questions that had previously been moral, social or cultural into legal questions, which may be debated and decided in courts of law." Perhaps most importantly, Gavison believed that the three fundamental aspects of Israel's vision – Jewish, democratic, and respecting of human rights – were already well established in the law, and that the vagueness in the meaning of these terms is an asset rather than a detriment to Israeli society. There was a danger, according to Gavison, that the debate, if it intensified, would foster the sense of a binary between the state's Jewish and democratic values when they are not by definition contradictory (a point made by a number of contributors here and an opinion shared by many Jews in the Diaspora as well).

If, however, there was a clear binary in 2014, it was between how Israel's Jewish and non-Jewish citizens viewed this question. A poll released December 9, 2014 by the Israel Democracy Institute found that 73 percent of Israeli Jews believed there was no contradiction in Israel being both a Jewish and democratic state, but 83 percent of Israeli Arabs believed that there was.[17] While Jewish and non-Jewish Israelis are more integrated in Israeli society than many outside of Israel perceive, it is nonetheless clear that the meaning of the state and its system of government differs almost diametrically between the two groups – and includes dramatic fissures within each group. Looming all the while in the background, and unquestionably adding a sense of urgency to the debate, was (and is) the fact that the Palestinians still do not have a state, and that the two sides were (and are) at an impasse about how, when, and whether a Palestinian state will come into being. Perhaps unsurprisingly, the past and future

---

17 "The Peace Index," The Israel Democracy Institute, http://en.idi.org.il/tools-and -data/guttman-center-for-surveys/the-peace-index/.

of the conflict between Israelis and Palestinians is embedded as the continuous subtext in the debate about how to define Israel.

THE NATION-STATE LAW IN THE 20TH KNESSET

Based on the elections held in March 2015, Benjamin Netanyahu managed to form a narrow coalition of sixty-one members, which included parties favoring a nation-state law, such as Bayit Yehudi, and those that vocally did not, such as United Torah Judaism.[18] The election results led to a narrower and more religious governing coalition in the 20th Knesset than the previous, and included Haredi parties who had previously objected on principle to what they perceived to be the encoding of a national, and therefore secular, understanding of Jewishness into the state's DNA that might come with a nation-state law. The coalition agreement for the new government stipulated that a nation-state bill would be passed, but it also gave each party veto power over the law's wording. One government official told me at the time that the Haredi veto guaranteed that no bill would be passed during this government's term.

Yet, even so, Likud Knesset member Ze'ev (Benny) Begin took up the issue again with a proposal (2015, P/20/1587) for a concise definition of the state's identity, shorn of most of the articles from previous drafts. The first clause of this new bill paraphrased the Declaration of Independence in stating simply, "Israel is the nation-state of the Jewish people, based on the foundations of freedom, justice and peace as envisioned by the prophets of Israel, and upholds equal rights for all its citizens." A month later Dichter also submitted a new version of his bill (2015, P/20/1989) in an attempt to bring attention back to the issue. Dichter's new law made a number of significant changes to his original proposal, in articles and wording, and

---

18 The former foreign minister and leader of Yisrael Beiteinu, Avigdor Lieberman, cited the removal of the nation-state bill from the legislative agenda as a key reason for keeping his party out of the new government, but Netanyahu did later bring Lieberman and his party into the governing coalition.

included an almost entirely new and expanded Explanatory Notes section. The newer Dichter bill shifted the explanatory emphasis from the past – historic justification – to the present purposes of 1) strengthening the ties between Israel and world Jewry, and 2) complementing Israel's commitment to human rights with its commitment to the Jewish people. The bill also had an override clause in its section on Basic Principles which subsumed all other laws and all other Basic Laws under the primacy and exclusivity of Jewish national self-determination.

After a delay of two years, Dichter's 2015 bill passed the Ministerial Committee for Legislation and, in the summer of 2017, managed to be read, re-drafted, and reread on the Knesset floor. In addition to Dichter, the bill had the vocal support of Yariv Levin and Ayelet Shaked, who have served respectively as minister of tourism and minister of justice throughout the 20th Knesset. A new version of the bill based on compromises reached in a special committee headed by Member of Knesset Amir Ohana was proposed on March 13, 2018, and passed the first Knesset reading on May 1, 2018 (see 2018, P/20/1989). In addition to several minor changes and the significant removal (at the recommendation of the attorney general) of the clause marking the supremacy of this law over all previous legislation, one further substantial revision was made in the drafting process: a section on the law's "Purpose" was removed, and with it reference to "the State of Israel's values as a Jewish and democratic state in the spirit of the principles in the Declaration of the Establishment of the State of Israel."

When, in 2014, Prime Minister Benjamin Netanyahu attempted to advance his bill, it was opposition among coalition partners Hatnua (led by Livni) and Yesh Atid (led by Lapid) that halted its advance. In 2018 it seemed that Levin, Dichter, Netanyahu, and Shaked would again be blocked from within their coalition, though this time from the religious United Torah Judaism and Shas parties (regarding the perspective of the ultra-Orthodox towards the bill, see Kalman Neuman's essay) and the centrist Kulanu party. The Haredi parties in particular voiced opposition to the idea of enshrining the state's secular Jewish identity in law. These parties only agreed to vote in a first reading of the bill if it would be immediately shelved and not brought up for the second and the third readings necessary to make the bill law.[19]

On the evening of April 30, 2018, the Knesset plenum held a special session to mark Herzl Day, the Israeli holiday celebrating Zionism's early statesman. Yariv Levin took the opportunity to say, "the nation-state law is an expression of Herzl's vision in its most distilled form." Isaac Herzog, the Zionist Union opposition leader, in response called the law "a blatant slap in Herzl's face."[20] Needless to say, it is difficult to know what Theodor Herzl, who died in 1904, might have thought about the nation-state law. But some might argue that there are elements in the nation-state law – both the proposals and the one that passed – that seem difficult to square with Herzl's strident secularism and well-known democratic utopianism. Though the vote on the nation-state bill was also scheduled for the same day, April 30, the members of Knesset remained conducting business until 3:45 AM on May 1, when the first reading of the nation-state law passed by sixty-four votes to fifty, but deferred the second and third readings, as agreed within the coalition, to an unspecified date in the future. On the same day, however, the Knesset successfully passed into law an amendment to the 1980 Foundations of Law Act, so that the law now refers judges in cases where a lacuna in the law exists to "the principles of freedom, justice, integrity and peace in Hebrew law and in the heritage of Israel."[21] Thus, even before the nation-state law passed, the process and debates it initiated resulted in a key element

---

19 Other Basic Laws – on legal rights, social rights, and freedom of expression and association – passed first readings in 1996 but have remained in the Knesset's Constitution, Law, and Justice Committee since.

20 Knesset Press Release, April 30, 2018, 6:55 PM, http://main.knesset.gov.il/News /PressReleases/Pages/press30.04.18ll.aspx.

21 Knesset Press Release, May 1, 2018, 3:45 AM, http://main.knesset.gov.il/News /PressReleases/Pages/press01.05.18a.aspx. It should be noted that the prior obligation to supplement Israeli law by invoking the principles of "Israel's heritage," which was in the 1980 Foundations of Law Act, has not been widely used by Israeli courts. Justices can achieve this result by any interpretation that does not find a gap in the law which would trigger a need to supplement it.

of the proposals separately becoming law, by giving judges more leeway to use Jewish sources in making decisions.[22]

Whatever the intentions of the coalition members who voted for the first reading of the law on May 1, 2018 may have been about postponing its passage, negotiations continued about the wording of various clauses and in July the prime minister made clear that he was seeking to have it passed. In order to do so, substantive revisions were made to the law between its first and final readings. Considerable opposition coalesced against an article that had appeared in many proposals, including the very first submitted draft in 2011, allowing for closed religious or national communities. In the first reading of the final bill, article 7 (b) read, "The state may allow a community composed of one religion or one nationality to maintain a separate residential community." Attorney General Avichai Mandelblit, Deputy Attorney General Raz Nizri, and Knesset legal advisor Eyal Yinon all warned that this article could be used to justify discrimination, and so did not pass constitutional muster and the Supreme Court could therefore overturn it.

In a highly unusual move, President Reuven Rivlin addressed a formal letter to the Knesset and the prime minister outlining his concerns with the closed community clause. In this letter Rivlin questioned whether this clause truly reflected "the meaning of the Zionist vision" and asked that members of Knesset "look inward, into the depths of Israeli society: are we willing in the name of the Zionist vision to lend a hand to discrimination and exclusion of a man or a woman based on their origin? The bill before you allows any group, in the broadest of terms and without any monitoring, to establish a community with no Mizrahi Jews, Haredim, Druze and members of the LGBT community."[23]

The position of president is largely ceremonial as the head of state,

---

22 It was agreed at the same time that if taken up again, the nation-state law would use the amended version of the Foundations of Law Act. The final version however did not include the provision on Hebrew law.

23 Notably, Rivlin did not mention Arab Muslims or Christians. The full text in English is in Hezki Baruch, "Rivlin Intervenes in Nationality Law," *Arutz Sheva*, July 10, 2018, https://www.israelnationalnews.com/News/News.aspx/248697.

and is elected by the Knesset not the citizens, and so it is extremely rare for the holder of that position to seek to intervene on a legislative matter. Adding to the chorus of pointed opposition to 7 (b) were other prominent Jewish figures such as outgoing chair of the Jewish Agency, Natan Sharansky, and the philanthropist Charles Bronfman, who signed a letter opposing the bill written together with Susie Gelman, chair of the New York based Israel Policy Forum.[24] Though supporters of the clause reacted vocally to the criticism at heated committee meetings, the pressure proved effective, as the prime minister worked with Minister of Education Naftali Bennet to craft alternative wording. Both clauses in article 7 – on heritage preservation and closed communities – were removed and replaced with a single, and highly ambiguous, clause: "The state views the development of Jewish settlement as a national value, and shall act to encourage and promote its establishment."

Other adjustments were made in order to get the law passed. The head of the special committee responsible for the nation-state law, Amir Ohana, successfully had the clause on Hebrew law dropped from the final version because he feared it could be used to discriminate against members of the LGBT community.[25] In exchange, the Bayit Yehudi faction had "religious" (*ha-datit*) added to clause 1 (b), so that the final version read that in Israel the Jewish people "exercises its natural, cultural, *religious*, and historical right to self-determination."[26]

Members of the coalition's Haredi parties, Shas and United Torah Judaism, were concerned about a variety of issues, from empowering Diaspora Jewry (associated with the more liberal American

24 See Raoul Wootliff, "Sharansky: Jewish State Bill will 'drive a wedge' between Israel and the Diaspora," *Times of Israel*, July 11, 2018, https://www.timesofisrael.com /sharansky-jewish-state-bill-will-drive-a-wedge-between-israel-and-diaspora/; Susie Gelman and Charles Bronfman, "Statement on the Nation-State Bill," Israel Policy Forum, https://israelpolicyforum.org/2018/07/11/statement-on-the-nation-state -bill/.

25 Jonathan Lis, "Mekhashesh le-pegiy'a be-LHTB"im: Ohana mitkaven livlom et sa'if ha-mishpat ha-'ivri ba-khok ha-le'om," *Haaretz*, March 1, 2018, https://www.haaretz .co.il/news/politi/1.5585879.

26 Emphasis added.

denominations), to defining the state as Jewish, to excluding more specific provisions on religious protections. To allay some of their concerns, the wording of 6 (b), on the state's connection to the Jewish people, was changed to specify that the state shall work to preserve this connection "in the Diaspora" (ba-tfutsot) rather than wherever Jews lived, to indicate that the state will orient its action outwardly rather than accommodate Israeli Jewish religious life to changing norms elsewhere.

Members of the coalition's centrist party, Kulanu, had expressed reservations about the absence of reference to equality or democracy in the law. This faction seems to have received little in negotiations, as no such reference – which did appear in other versions – was added to the final text. Nonetheless, the law passed in the end with the votes of all the parties in the coalition, as it would appear that few were willing to expend the necessary political capital to oppose it.

REACTION TO THE LAW'S PASSAGE

The final debate on the law in the Knesset lasted over eight hours, and passed in the early hours of the morning of July 19, 2018, by sixty-two votes to fifty-five, with two abstentions. After the vote, some lawmakers tore up the text of the law while shouting "apartheid," while others triumphantly took selfies with the prime minister (one of which was much satirized and lampooned in the Israeli press).[27] Prime Minister Netanyahu described the law as "a pivotal moment in the annals of Zionism and the State of Israel," and continued, "This is our state - the Jewish state. In recent years there have been some who have attempted to put this in doubt, to undercut the core of our being. Today we made it law: This is our nation, language and flag."

---

27 One cartoon by the illustrator Avi Katz which appeared in the *Jerusalem Report*, a biweekly magazine of the *Jerusalem Post*, depicted the legislators from the selfie picture as pigs, with the caption quoting George Orwell's *Animal Farm*, "All animals are equal but some animals are more equal than others." Despite having approved the cartoon's publication, the *Jerusalem Post* fired Katz in response to public criticism, only further enflaming the controversy.

Avraham Dichter linked the law's passage to the founding Zionist congress in Basel and said that as a result "No minority will be able to change the state's symbols."[28] Yariv Levin proclaimed "a historic and defining moment in Israel's history – a historic and significant law." Amir Ohana described the legislation in the most monumental terms: "This moment will be remembered in the history of the Jewish nation. We are laying down one of the cornerstones of our existence... After 2,000 years of exile, we have a home."[29]

Opposition lawmakers, unsurprisingly, articulated a different view. Members of all the opposition parties attacked the law variously as "racist," as a "black flag," as denying the Palestinians the right of self-determination, and as sticking a finger in the eye of minorities such as the Druze, who serve in the Israel Defense Forces. Yoel Hasson, a member of Knesset from the Zionist Union who earlier in his career had been national head of Betar (a youth movement associated with Zionism's right wing), asked "What paper do we need so that we will know or feel or understand that this is the state of the Jewish people?" Hasson answered his own question as follows: "This is a document of a sick person... and insecure person." Benny Begin, who abstained from the vote, said "I will not oppose the law, however, I cannot support it either." But Begin also warned his own Likud party bluntly, "Nationalism that does not pay heed to human rights deteriorates to ultranationalism. Beware of this detachment [my] friends."

The law immediately evoked significant international attention, especially among American Jews, a number of whose prominent religious and communal leaders spoke out against it. Rabbi Rick Jacobs, President of the Union for Reform Judaism (the largest American Jewish denomination), released a statement calling the law's passage "a sad and unnecessary day for Israeli democracy," and Ronald Lauder, the current president of the World Jewish Congress, wrote, "as a loving brother, I ask Israel's government to

---

28 Absent this law, how a minority could change the state's symbols is unclear.
29 All of the quotations from this and the following paragraph are from the Knesset press release, "Knesset passes Jewish nation-state bill into law," July 19, 2018, https://knesset.gov.il/spokesman/eng/PR_eng.asp?PRID=13979.

listen to the voices of protest and outrage being heard in Israel and throughout the world. As president of the World Jewish Congress, I call upon Israeli leaders to rethink their destructive actions during this summer of disharmony."[30] The law's passage was also covered extensively in the international press, and especially in the major liberal-oriented American and British newspapers and magazines.[31] *The New York Times* in particular published an article about the law's passage as front-page news, and subsequently, in addition to several further news articles, has published six opinion pieces on the topic.[32] For a single piece of legislation passed in a small country on a fairly abstract matter – how to define the state – the coverage has been intense. In the surest sign that the issue saturated the American public, the satirical online magazine *The Onion* published a mock news story with the title "Israel Passes Law Cementing Itself as Exclusive Nation-State of Benjamin Netanyahu."[33]

Within Israel, various groups and parties have filed legal petitions against the law for the Supreme Court to consider its constitutionality. The loudest and best organized opposition to the law, however, has come from the Druze community. Members of the Druze com-

---

30 See "URJ President Rabbi Rick Jacobs Statement on Israel's Nation-State Law," URJ Press Release, July 18, 2018, https://urj.org/blog/2018/07/18/urj-president-rabbi -rick-jacobs-statement-israels-nation-state-law; Ronald S. Lauder, "Israel, This Is Not Who We Are," *The New York Times*, August 13, 2018, page A27, and https://www .nytimes.com/2018/08/13/opinion/israel-ronald-lauder-nation-state-law.html. The American Jewish Committee (AJC) also issued a press release, with milder language expressing concern that "two elements of this new Basic Law [on the status of Arabic and Jewish settlement] put at risk the commitment of Israel's founders to build a country that is both Jewish and democratic." See "AJC Criticizes Knesset Adoption of Nation-State Bill," AJC, July 18, 2018, https://www.ajc.org/news/ajc-criticizes -knesset-adoption-of-nation-state-bill.

31 See articles in *The Washington Post, Vox, The Atlantic, Newsweek, Time, The Independent, The Guardian, The Financial Times,* CNN.com, BBC.com, NPR.org, France24.com and many others.

32 Since the law passed, *The New York Times* has published four opinion pieces against the bill (by Ronald Lauder, Omri Boehm, Sayed Kashua, and Martin Peretz), and two in its defense (by Bret Stephens and Naftali Bennett, Israel's minister of education).

33 "Israel Passes Law Cementing Itself as Exclusive Nation-State of Benjamin Netanyahu," *The Onion*, August 2, 2018, https://www.theonion.com/israel-passes-law -cementing-itself-as-exclusive-nation-1828058658.

munity are subject to conscription in the Israel Defense Forces and many stress their loyalty and contributions to the state. Three Druze members of Knesset sit in the current governing coalition, including the minister of communications, Ayoob Kara. One of these members, Akram Hasson from the Kulanu party, called the law "a stab in the back" because it did not include a reference to equality.[34] The law provoked a massive and popular outcry among the Druze public, many of whom felt the law excluded them from state sovereignty and, by failing to specify legal equality for all citizens, demoted their status within the state. They were also concerned about the demotion of Arabic and the article on Jewish settlement, given that many Druze already feel that they face discrimination in land and housing rights.

On the evening of Saturday August 3, tens of thousands of people (the widely varying estimates ranged from 50,000 to 120,000), Druze and Jewish, filled Rabin Square in Tel Aviv, waving Druze and Israeli flags, chanting *"shivayon"* – equality – and listening to speeches from prominent Druze and Jewish opponents of the law, such as the mayor of Tel Aviv, the Druze spiritual leader Sheikh Mowafaq Tarif, several retired Druze and Jewish generals, and former heads of the Mossad and Shin Bet security services. Behind the stage, city hall was lit up in colors alternating between the multicolored Druze and blue and white Israeli flags. The mood, the speeches, and the attendees seemed to blend patriotism and frustration. One large multigenerational Druze family who had come in for the protest from Daliyat al-Karmel and were holding Israeli flags told me that they were not opposed to the law, but rather opposed a definition of the state's identity that did not include equality for all, not just the Druze. A group of young men who had come in from the town of Hurfeish, all of whom had served in the military and two of whom were still professional soldiers as engineers in the air force, stressed their sense of insult and frustration. As one told me, the young Druze

---

34 Adam Rasgon, "Druze Revolt," *Times of Israel*, August 8, 2018, https://www
.timesofisrael.com/druze-revolt-why-a-tiny-loyal-community-is-so-infuriated-by
-nation-state-law/.

generation does not, like its parents, accept everything as perfect and is not willing to accept anything short of equality for all of Israel's citizens. Another said that the Druze's unquestionable loyalty and service to the state put them in a position to protest and demand equality with greater confidence than others in the Arab minority.

The cover of Israel's largest circulating newspaper, *Yedioth Ahronoth*, the next day featured exclusive coverage of the protests, with the main headline reading "The Cry of Brothers" (*za'akat ha-akhim*).[35] The government responded to Druze concerns about the law with empathy, meetings, and a willingness to legislate a separate law related to the status of the Druze and Circassians (who also serve in compulsory military service), and potentially other minorities. Naftali Bennett, the education minister, even expressed a degree of regret about the law because of the Druze response and claimed the government now had a responsibility to "heal the rift."

Despite the sentiment among participants I spoke to about the need for equality for all rather than special privileges for certain minorities, the speeches at the rally, and often also the response of Jewish opponents to the law, repeatedly emphasized the sacrifice of the Druze, Circassian, and Bedouin (who are exempt from military service, but are recruited as volunteers), and often conspicuously failed to mention Arab or Palestinian citizens more generally. Even President Rivlin in his letter to the Knesset warned of the potential for article 7 (b) to lead to discrimination against Middle Eastern Jews, Haredim, Druze, and the LGBT community – essentially those who may be incidentally affected – without mentioning the real target of the article at issue, the broader Arab community. Such selective sympathy has confirmed for many Palestinian citizens the previously held sentiment that equality within the state is not liberal and democratic, but rather hierarchical, with individual and group rights contingent on factors such as "loyalty" – as demonstrated by military service – and adherence to the state ideology. Thus while many in the broader Muslim and Christian Arab communities in Israel oppose the law, the general sentiment has been not one of disillusionment

---

35 See *Yedioth Ahronoth*, August 5, 2018, with full coverage on pages 1–5.

or betrayal, as among many Druze, but one of affirmation that the state is moving away from its liberal ideals and willing to make de jure the dominant standing of the majority.

Compared to the protest organized by the Druze community, far fewer people attended a joint Arab and Jewish protest held on Saturday evening August 10, initiated by left-wing political parties and civil rights groups, which marched from Rabin Square to the Tel Aviv Museum of Art (the highest estimates were at 30,000). At that protest, marchers carried signs with the words "equality," "democracy," "rights," "justice," and "resist apartheid," written in Hebrew and Arabic. Some youths carried Palestinian flags and posed for photographs for journalists, while many young people and families sat in groups and chatted when the march reached its destination. The speeches were angry, but the atmosphere among attendees was mainly festive and resistant, suggesting the Arab-Jewish protest represented more of an opportunity to vent than a realistic hope to change the law.

The opposition in the Knesset similarly sought a symbolic opportunity to voice their objection to the law, gaining the twenty-five signatures necessary to recall the parliament from summer recess for a debate in the plenum. At that debate, opposition leaders Tzipi Livni and Yair Lapid focused on the Declaration of Independence and what they considered the nation-state law's betrayal of those values (several activists were removed from the public gallery for holding up copies of the Declaration). Members of the Joint List such as Yousef Jabareen and Ayman Odeh argued that the state must be for all citizens – Jews and non-Jews – with Jabareen reading segments from Martin Luther King's August 1968 "I have a dream" speech. And the official response from the government, by Ze'ev Elkin, attempted to call out the opposition for hypocrisy and questioned why Livni and Lapid did not push harder for a law giving constitutional status to the Declaration of Independence, if that was what they wanted, when they were members of the last government.[36] The clear purpose

---

36 Knesset plenum debate (special session), August 8, 2018 (I was present). A brief synopsis can be found in the Knesset press release, "Knesset debates Jewish nation-state

of this debate, however, was for the parties to position themselves for elections.

Different forms of opposition to the law have continued in various sectors of Israeli society: forty former ambassadors signed an open letter against it, Chief Rabbi David Lau suggested it should be amended to satisfy the Druze (but otherwise supports it), and President Reuven Rivlin has continued to speak out against the law, calling it "bad for the State of Israel and bad for the Jews."[37] In response to the criticism, the prime minister and members of Knesset who support the law have defended it as changing nothing in practical legal terms (despite the hyperbolic language used at the time of the law's passage), focusing instead on its symbolic value. As for Israeli public opinion, a poll taken the week after the law passed indicated that a narrow majority of Israeli Jews (52 percent) believed the law was necessary, and a strong majority of 60 percent of all Israelis believed the law should have included a clause on equality. Interestingly, Israeli *Jews* were quite divided on the status of Arabic as an official language: while 51 percent supported the change in the law, 40 percent opposed it, preferring Arabic remain an official language.[38]

For many in the Jewish Israeli public, whether they favor or oppose the law, it is unlikely to affect their lives in the short term. The law has also shared the spotlight with other debates that have raged simultaneously in 2018, over religion and state and gay rights. In particular, the demand for equal surrogacy rights for gay couples was also a focus of Israeli human rights activism over the summer

---

law in special session," August 8, 2018, https://knesset.gov.il/spokesman/eng/PR _eng.asp?PRID=13995.

37 Itamar Eichner, "40 Former Israeli Diplomats Come Out against Nationality Law," *Yedioth Ahronoth*, August 5, 2018, https://www.ynetnews.com/articles/0,7340,L-5322838,00.html; Amihai Attali, "Chief Rabbi Demands Nation-State Law Amendments," *Yedioth Ahronoth*, September 2, 2018, https://www.ynetnews.com/articles /0,7340,L-5339820,00.html; "Israel's President: Nation-State law is 'Bad for Israel and Bad for the Jews,'" *Times of Israel*, September 6, 2018, https://www.timesofisrael .com/president-nation-state-law-bad-for-israel-and-bad-for-the-jews/.

38 Tamar Hermann and Ephraim Yaar, "60% of Israelis Think the New Nation-State Law Should Have Included 'Equality," Press Release by the Israel Democracy Institute, July 31, 2018, https://en.idi.org.il/articles/24311.

of 2018, in response to a new surrogacy law that extended specified rights to mothers only. To what extent public opinion on the nation-state law may shift, whether the opposition will revive amending or abrogating the nation-state law in the fall 2018 session of the Knesset, whether the government will pass a new law relating to the protections and status of minorities, or whether elections will come sooner rather than later, remain at this point – September 2018 – still to be seen.

ISRAEL'S NATION-STATE LAW IN COMPARATIVE CONTEXT

The timing of recent bills regarding Israel's character, and ultimately the passage of the nation-state law, cannot be divorced from electoral politics. But, in the more than 130 years since Zionism first emerged as a political idea, and the 120 years since the First World Zionist Congress, there has consistently been an enormous diversity of opinion about how to interpret the Jewish component of what would be the Jewish homeland or state. As a movement, Zionism always included individuals, streams, and parties with widely diverging ideological perspectives: socialist and liberal; traditional; self-consciously heretical; utopian and practical; those who sought spiritual or religious redemption, and those who simply sought a home free of anti-Semitism – each with a different perspective on Judaism and Jewish nationality. The ambiguity in the Declaration of Independence about what it means for Israel to be a Jewish state left open the possibility of multiple interpretations that proved especially useful in maintaining strong ties to the Jewish Diaspora and helped the state to absorb waves of migrants from different parts of the world – Europe, Arabic-speaking countries, Iran, Ethiopia, and the Soviet Union, to name just a few – with dramatically varying religious traditions and commitments.

Naturally, constitutional ambiguity and the diversity of Israeli society have also created differences of opinion as to the benefits of clarifying the state's vision and, if attempted, what aspect or aspects should be emphasized (and one can see such diversity in the draft bills that were proposed). Furthermore, it is important to reiterate that arguments for increasing civic cohesion through such legislation look very different to the one-fifth to one-quarter of the state's population that is not Jewish. This yawning gap in perspective regarding the state's identity both in the present and going forward is evident in the contributions in this volume.

Israel's declarative founding document cites the state's purpose as providing a refuge for Jews, establishing Jewish sovereignty, and reaffirming the Jews' connection to their biblical birthplace. While the state grants equal voting franchise to all Israeli citizens, regardless of religion or nationality, the state also makes distinctions between citizens, and potential citizens, in important ways. Most significantly, Jews from anywhere in the world qualify for citizenship with few restrictions. Furthermore, the state, given its ideological purpose, supports – both monetarily and through the state's imprimatur – Jewish cultures and languages, religion, and identity construction. There is an understanding in Israel, reflected in its politics and daily life, that the government and state must serve not merely the interests of Israeli citizens, but also the interests of Jewish Israelis and global Jewry; as one often hears, Israel is the Jewish state. The obviousness of Israel's Jewish identity explains why the debate over a nation-state law was of lesser interest to the Israeli public than it was to its political and intellectual classes. Nonetheless, the persistence of political will to clarify in writing the identity of the state suggests that, at least among many lawmakers, more clarity was needed, and perhaps still is.

In the broader context of comparative constitutionalism, among states that, like Israel, came into being in the twentieth century, how typical or atypical would Israel's nation-state law be? There are many comparisons to be made between Israel and other states that gained independence in the mid-twentieth century and in the 1990s. One scholar who supported the law drew comparisons between Israel's proposed nation-state bills and the Latvian and Slovak constitutions, which, he argued, explicitly place the right to self-determination in the hands of the majority national/religious/linguistic group.[39] He and others have also argued that Israel's protections for minority languages and religions are more sweeping and liberal than is the norm for European states. Readers can judge for themselves as these constitutions are publicly available, but the Slovak constitution states explicitly that "state power derives from the citizens" (i.e., not the Slovak people) whereas the Latvian constitution speaks somewhat more vaguely of sovereignty being vested in "the people of Latvia."[40] Nonetheless, it is certainly true that many European constitutions, especially in their preambles, locate the historical justification for the state in the unique history of the dominant national group. Furthermore, matters of religion and state are not more intertwined in Israel than in many other liberal democracies. Greece's constitution, for example, put into force in 1975, was passed "In the name of the Holy and Consubstantial and Indivisible Unity," and includes a clause naming Eastern Orthodox Christianity, with "Our Lord Jesus Christ at its head," as the "prevailing religion."[41]

States such as Pakistan and Indonesia, founded on a secular-national understanding of Islam, have, similar to Israel and Judaism, struggled since their establishment to articulate in writing what Islam should mean to the state. Pakistan's constitution includes "Islamic provisions," speaks of an "Islamic way of life," and also of strengthening Pakistan's bond with the Muslim world.[42] Pakistan's

---

39 Eugene Kontorovich, "The Legitimacy of Israel's Nation-State Bill (I): Comparative Constitutionalism," *The Washington Post* (The Volokh Conspiracy blog), December 9, 2014, https://www.washingtonpost.com/news/volokh-conspiracy/wp/2014/12/09/the-legitimacy-of-israels-nation-state-bill-i-comparative-constitutionalism/?utm_term=.506b20d765dc; Eugene Kontorovich, "The Legitimacy of Israel's Nation-State Bill (II): Diplomatic Considerations," *The Washington Post* (The Volokh Conspiracy blog), December 10, 2014, https://www.washingtonpost.com/news/volokh-conspiracy/wp/2014/12/10/the-legitimacy-of-israels-nation-state-bill-ii-diplomatic-considerations/?utm_term=.8de1a67b0ef2.

40 See "Constitution of the Slovak Republic," https://www.prezident.sk/upload-files/46422.pdf and "The Constitution of the Republic of Latvia," http://www.saeima.lv/en/legislation/constitution.

41 See "The Constitution of Greece," https://www.hellenicparliament.gr/en/Vouli-ton-Ellinon/To-Politevma/Syntagma/.

42 See "The Constitution of the Islamic Republic of Pakistan," http://www.na.gov.pk

constitution, however, also declares Islam the state religion, and gives specific protections to a number of other legally recognized religions, whereas none of the proposed nation-state laws sought to make Judaism Israel's state religion (though more than anything this had to do with resisting the equation between Jewishness and religion). India's constitution makes distinctions between citizens based on religion by preserving considerable autonomy for the state's religious groups, but, at least on paper, is structured far more toward equality for all citizens than is either Pakistan's constitution or Israel's nation-state law in its proposals and final form (David Myers makes further comparisons in his essay, including to Turkey and Armenia).[43]

Some aspects of Israel's constitutional history and current constitutional debates are indeed comparable to those of states that gained independence in the twentieth century. It is typical and even normal for Israel's lawmakers to seek a constitutional document (if not a constitution) that lays out the vision, identity, and meaning of the state. In addition, Israel is not alone in struggling to determine the meaning of citizenship in a nation-state, the proper place of religion in the state and in its laws, and how to balance a commitment to the religious and national culture of the majority with the post-enlightenment language of civic equality that has tended to pervade constitutional preambles and articles since the late eighteenth century. It is also not alone in finding elements of protected or state-supported religion as running contrary to liberal ideals. As Tanya Zion-Waldoks points out in her essay, without addressing the gender inequality at the heart of religious personal status laws – which exists in many states – any discussion of clarifying the state's identity will only serve to calcify legal sex discrimination. In this regard Israel is no different from those other states that have sought modern, and even secular, constitutions, while carving out space for

---

/uploads/documents/1333523681_951.pdf.
43 See "Constitution of India," https://india.gov.in/my-government/constitution-india /constitution-india-full-text.

religious traditions, especially concerning marriage, that in effect preserve a legal space for female inequality.[44]

A key purpose of any state's struggle to define itself constitutionally is to determine where sovereignty lies. And because every state is made up of different people and has evolved from a different history and legal culture, so every state will interpret the basis for the state's sovereignty differently. Based on the Declaration of Independence and the ideologies of the dominant political parties since its composition, Israel's independence is a product of the reconstitution of political control by Jews over the place of Jewish religious, historical, and national origins. Thus, the basis for Israel's sovereignty (not merely its independence, but the source of its authority and legitimacy), in the most common understanding of its declarative founding document, stems from the Jewish people. Such expansion of sovereignty to a collective beyond Israel's borders was strengthened in the recent versions of the nation-state bill, and even more so in its final version as passed. The Explanatory Notes in Dichter's 2015 bill stated that the Basic Law will "anchor Israel's deep moral commitment to Diaspora Jewry. Israel sees itself as a nation-state intended for all the Jews of the world who wish to immigrate and is committed to all the Jews of the world wherever they may be" (2015, P/20/1989). In the final bill's first reading, an article of the bill itself (and therefore with the force of law) stated that the "state shall act to preserve the bond between the state and the Jewish people wherever they may be," and committed Israel to preserving the cultural, historical, and religious heritage of Diaspora Jewry (2018, P/20/1989).[45]

As a state drawn demographically to a significant degree from Jewish refugees and their descendants, there is both an ideological

---

44 See Yüksel Sezgin, *Human Rights under State-Enforced Religious Family Laws in Israel, Egypt, and India* (Cambridge, UK: Cambridge University Press, 2013), and Michael Walzer, *The Paradox of Liberation: Secular Revolutions and Religious Counterrevolutions* (New Haven, CT: Yale University Press, 2015).

45 As mentioned above, the phrase "wherever they may be" in that article was changed before the law's final passage to "in the Diaspora" (*ba-tfutsot*) to indicate specifically that the state shall act outside of its own borders to preserve the bond between the broader Jewish people and the state.

(or "moral") and a practical logic to this commitment to the Jews in the Diaspora, which is indeed central to Israel's mission. The effect, however, of codifying the expansion of sovereignty over Israel to global Jewry (or arguably, the sovereignty of the State of Israel over global Jewry) is also to clarify to the significant minority of Israeli citizens who are not Jewish that the state's sovereignty resides with a collective that they cannot join (see Amal Jamal's essay). Here too we can find grounds for comparison in other states, such as the post-Soviet Baltic countries, which found themselves with a large minority of citizens who identified culturally, linguistically, and religiously with Russia. So, for example, the Lithuanian constitution places sovereignty in the Lithuanian nation, and extends citizenship to a global population of Lithuanians (thereby including the Lithuanian Diaspora in the nation, and extending sovereignty to those potential citizens), while maintaining within Lithuania state-supported independent "ethnic communities of citizens" whose kin are not similarly entitled to the same benefits as ethnic Lithuanians.[46] Whether such an example is worth following, is a different question altogether.

What is perhaps particular (or perhaps is not) to Israel's current constitutional struggle is that one might interpret the very impetus to put its identity to paper as an attempt to reaffirm boundaries between the sovereign majority and everyone else. For the more strident proponents of a nation-state law, the Jewish identity of the state is under threat from those who argue for a "state for all citizens."[47] A constitutional counterbalance to existing laws enshrining

---

46 "Constitution of the Republic of Lithuania," especially articles 2, 32, and 45, http://www3.lrs.lt/home/Konstitucija/Constitution.htm.

47 Fifteen lawmakers submitted to the Knesset on May 30, 2018, a law drafted by Yousef Jabareen, entitled Basic Law: A Democratic State, Multicultural and Egalitarian, and a similar bill was submitted by three members of Knesset entitled Basic Law: A State for All Its Citizens on June 4, 2018. Knesset Speaker Yuli Edelstein disqualified the latter bill from discussion on the Knesset floor, but the bill's sponsors (Jamal Zahalka, Haneen Zoabi, and Joumah Azbarga) have petitioned the High Court of Justice for a ruling on the matter. See Jonathan Lis, "Knesset Council Bans Bill to Define Israel as a State for All Its Citizens," *Haaretz*, June 4, 2018, https://www.haaretz.com/israel-news/.premium-knesset-council-bans-bill-to-define-israel-as-state-for-all-citizens-1.6145333; *idem*, "Arab Lawmakers Ask Court to Overturn Ban on Debating Bill Calling Israel a State of All Its Citizens," *Haaretz*, June 13, 2018,

human rights and equality is necessary, according to those lawmakers, to protect the state's identity from erosion by an independent judiciary (states without an independent judiciary, in contrast, can put any ideals they like in a constitutional document). Speaking at a conference in February 2018, Justice Minister Ayelet Shaked insisted that a nation-state law was needed to counter demands for national (as opposed to civic) equality, and as ballast against the Supreme Court's expansive view of democracy. In this speech Shaked repeatedly emphasized that because universal values are already enshrined in Israeli law, the Supreme Court should be given a legal "tool" to prioritize, when necessary, the Jewishness of the state, even at a cost to democracy or equality.[48] Whether the court will decide cases before it differently now that it has been provided such a tool is unclear and likely will depend on the case and the composition of the bench. Despite critics who say otherwise, the court has in the past taken the well-being of the Jewish collective into consideration when rendering decisions, a fact equally true both before and since Barak's constitutional revolution.

There are, in contrast, also those who see Israel's primary constitutional challenge as finding a way to articulate how Israel can be *both* a Jewish state and a state for all its citizens. To do so however requires identifying what is Jewish and what is democratic about the state in a way that makes all citizens the bearers of the state's sovereignty. The difficulty in articulating how, within a Jewish state, sovereignty can lie with all citizens – including those opposed to the state's governing ideology – and, at the same time, how the state can

https://www.haaretz.com/israel-news/.premium-arab-mks-ask-court-to-overturn-ban-on-debating-israeli-identity-bill-1.6172091; and Gideon Allon, "Arab MK Drafts Bill to Counter What He Calls 'Jewish Supremacy,'" *Israel Hayom*, January 31, 2018, http://www.israelhayom.com/2018/01/31/arab-mk-drafts-new-law-to-counter-jewish-supremacy-bill/.

48 Revital Hovel, "Justice Minister: Israel Must Keep Jewish Majority Even at the Expense of Human Rights," *Haaretz*, February 13, 2018, https://www.haaretz.com/israel-news/justice-minister-israel-s-jewish-majority-trumps-than-human-rights-1.5811106; Yonah Jeremy, "Fight over Jewish Nation-State Bill Smolders," *Jerusalem Post*, February 12, 2018, http://www.jpost.com/Israel-News/Fight-over-Jewish-nation-state-bill-smolders-542420.

hold as its primary purpose Jewish national self-determination, has led most who favor this dual vision also to favor avoiding legislation on the matter completely (even if they support a nation-state law in theory). This was the position of Tzipi Livni, who articulated to me that "if we want to translate the 'Jewish democratic state,' the meaning is 'nation-state for the Jewish people with equal rights for all its citizens.' *This* [the nation-state] is the 'Jewish' and *this* [equal rights for all citizens] is the 'democratic.'"[49] Reuven Rivlin has argued during his presidency that instead of Israelis thinking about the state in terms of majority (Jewish) and minority (Arab), or even Zionist and non-Zionist, today's Israel is composed of four "tribes" of approximately equal size: secular Jewish, Jewish national-religious, Arab, and Haredi. As each tribe becomes more isolated from the others – especially in systems of education – the only way to build bridges between them, in Rivlin's formulation, is to acknowledge a multi-ideological Israeli identity that resembles the multicultural civic nationalism of a growing number of states.[50] In essence, the creation of a shared Israeli identity must recognize difference.

Where and if Palestinians who are not Israeli citizens fit into this formula, or in fact any formula, is not clear. Livni suggested to me that such a simple premise – how Israel is Jewish, and how it is democratic – is in fact problematic because of the absence of a Palestinian state with its own borders and constitutional grounding. As long as this political conflict remains unresolved and Israel's borders remain undetermined, an argument will also remain, upheld by proponents of the nation-state law, to create a legal bulwark against the erosion of the state's Jewish identity – and indeed to keep the state's sovereignty under the control of the Jews – even if at the expense of some aspects of the state's democratic character.

As several essays in this volume point out (see in particular those by Israel Bartal, Nir Kedar, and Yehudah Mirsky), Israel today is more

---

49 See in this volume "On the Meaning of Israel as a Jewish and Democratic State: A Conversation with Tzipi Livni."

50 "President Reuven Rivlin Address to the 15th Annual Herzliya Conference," June 7, 2015, http://www.president.gov.il/English/ThePresident/Speeches/Pages/news _070615_01.aspx.

religious, less socialist, and less European than it was in the early years of independence. It is also ethnically (by place of origin) and culturally more diverse. The impetus to enshrine the state's Jewish national identity in the law seems connected to a sense among its proponents that the percentage of Israelis – whether religious or secular, Jewish or non-Jewish – who see the state's identity in Jewish national terms is in decline. Benny Begin, who crafted his own law, perhaps best captured this sentiment in his essay when, in explaining the necessity of a nation-state law, he paraphrased Cardinal Richelieu, who said, "if it is self-evident, write it down," and added, in his own words, "if it is not self-evident, all the more so."

CONCLUSION – PROBLEMS OF INTERPRETATION

Israel's democratic infrastructure includes a parliament and local governments elected by an equal franchise of all adult citizens, an independent judiciary, a free press, and many liberal protections for individual rights guaranteed by its regular and Basic Laws.[51] But the preponderance and electoral power of one group that associates with the state's national and religious ethos, in contrast to a minority that largely does not, has led to a number of democratic caveats, made worse by the context of an ongoing military and political conflict. Today, many Palestinian citizens of Israel already feel their interests to be inadequately represented by the state and government and their treatment in the courts to be unequal. Since the nation-state law

---

51 Some, such as Ilan Pappé, have argued that Israel is not currently a democracy, and has not been one historically (see *Ten Myths about Israel* [London; New York: Verso, 2017]), but such critiques tend to focus on instances of government abuse or unequal treatment of citizens. These examples may, for Pappé and others, be enough to disqualify Israel's claim to be a democracy, but it is difficult to deny that all citizens in right and practice participate equally in the democratic governance of the state. Aharon Barak, in contrast, has recently composed a more nuanced assessment of the nature of Israeli democracy and its challenges ("Individual Freedom in a Jewish and Democratic State," *Haaretz*, March 25, 2018, https://www.haaretz.com/opinion/.premium-individual-freedom-in-a-jewish-and-democratic-state-1.5935245).

does not take away any specific right, it undermines the democratic rights of Palestinians only as specific clauses may be interpreted in the future by the courts. And in certain respects, specifically the provisions on the guarantees to the use of Arabic and the right to celebrate culturally specific days of rest, it affirms elements of their collective rights. But those rights, even if guaranteed, are qualitatively lesser than those of the Jews within the state – Hebrew is now the sole state language and the Jewish Sabbath is the regular day of rest. As such, the law establishes a clear hierarchy within the state ethos of culture, religion, law, and self-determination that cannot but be interpreted by Palestinian citizens of Israel as an erosion of their equal status.

The most fervent opponents and supporters of the law seem to talk past one another, though they are, strangely enough, in greater agreement on the law's purpose than the more moderate opponents and supporters in the middle. The members of Knesset from the Arab Joint List argue that the law's purpose is to enshrine the inferior status of non-Jewish citizens in the state – even using the term apartheid – while the prime minister and especially members of Knesset from Bayit Yehudi respond, seemingly in confirmation, that "this is *our* state, and there can be no equality in self-determination."[52] Many in the opposition, however, are not philosophically opposed to the idea of such a bill but oppose it in its current form: because it fails to mention equality or democracy, because of the timing, or because of the benefits weighed against the cost to social cohesion. And the dominant government position among members of the largest party, the Likud, is that human rights and civil equality are already protected by the law, and the new bill includes specific stipulations (such as on the status of Arabic) that guarantee no erosion of individual or collective rights for minorities.

That the law has produced so many varying and sometimes dia-

---

52 In the Knesset debate on August 8 Yousef Jabareen made explicit comparisons to South Africa under apartheid; in their responses both Bezalel Smotrich and Amir Ohana said explicitly that there can be no equality among nationalities and that "this is our land" (Smotrich) and "this is our state" (Ohana). These remarks do not appear in the synopsis in the Knesset press release, but I was present for them.

metrically opposed interpretations of its significance reflects the ambiguity of its key articles and, most of all, the different historical experiences of the state's citizens. Certainly there are people who oppose the constitutional codification of the state's symbols, days of rest, and calendar without simultaneous recognition of those of the state's minorities (as Yousef Jabareen does in this volume). But all such aspects have long been established in Israeli law and are facts of life in the state.

The contention primarily surrounds the articles dealing with the state's *identity*, such as those in the Basic Principles, on Language, on the Connection to the Jewish People, and on Jewish Settlement. Take article 1 (c): "The right to exercise national self-determination in the State of Israel is uniquely that of the Jewish people." If one is Jewish and feels the identity of the state has been under attack in recent years by the courts, "leftists," minorities, academics, and foreign countries, then this clause is a blunt and necessary reiteration that Israel's purpose is to act as a vehicle for Jewish self-determination and the protection of Jewish people (see in this volume the essay by Amnon Lord). Other Jews less worried about playing defense may feel that the article is unnecessary because it simply restates an obvious fact benignly and with little consequence, or that it is harmful because it restates an obvious fact with the unfortunate consequence of unnecessarily alienating the state's minorities; many in the opposition bemoan that the true purpose of the clause is political rather than ideological or practical. If one is not Jewish but feels a deep sense of connection to the state as a citizen, such as is the case for many Druze, then the clause may feel like a form of intentional exclusion from collective sovereignty that creates a fissure in the social contract. And if one is a Bedouin or a Palestinian-Arab Muslim or Christian who already feels their status to be unequal and eroding within the state, then, the clause may be read as constitutionally enshrining the superiority of the majority ethnic group in a way that opens the door for legislation and court decisions that will in turn allow for further discrimination and privilege Jewish self-determination over the civil rights of non-Jews. All of these readings are viable when one accounts for the different experiences of the state's citizens. The different interpretations would break down similarly if we considered the clauses calling Jewish settlement a "national value" or designating Hebrew the "state language" and Arabic a language with "special status."

The most fervent supporters and opponents of the law also tend both to emphasize the uniqueness, respectively for better and for worse, of Israel as a state (though the idea of Israel's uniqueness is shared widely in both the government and the Israeli public). The historical circumstances which gave rise to Israel as a sovereign Jewish nation-state were indeed singular – as have been its ongoing military conflicts – and the society and government it produced follows its own particular logic. But what state today does not claim a unique history and does not possess its own political culture that responds to its particular social needs? While Israeli society is unique, its laws, like all laws, can be dissected for consistency with the legal culture that produced them and compared to those of other states. In this regard the law's supporters can make a fair claim that most if not all of the articles in the final nation-state law merely make de jure what already existed in Israeli society de facto, and that comparable, if perhaps not identical, language can be found in the constitutional documents of other democratic states. At the same time and by the same standard, the law's detractors can also make a fair argument that the law constitutionally encodes the privileges and status of the majority in a way that is inconsistent with both Israel's own Declaration of Independence and its subsequent legal history and runs counter to the trends of international human rights law since at least the 1990s. Whether Israel's nation-state law proves to be a forewarning of growing legal majoritarianism to come, a symbolic triumph with little consequence, or opens the door to a conversation – and perhaps more laws – about the meaning of equality in a Jewish state, will be up to generations of Israel's courts, lawmakers, and citizens to determine.

Rally in Tel Aviv's Rabin Square organized by the Druze community, August 4, 2018. Photo by Simon Rabinovitch.

Protesters and counter-protesters face off at an Arab-Jewish march against the nation-state law in Tel Aviv, August 11, 2018. Photo by Simon Rabinovitch.

PART I. SOURCES

Constitutional Anchoring of Israel's Vision: Recommendations Submitted to the Minister of Justice (November 19, 2014)

Ruth Gavison

ABSTRACT

Context

This work has been written against the background of bills designed to anchor the vision of the state in a Basic Law. My mission was to examine the question of the constitutional anchoring of Israel as a Jewish and democratic state.

Society, State, and Vision

- A shared vision is critical for a society whose members are required to make sacrifices for its existence and contribute to its flourishing. The core vision of a state includes the basic values that lend a unique character to its society.
- Israel is a nation-state whose vision includes three main components: Jewishness, democracy, and human rights.
- Each of these three components is a vital feature of the vision of the state, and they all complement each other. There is a broad agreement within the Jewish public on a vague and thin conception of this vision. The component of Jewishness in the vision of the state is not easy to swallow for members of Israel's Arab minority. At the same time, the complex vision of Israel regards them as equal citizens, and as full partners in the state.

- The full vision, in its entirety, is vital for the strength and success of the state. Such strength and success of the state are in turn essential to the welfare of all of Israel's residents, irrespective of nationality or religion.
- A distinction should be made between the broad acceptance of the core of the vision, and disagreements within Israel's society over varying interpretations of the vision and its practical implications for social life.
- Israel manifests deep political, social and ideological disagreements. Most of them are not about the core vision itself. They relate to its interpretations and implications.
- The state has an interest in strengthening the broad acceptance of the core vision of the state.

Constitutional Anchoring of the Vision

- The vision of a state is usually articulated in the preamble of a constitution. It has declaratory, expressive and educational functions. In this way the core vision is distinguished from the constitutional arrangements that give it practical meaning. Israel does not have a full constitution. The present bills aim to establish a separate constitutional anchoring of the vision by itself. There are three types of law under discussion: some (e.g., the Begin proposal) are full **vision laws** (Basic Laws seeking to anchor the full vision of the state, including all three components); some are **Jewish nation-state laws** (Basic Laws which by name and content seek to provide constitutional anchoring only for the Jewish component of the vision); and the **Declaration law** (an instance of a vision law, that would anchor the Declaration of the Establishment of the State, also called the Declaration of Independence, in its entirety).
- Questions of vision are not legal questions, and should not be decided by law or in courts. A separate anchoring of the vision would transfer the locus of discussion about disagreements on interpretations of the vision from the public and political arenas to the courts. Against the background of Israeli constitutional

reality, in which the status of Basic Laws and judicial review under them is controversial, this process will enhance uncertainty and disagreement.

- Debate and discussions concerning interpretations of the shared vision are inevitable, desirable, and contribute to the freedom and openness of society. A move to anchor the vision will put the vision itself as the focus of disagreement, and create the impression that the debate can and must be decided once and for all.

- A **Jewish nation-state law** may upset the balance among components crucial for maintaining the full vision. Moreover, such a law seeks to anchor in a Basic Law arrangements that are not part of the core of the vision. Consequently, it may limit the broad agreement concerning the Jewish component in the core vision.

- The **Declaration of the Establishment of the State** (hereafter, the Declaration) does reflect the complex vision articulated by the founders of Israel. This Declaration, deliberately left outside the law thus far, obtained its meaning in the historical context wherein it was adopted, and enjoys broad support in Israel. It is better to leave it untouched, and not subject it to controversies that will inevitably arise as a part of a campaign to enact it as a Basic Law, in totally different social and political circumstances.

Main Recommendations

- To act in a variety of ways – both cultural and educational as well as legal and legislative – to bolster the broad endorsement of the core vision of the state, in three circles of solidarity: the civic collective in Israel, including all citizens; the Jewish majority in Israel; and Jewish communities around the world.

- To refrain, at this stage, from additional constitutional anchoring of the core vision through legislation, in part or as a whole.

- If legislation to provide constitutional anchoring of the vision of the state is initiated, the law and the process of legislation should both reflect the magnitude of the mission. An attempt should be made to seek a law that will strengthen solidarity and not deepen rifts, so that the vision of the state will be strengthened and not weakened by the legislation. The legislation and the law should highlight civic solidarity in Israel; should enhance Jewish solidarity in Israel and abroad; and should manifest a fair, generous and inclusive attitude to the members of the Arab minority.

INTRODUCTION

In August 2013 you [Minister of Justice Tzipi Livni] commissioned me – with the agreement of all coalition factions – to examine the proper way "to formulate a constitutional arrangement dealing with the nature of the state…and anchor the components of its identity in a way that would integrate these values, the Jewish as well as the democratic."[1] The request was prompted by a number of bills seeking to anchor the vision of the state in a Basic Law, and the heated public debate surrounding them. I thank you for the trust you have placed in me.

To perform my task I have studied materials concerning theories of state, processes of constitutional anchoring, and the vision of the State of Israel and its constitutional history. I have met with the MKs who proposed the bills, consulted with experts in Israel and abroad, and discussed the matter with many people from different sectors of Israeli society. I participated in conferences on the subject, representing a broad range of attitudes to the question. I have received memoranda and reports from various individuals and organizations. Throughout I have enjoyed the diligent and effective support of my team and of the Ministry of Justice. I thank the many who have helped me in this task.

I chose to define my task broadly. The disagreements surrounding the proposed bills do not concern only the issue of legislation. They relate also to the vision of the state itself, its substance and its function. Israel does have a vision, and it has pursued it with considerable success. Its canonical formulation, often mentioned and

---

1 "A Procedure to Constitutionally Anchor the State's Identity," Ministry of Justice, http://index.justice.gov.il/StateIdentity/Pages/default.aspx.

invoked in many contexts, is the one contained in the Declaration of the Establishment of the State: Israel is the realization of the Zionist dream of the rebirth of the Jewish people in its homeland. The state is Jewish, democratic, and respects the basic liberties of all its residents.

Israel's success as a state depends on two circles of solidarity. The first relates to its ability to persist and win the battle over its existence as a Jewish state, based on a strong solidarity among the Jews in Israeli society (and with world Jewry); the second is its ability to create a civic partnership among all its citizens, based on its being a free and democratic society respecting their rights. Constitutional anchoring of the vision is one way of promoting it. I wanted to examine the question of the vision itself, not just its constitutional anchoring.

This paper is a concise statement of my recommendations. I start with the question of the vision of the state. I then look at some difficulties involved in an attempt to anchor it in a Basic Law. I have added some observations in case the Knesset decides to proceed with legislation nevertheless. I conclude with a few general recommendations, based on an analysis of the arguments presented by the advocates of the bills. At a later stage I will submit a longer report (in Hebrew), in which some of these points, as well as the description of my work, will be developed at greater length.[2]

THE VISION OF THE STATE OF ISRAEL

According to the founders of the state, and in most formulations that followed theirs, the vision of Israel is clear, and includes three distinct components:

- Jewish character;
- Democratic character;
- Protection of human rights.

---

2 This longer report is the book of 2015 in the "Reports" section of the suggestions for further reading.

Let me expand: Israel is a **democratic** state, in the sense that sovereignty in it is vested in all its citizens, irrespective of religion or national origin, on the basis of liberty and equality; it protects the **human rights** of all its residents; and it is the political framework that allows Jews to realize their **right to self-determination** and to political, cultural and religious independence, based on their being a stable and strong majority in the country. The basic commitment to these three components of the vision, each one and all three of them together, integrated and complementing each other, is **the core of the vision of the state.**

In Praise of Minimalism and Vagueness

The power of this vision lies in its vagueness. There are very few arrangements that the vision requires, and very few that are negated by it. This is because each of its components is vague, and its meaning is deeply contested; it is also because the relationships among these components, and the implications each of them may have with regard to the implementation of the others, are many and varied. At the same time, the vision offers a compass that can serve most of Israeli society.

The Declaration chose not to render the vision of the state in terms of a legally binding formulation, and did not provide detailed interpretations. It presupposed that the three components of the vision complemented one another.

In contrast to this presupposition, there is a tendency in contemporary public and political discourse in Israel to present the vision of the state as trapped between two contradictory poles: a "particularistic" tribal pole, which is the essence of the "Jewishness" of the state, as against a "universalistic" or humanistic pole, which is the main pillar of democracy and human rights. The enactment of the expression "a Jewish and democratic state" in the 1992 Basic Laws, and the public debates that followed it, contributed much to this picture of the state moving between two competing poles. This tendency was strengthened by the undeniable fact that while Israel is the only Jewish state in the world, democracy and human rights are ideals shared by many other states.

This impression of a contradiction between two poles is misleading. There are at least three distinct components in the vision: Jewish distinctness, democracy, and human rights. These derive their basic legitimacy from different sources. Within each of them, as well as among them, there are many tensions.

The Jewish character of the state is indeed a particular matter related to Jews and Judaism, however we may define these terms. The core of this component in the vision of the state is the ability of Jews to exercise in their homeland a state-level right of self-determination. This self-determination permits them to decide what form Judaism will take in Israel. This component of the vision concerns the Jewish collective, whose members are Jews. Its nature is defined by Judaism – in its cultural, religious and historical dimensions.

Democracy is the principle that sovereignty of the state is vested in all its citizens, irrespective of religion, nationality, or gender, on the basis of liberty and equality. The core idea is that it is a government of the people, by the people, and for the people. The constituency of this component of the vision is the civic collective, the *demos*. The arrangements of the state are determined by "We, the People," in which all citizens have one, equal vote.

Human rights are derived from the basic principle that all persons are entitled to human dignity. Human dignity may be the right of all persons *qua* persons. In religious theories of human rights it may be based on the belief that all persons were created in the image of God (this formulation reflects the religious basis of some human rights theories. A non-religious account may say that all persons, *qua* persons, are entitled to human dignity). Human rights thus reflect the duty imposed on states, societies, and all individuals to treat individuals respectfully. The constituency of human rights is not ethnic-national or even state-civic, but is humanity as a whole (when human rights are protected by the law of the state, these rights are legal rights as well).

The meaning of the vision of the state, based on the three components – Jewish character, democracy, and human rights – is the freedom of Israeli society to determine the detailed arrangements governing its affairs, substantive as well as institutional, subject to the bona fide aspiration that the arrangements meet the demands imposed by these three ideals. When the meaning given to these components of the vision is indeed thin, they can be reconciled and they in fact reinforce each other. Jews are a stable majority in Israel, and most of them see the state as their national home. The Jewish character of the state thus also reflects its being a democracy, since the denial of the Jewish character of the state would also frustrate a basic preference of the majority. Such denial would be justified only if the preference itself were illegitimate. This essay – along with the law of nations, liberal political theory, and the Declaration of the Establishment of the State – rejects this view. Thus, in Israel, democracy supports the Jewish character of the state. Human rights are justified by universal moral principles. They are a constraint on what states and societies may do to individuals and to groups. However, they cannot sustain and inspire a whole culture and a way of life. All great cultures address the rights of men *qua* men ("Beloved is man for he was created in God's image") as well as other considerations, including particular interests and social concerns of the nation in question. The practical power of human rights in any state is greatest when they are supported by norms and agents external to the state and its particular culture(s), as well as by insights and imperatives coming from within the culture(s) themselves. This is true for the State of Israel, and for the cultures constituting the sectors of Israeli society.

Jewish character, democracy, and human rights are all very vague and contested. The richer the meaning given to any of these components the more it is likely that there will be a disagreement about whether a specific arrangement meets the demands of the vision, and the greater the likelihood of tension and even contradiction between the components of the vision. Thus, if a Jewish state means a Jewish theocracy, this state may not accept the sovereignty of the *demos*, or the rights of individuals and groups to freedom of religion and freedom from religion. A Jewish state seen as a rigid ethnocracy may indeed legitimate discrimination against all non-Jews. It thus may not protect the rights of individuals and minorities to equality, liberty, and culture. A civic, neutral democracy may not facilitate the promotion of the rights of Jews to self-determination (and the rights of minorities to culture), and might lead to an underestimation of the importance of non-civic identities to individuals and groups (minorities and majorities alike). An expansive interpretation of the human rights discourse, combined with a broadly interpreted power of the courts to invalidate legislation allegedly violating such rights, might weaken the power of individuals and groups living in the country to determine the arrangements and practices prevailing in it.

The Challenge of Civic Cohesion

The tendency to see a conflict between Jewish character and democracy has a special meaning for the Arab minority in Israel. Its members find it easy to promote ideals of democracy and human rights (even though some groups within this minority may be reluctant to endorse some interpretations of human rights and democracy, for religious or cultural reasons, just as these are rejected by some groups of Jews). It is unlikely that Arabs will find it equally easy, however, to identify with the Jewishness of the state.

The disagreement between Jews and Arabs thus concerns not only the interpretation and the practical implications of the vision, but the vision of the state itself. Arabs are a minority within Israel, but they belong to the majority in a region in which Jews are a minute minority (the Middle East). Between the two groups there is an unresolved conflict, including a struggle concerning the existence of the state itself. Since 1967, the disagreement also involves the political future of the territories captured by Israel in the Six-Day War, and the legitimacy of Jewish settlement in them. Among Arab political leaders in Israel there are those who emphasize identification with the Palestinians, including the goals of those denying Israel's right to exist, more than civic cohesion within Israel. Some of Israel's Jewish leaders, for their part, emphasize national antagonism more than civic partnership. Such positions reinforce each other.

The picture becomes even more complex since Jewish-Arab tension exists independently of the question as to whether the Jewish character of the state is a matter of nationalism, culture, religion, or a combination thereof. There are internal debates within the Arab minority in Israel concerning issues of identity, the relationships between religion and national identity, and the role of individuals in the communities to which they belong. However, these debates are often played down due to the high visibility and significance of the national conflict. For our present purpose, it is important to stress that the claim of a Jewish character of the state is usually not countered by claims to neutrality or to "a state of all its citizens," in the sense of privatizing all non-civic identities (as in France). Rather, it is countered by claims of different, possibly incompatible, identities and meanings (religious, national or a combination thereof). Many of the leaders of the Arab minority in Israel do not advocate a neutral, civic state; they aspire to reconstitute Israel as a bi-national or a multicultural state. What is common to the visions that one can identify within the Arab minority – a bi-national state, a civic neutral state, or a part of an Arab-Islamist state – is that all of them deny Israel as the nation-state of Jews. (To be clear: even if members of the Arab minority in Israel were to desire a civic, neutral state, Jews might still insist that Israel should be the nation-state of Jews).

This ideological and identity-based conflict plays out against the background of a complex social reality. The large majority of Arab citizens of Israel are well-integrated into life in Israel, and do not take part in hostile activities against the state. They exhibit varied and complex attitudes towards their Israeli citizenship. There is extensive and expansive Jewish-Arab activity within Israeli civil society to enhance civic cohesion. The extent and sophistication of these attitudes and activities are often played down due to the context of the conflict and the tendency of the discourse in Israel towards polarized presentations of reality. These facts also obscure the presence in Israel of many individuals and groups who are neither Jews nor Arabs, who are full members of the state. In fact, Israeli society exhibits impressive and important elements and achievements of pluralism, integration and partnership.[3]

To achieve a measure of civic cohesion Israel needs to strengthen

---

3 To support the complexity of the picture, see the annual reports of Jewish-Arab relations in Israel of Sammy Smooha.

the political framework of the state in a way that will facilitate significant partnership of all citizens in building the state and the nation, without distinction of national origin or religion, and to strengthen the feeling of membership and inclusion of all – despite the fact that the country is not fully and exclusively civic and neutral. This is a central and essential challenge. The strengthening of civic cohesion is a clear implication of the component of democracy in the vision of the state, based on an equal and inclusive citizenship. However, it is also required by the very task of the state – irrespective of regime – to serve the people living in it, and to promote their welfare.

The Challenge of Jewish Solidarity

"Jewish" and "democratic," in the internal Jewish debate concerning the vision of the state, are also often represented as being at odds with each other. On the one side stands a humanist-secular-liberal conception (either national-Hebraic or neutral and post-nationalist), committed to individuals and their rights (democracy), while on the other side stands a halakhic Jewish conception (Jewish state). There are those who claim that Israel as a "Jewish state" is tantamount to a Jewish theocracy, incompatible in principle with democracy. According to this view, there is a necessary contradiction between the Jewish and the democratic nature of the state. Accordingly, Israel must give up either the Jewishness of the state (according to a purist secularist conception) or give up its democratic nature (according to a purist religious conception).

The binary presentation of "Jewish" versus "democratic" in the internal Jewish debate is also misleading. It does not do justice to the deep and persistent debate among Jews about the nature of the State of Israel, the essence of Judaism, and the way in which the state should reflect its Jewish character. This presentation tends to foment hostility, distrust, and animosity among those who are allegedly the carriers of conflicting Jewish visions for the state: observant Jews and non-observant ones; nationalists versus cosmopolitan humanists.

The majority of the Jewish population of Israel, including the

majority of the Orthodox leadership, does not see the Jewish character of the state as a move towards theocracy. In the 1948 Declaration
it was made clear that the Jewish character of the state consisted in
the exercise of the right of national self-determination of the Jewish
people. In fact, the Jews, both in Israel and outside it, exhibit a great
variety of approaches to religion, to the essence of Judaism and its
continuing importance, and to the relation between Judaism as a
religion, civilization, or nation and democracy on the one hand and
human rights on the other. Similarly, they hold a variety of opinions
on the question of how the Jewish character of Israel should be
reflected in its public sphere. Pluralism in these matters cuts across
group identities: there are observant Jews who advocate the privatization of religion in Israel, and there are secular Jews who struggle
for maintaining a cultural Jewish presence in Israel's public sphere.

Debates concerning the Jewish component in the vision of the
state are inevitably tied both to the debate about the legitimacy
of Israel as a nation-state as against civic and neutralist visions,
or post-national and post-Zionist ones, as well as to the political
debate concerning the future of the settlements and the conflict
with the Palestinians. Against this background it is important to
note that, while it is mainly secularists who hold civic-neutral and
post-national attitudes, a large majority of Jews, in Israel and abroad,
including most of those who are not observant, regard Israel as
the place where Jews exercise national self-determination. On the
matter of the future of the occupied territories, the picture is more
complex. There are secularists who support the vision of a Greater
Land of Israel, and there are Orthodox Jews who support the vision
of two states for two nations. What is important for our purposes is
that the advocates of both these political visions often justify their
positions by the wish to maintain Israel as a state which is Jewish,
democratic, and supportive of the human rights of all. All of this
suggests that a discourse emphasizing the apparent contradictions
among the three components of the complex vision blurs the fact
that the great majority of Jews in Israel, and thus a majority of Israeli
citizens (as well as a majority of Jews around the world), endorses
the complex vision of all three components and wants to combine

them. Consequently, as far as the Jewish majority is concerned, the debate is not about the possibility – conceptual or practical – of justifying and combining the three components, but rather about questions relating to their practical interpretation: what is the relative weight of each of the components in comparison with the other two components? Should arrangements pertaining to the implementation of the components of the vision be regulated, in whole or in part, by the state itself? If so, in what form? Who should be making decisions on such matters? Through what sort of process should such decisions be made?

The challenge of maintaining Jewish solidarity, in Israel and abroad, requires a sense of all-Jewish kinship aimed at defending the right of Jews to protect their lives, welfare, and identity, and an agreement that the existence of Israel as a Jewish state is a central manifestation of that right. The deep intra-Jewish debate over the meaning of the vision of the state and its implications should be conducted in ways that do not tend to undermine – intentionally or indirectly – Israel's ability to maintain itself as a state in which Jews exercise their right to freedom and independence.

The Centrality of a Thin, Integrated Vision and Its Institutional Implications

Like every complex vision, that of the founders of Israel has its internal tensions. However, only this complex vision can meet the needs and concerns of Israel's heterogenic society. Israel is a democracy committed to the human rights of all its citizens, and it should remain so. Democracies, however, do not have to be civic, secular, or neutral; and human rights cannot determine all aspects of social life. Arrangements seeking and facilitating the implementation of the right of Jews to national self-determination can be part of a vision in which the other components are a robust and lively democracy and respect for the rights of all individuals and groups living in it. Moreover, a state established and maintained to permit the national rebirth of the Jews, which, since its inception, has been in a struggle with its neighbors concerning its existence and identity; which has a large Arab minority which does not share its vision; and which is related to important Jewish communities outside its borders – cannot be civic or neutral. A civic and neutral democracy is neither required nor is it suitable to the reality of Israeli society.

To conclude: **The vision of Israel must remain complex: Jewish character, democracy, and human rights. The Jewish majority in Israel cannot and should not give up the component of the Jewish character in the vision of the state. More importantly: keeping this component and recognizing it as an essential part of the vision of the state is critical to the viability of the state, and to its ability to provide security, welfare, and protection of the rights of all its citizens and residents.** In our time and region it is clearer than ever that functioning, effective, and vital states are essential to protect the rights of all those living in them to life and to flourishing. All those living in the country have a stake in keeping Israel functional and strong.

Israel must insist on the protection of the core of all components of its vision – Jewish character, democracy, and human rights – and put this commitment at the center of its shared political framework. However, it is not thereby committed to any specific interpretation of the implications of this core vision with respect to the practical aspects of social and political reality. Here are a few important guideline principles concerning the debate on the interpretation of the vision and its practical implications:

- Not every determination in interpretive debates on practical arrangements related to components of the vision is a violation of the core of the vision.
- Not all debates about the interpretations of the components of the vision have to be resolved. When a formal resolution is not required, it is better to avoid it. Rich social and cultural practices, invoking a shared political culture, are better than resolutions. The state should permit them and encourage them.
- At times, decisions involving value judgments of different groups, or institutional arrangements and competences, must be made.

In such cases, the state cannot avoid a resolution, which may be controversial. Usually, such arrangements are neither required by any of the components of the vision, nor are they inconsistent with them. The power of the vision – integrating all the components – lies in its vagueness.

- Social arrangements reflect resolutions seen as suitable to a particular time and place. It is advisable to permit adaptation of such resolutions to changing circumstances. It follows that low visibility and flexible arrangements are preferable to more entrenched arrangements enjoying higher visibility. Decentralized arrangements, resting on social agreements, are preferable to those based primarily on coercion and legal enforcement.
- Special care and restraint should be taken with resolutions involving a high symbolic and declaratory import, in both content and in the explanatory statements. Minimalism in both may help to maintain the delicate fabric of Israeli society (and enhance relations between Israel and others).
- When decisions concerning the implications of components of the vision must be made, the institutional question – who decides, and in what kinds of processes – becomes critical. When questions of identity, meaning of life, and conceptions of the good are involved, it is better that decisions and deliberations are undertaken through public and social debate rather than in legal discourse and by courts and lawyers. If a legal resolution is required, it is better made by the legislature, in processes of negotiation and compromise, and not by courts invoking a discourse of rights.
- When a complex vision is being interpreted, it is critical to give a minimalistic, vague reading to **all** components of the vision. The interpretation of the vision and the relationship among its components are not legal questions. Social, cultural, and community processes of implementation are essential both to endorsing the vision and distinguishing between its core and its practical implications. Society should determine the relative level of richness and thickness of the components dynamically. Social, ideological, and political forces working within a shared

framework of checks and balances will facilitate the maintenance of a delicate and dynamic balance among them.

- It is nonetheless important to publicly support the core of the vision, and to enforce it when necessary. An independent and strong court, interpreting the law without bowing to the preferences of government, is an essential ingredient in upholding the vision of the state. An ongoing dialogue should take place among interpreters of the vision, so that none of these institutions and agencies may claim a monopoly or a "last word" in making such determinations.

- There is a built-in tension between a broad human rights discourse coupled with an expansive power of judicial review and the ideal of democracy. Protection of human rights is critical to protecting individuals from the state or the majority. Undue expansion of rights, however, may take the decision concerning arrangements suitable for society out of the hands of society itself, and relegate it to an unelected judicial agency. Such a result is of special concern if the court's value judgments are very different from those regarded as central by the majority of the public's elected representatives. The relationship between legislatures and courts in a democracy is a basic constitutional question, including institutional determinations of powers, appointments, and procedures. Answers given to these questions may depend in turn on the social and professional ethos concerning the right way to act. In this matter, too, a minimalistic conception is desirable: democracy is consistent with an entrenched constitution, including a bill of rights and a judicial power to invalidate Knesset laws, but it does not require any of these things. The protection of human rights may be aided by a bill of rights and judicial review, but it can be and has been achieved without them.

A CONSTITUTIONAL ANCHORING OF THE VISION?

Upon the foundation of the state, the founders drafted a powerfully evocative vision, one that reflected a firm Israeli endorsement of the right of Jews to political and cultural independence, combined with a no lesser commitment to democracy and to basic liberties "in the spirit of the prophets of Israel." They decided not to give their Declaration legal force, and later decided to refrain from enacting a full constitution at that stage. In the early years of statehood, the Supreme Court decided not to grant the Declaration a legally binding force.

Two Basic Laws dealing with human rights, (as amended in 1994, hereafter the 1992 laws) mention "the values of Israel as a Jewish and democratic state," and invoke "the principles in the Declaration of the Establishment of the State." They have been described as a "constitutional revolution." In 1995 the Supreme Court in a seminal judgment ruled that the new Basic Laws grant the court the power to invalidate laws inconsistent with them. Moreover, it was held that the passage of the 1992 laws radically changed the status of "old" Basic Laws, so that all of them now became super-laws, overriding regular laws even if they are not entrenched.

Since then the courts have had the power to review and invalidate not only the government's policies (as they always did), but statutes of the Knesset itself. In addition, prolonged trends of the relaxation of the requirements of standing, and of the limits on the doctrine of non-justiciability, as well as expansion of the grounds for review (adding the grounds of reasonableness and proportionality; all these trends together were dubbed "judicial activism"), resulted in a significant broadening of the scope of judicial review over decisions of the government and the Knesset. In addition, many judges used an expansive human rights discourse, and derived human rights such as a right to equality and to family unification from the vague "right to human dignity," despite the fact that the Basic Law explicitly and deliberately excluded these rights from constitutional protection. Laws were reviewed, and some were invalidated, on this controversial basis.

The constitutional revolution triggered attempts to complete the constitutional process by either enacting a full constitution or by completing the enactment of Basic Laws. A number of draft constitutions were proposed, reflecting different ideological and constitutional attitudes, most of them endorsing the basic vision of the state.

The bills that have triggered this essay are, in part, the result of the failure of these attempts to complete the constitutional drive. The draft "Jewish nation-state laws" (those stressing the Jewish character of the state) and the Declaration law (proposing anchoring the Declaration, and incorporating the full vision including democracy and basic liberties) are meant to strengthen the endorsement, within Israel and with a view to the entire world, of the vision of the state, including its Jewish character. The supporters of these laws argue that the legislation will reflect a united stand of the Jewish population behind the integrated vision of the state. It will emphasize Jewish solidarity, and will be a response to the campaign to de-legitimate the state. These are all important goals. In addition, the advocates of the "Jewish nation-state laws" argue that they are important as a response to the fact that the constitutional revolution strengthened the components of democracy and human rights in the vision, thus contributing to the weakening and marginalizing of the component of the Jewish character of the state. Critics of the laws argue that, if the "Jewish character" component is enacted, it will make democracy and human rights secondary to the Jewish character of the state. They argue as well that the laws are designed to alienate the Arab minority and legitimate discrimination against it, and that they will strengthen religious and theocratic forces in the state. The critics argue that the other two components of the vision – democracy and human rights – are the ones that have been eroded and need additional support. Some critics of "Jewish nation-state laws" extend their objections to proposals of "vision laws" (laws to anchor the full vision of the state, including all three components) as well. It seems that these latter objections reflect a reluctance to see even a balanced entrenchment of the full vision, preferring the present open-ended ambiguity. Let me repeat: most Jews, in Israel and abroad, accept the characterization of the state as Jewish and democratic, and are willing to fight for it. Many of them, however, do not support the enactment of such a declaration without what they see as an adequate response to their concerns regarding issues such as the status of the Arab minority, the future of the occupied territories, state and religion matters, and the relations between Israel and the Diaspora.

Political, social, and cultural processes, as well as the 1992 laws, have indeed raised challenges to the vision of the state, including some erosion in the endorsement of the component of its Jewish character. Nonetheless, a constitutional anchoring of the vision is not necessarily an effective way to deal with these challenges. As we have seen from developments until now, the legislative process itself – especially if legislators seek a quick and decisive process built on power balances, rather than a meaningful social process of deliberation and debate among all sectors of the Israeli population and with Jewish communities abroad – will be polarizing and con-flictual. It will increase adversity and will not encourage cohesion and solidarity. Even if the legislation is passed, its contribution to strengthening the vision, especially of the Jewish component, is questionable, whereas the dangers it entails are many and evident.

Arguments against Constitutional Anchoring of the Vision of the State

There are two types of proposed bills before the Knesset. Some of the reasons adduced here apply to all proposals of constitutional anchoring of the whole vision or of just its Jewish component, while others specifically concern laws stressing the Jewish identity of the state (Jewish nation-state laws).

VISION QUESTIONS ARE NOT LEGAL QUESTIONS

Legislation transforms questions that had previously been moral, social, or cultural into legal questions, which may then be debated and decided in courts of law. Law is an important social institution, allowing society to resolve disputes according to general and public laws and norms. At the same time, legalization may direct matters for which it is preferable to seek a dynamic and ongoing social, political, and cultural regulation, without a once-and-for-all clear determination, into the legal and the judicial systems. The danger is especially great for those "big" subjects of social and cultural debates which are eminently unsuitable for a legal determination. The problem is twofold: first, legislation invites a resolution and not the continuation of a conversation. Second, legislation invites judicial determination, based on the interpretation of the law and a human rights discourse, instead of dynamic resolutions based on ongoing negotiations among social, cultural, and political forces.

CONSTITUTIONAL ANCHORING OF VISION SHARPENS DISAGREEMENTS THAT ARE BETTER MITIGATED

Societies in which there are many deep rifts on a number of subjects, and in which various groups seek to pull the vision in contradictory directions, need a space of flexibility that will permit the discussion and regulation of practical issues in ways that will not force individuals and groups to separate themselves from the larger society. Problem-solving often permits differing opinions to converge in identifying the practical challenge and finding acceptable ways of dealing with it. Thus, we do not have to decide whether Judaism is a religion or a nation, or whether Jewish religion is the rules of the *Shulkhan Arukh,* to decide about an adequate arrangement on matters of marriage and divorce or the character of the Sabbath in Israel. Similarly, we do not need a constitutional anchoring of the status of Hebrew and Arabic in Israel in order to continue to seek and maintain a reality in which there is respect for both languages, with Hebrew retaining the dominant position. In many cases, a decent reality is better than a new Basic Law.

ENACTING A VISION MAY REQUIRE A RESOLUTION OF ISSUES THAT SOFT AND VAGUE PRINCIPLES OF VISION LEAVE OPEN

The proposed legislation is all on a high level of generality. At the same time, some of the proposals include resolutions of matters that at the moment are not regulated at the level of a Basic Law. All such resolutions are extremely controversial. The Jewish nation-state laws all emphasize that Israel is the nation-state of the Jewish people. Some interpret the emphasis on Jewish self-determination as a willingness to give up the demand that society and the public sphere in Israel will have cultural Jewish characteristics, religious or national. In the past, this was a reason invoked by religious parties to object to such proposals. (In the meetings we held in preparation for writing these recommendations we did hear such criticism from both ultra-Orthodox and national-ultra-Orthodox. Indeed, some of the leaders of National Orthodoxy think that the erosion in support for Jewish self-determination justifies its endorsement even if this may lead to some weakening of the legal recognition of religious and traditional elements in the public sphere). Similarly, the advocates of the Jewish nation-state laws and the vision laws both claim that they wish to revive the vision of the Declaration. However, the very fact of a new proposed Basic Law, and emphasis on the Jewish component (as in the Jewish nation-state laws) are perceived – whether or not this is their intention – as weakening the commitment to human rights and democracy, especially to the detriment of the Arab minority. Thus, the arrangements proposed with regard to the status of Arabic in Israel generated enormous controversy, despite the fact that the proposals did not seek to change the existing reality.

The same applies to the relations between Israel and Diaspora Jewish communities. The JPPI study revealed that commitment to Israel as "Jewish and democratic" is broad and deep in recognized Jewish communities, uniting people with all attitudes to matters of state and religion and to relations with the Palestinians.[4] This agreement is weakened, and requires more thought and deliberation, when specific arrangements are discussed.

Thus, it seems that the legislative process itself may sharpen disagreements and weaken agreement on the core vision. It is reasonable to assume that these disagreements will not be confined to the social and political systems within Israel, but will provoke debate and responses both in Jewish communities abroad and in the international community.

ENACTING A VISION LAW DEEPENS THE PERCEPTION THAT THE COMPONENTS OF THE VISION CONTRADICT EACH OTHER

Some of the goals of endorsing a vision are to influence public

---

4 "Jewish and Democratic: Perspectives from World Jewry," A Jewish Policy Institute Report (2014), http://jppi.org.il/uploads/jewish_and_democratic-eng.pdf.

discourse, to emphasize the distinction between the vision and its interpretation, and to broaden support for the vision itself while deliberating freely and democratically about disagreements concerning its interpretation. The impact of the legislation of a vision law, and especially a Jewish nation-state law, will, however, be the exact opposite. The process of debating the law before it is passed, and the law itself if passed, no matter what the specific formulation chosen, will be perceived as an intention to change the existing situation, and thus as a threat by those fearing that change may harm them. In other words, the process of legislation, and the law itself, will lead to a structured conflict situation, further sharpening the perception that the components of the vision contradict rather than complement each other. This perception was heightened by the inclusion of the expression "Jewish and democratic" in the 1992 Basic Laws, and by the way in which it was interpreted. This expression also contributed to blurring the distinction between democracy and human rights as components of the vision, and downplayed their complex relations. We should not repeat this mistake.

CONSTITUTIONAL ANCHORING DURING TIMES OF ORDINARY POLITICS AND DEEP DISAGREEMENTS WILL NOT SERVE ITS FUNCTION

The purpose of constitutional anchoring is to strengthen the distinction between the shared framework, which enjoys broad support, and specific arrangements, which may be fiercely contested. This is why it is common to enact entrenched constitutions when the political system is willing and able to act on the distinction between the shared framework and specific arrangements, and to transcend divisive disagreements in order to strengthen the shared vision.

This is not usually the case in Israel, and it is clearly not the case now. What we have in Israel now is only "ordinary politics." The Knesset is deeply divided over matters of security and peace, state and religion, and social policy. A specific challenge to the vision of the state is the debate, in Israel and abroad, concerning the future of the territories occupied in 1967, and concerning the impact of various attitudes to it regarding the ability of the state to maintain the core of its vision. True, these disagreements are all within the vision and not about it. However, their ideological intensity and their political visibility is a reason to be extremely cautious about constitutional anchoring of the vision of the state. In conditions of deep controversy, the process of legislating a vision law, and especially one of the Jewish nation-state law variety, may lead the country to campaign for and against the legislation; and this may be perceived as, and may in fact be, campaigning for and against the vision itself. The legislative process may lead, by its nature, to partisanship concerning the vision. It may weaken both civic cohesion and Jewish solidarity, instead of strengthening them.

A VISION BASIC LAW WILL NOT AFFECT THOSE DENYING THE LEGITIMACY OF THE JEWISH STATE

Supporters of the law are not naïve enough to aspire to directly change the views of those denying the legitimacy of the Jewish state. They want, instead, to bolster the position of those who support it, by expressing a firm and united endorsement of the vision. Indeed, such a firm stand is an important message to the deniers of the legitimacy of the state; it is a response to the need to strengthen Jewish solidarity. However, deeply contested legislation may not express inner strength. It may rather exhibit its opposite. It may well increase divisiveness, and give ammunition to claims made against the legitimacy of the Jewish state by its enemies, this time invoking statements made by Jews struggling against the legislation.

THE VISION OF THE STATE ALREADY HAS A SEMI-CONSTITUTIONAL STATUS

It is simply not accurate that the vision of the state – including the explicit and central affirmation of its being the state in which the Jewish people exercises its right to national self-determination – does not enjoy a special and unique status among the values of the state. True, this core vision is not stated formally and is not expressly anchored in a constitutional enactment. Yet, since the Establishment of the State, the vision filled, and it still fills, a critical role in education, nation-building, legislation, and policy-making. Often, this function has been served by the text of the Declaration. In this sense, the 1992 laws were not a revolution.

A NATION-STATE BASIC LAW WILL NOT "REPAIR" THE IMPACT OF THE "CONSTITUTIONAL REVOLUTION"

A central justification for the need to enact a Jewish nation-state Basic Law stresses the urgent need to "undo" the imbalance in the vision created by the "constitutional revolution." The argument is that, since the 1992 laws, the old balance among components of the vision has been changed, and democracy and human rights have received greater weight. The supporters of legislation want the law to influence decision-makers, especially jurists and judges, to return to the tendency of giving equal weight (or possibly a preference?) to the component of the "Jewish state."

The advocates of the Jewish nation-state law are right in stating that there have been significant changes in the discourse about the vision of the state, based in part on the impact of the inclusion of the expression "Jewish and democratic" in the 1992 laws. This expression indeed strengthened the claim that the two components could not be made compatible. However, the truly serious impact of the 1992 laws is not at the level of public discourse and the endorsement of the vision, but in the power given the courts to review and invalidate Knesset legislation, and in the expansion of the human rights discourse and the grounds for judicial review. These broadened powers permitted and facilitated the transfer of decisions – that up to 1992 were within the almost exclusive power of the political system – to the judicial system.

Arguments against this institutional tendency should be seriously heard and debated. However, the proposed Jewish nation-state Basic Laws do not deal with this issue in any way. They do not seek to change the legal situation concerning the powers of the courts, the status of the attorney general, or the representation of the state in litigation. There is no reason to expect that the law that may be enacted will limit lawyers and courts more than the present legislation. It may in fact have the opposite effect: it is a well-established principle that courts have the power to interpret laws of the Knesset and be their authoritative interpreters. Once the vision of the state becomes a full-fledged law, the power of the courts to interpret this law according to their inclinations and perceptions, as well as the legitimacy for doing so, will in fact increase.

A VISION LAW WILL NOT HELP DEAL WITH EDUCATIONAL, CULTURAL, AND ACADEMIC REALITIES

A state and a society cannot remain indifferent to significant voices which deny the legitimacy of their vision, or a part thereof. Indeed, the broad variety of groups and cultures in Israel does generate a very wide spectrum of attitudes toward the vision of the state, including some that challenge it and deny some of its components. One should not disregard or belittle the fact that claims denying the legitimacy of the right of Jews to self-determination in their homeland are becoming more pervasive and vocal.

It is therefore essential to develop a political culture in which these matters are discussed in an informed way and without sloganeering. It is of great importance to equip members of society, especially younger ones, with the information and resources necessary to deal with claims denying components of the vision of the state. Against the background of a broad consensus, a Basic Law could indeed be an anchor for such educational activity. In the absence of such a consensus, however, the enactment of a Basic Law could lead to the opposite result. Under such circumstances, it is preferable to deal with the challenges in a more focused way. The 1953 Public Education Law, for instance, includes a special section declaring its goals, which articulates a reasonable balance among the components of the vision. It is important to deepen ways of implementing these goals. Similarly, in the system of higher education both the schools themselves and the reviewing agencies have powers which can implement a needed balance between the strict guarantees of academic freedom and the need to make sure that tendencies to invoke that freedom in order to de-legitimate the state and its vision are checked. A Basic Law concerning vision cannot in itself provide a response to problems which are primarily ones of education and the transmitting of values in a society troubled – and which will continue to be troubled – by deep disagreements. More important, such education must in any case take place primarily within cultural and social communities. It cannot rest exclusively on the law or on the force of the state.

A Basic Law Concerning Vision and Completing the Constitution

Some of the advocates of the Jewish nation-state Basic Law claim that its enactment would "remove" the obstacles that have hitherto prevented completion of the constitutional project in Israel. Some of its critics argue that its passage would make such completion redundant. Neither argument is strong. Israel has not enacted a full constitution because of the absence of a political will to do so, based on disagreements concerning both the details of the vision, the basic rules-of-the-game for the state and society, the formulation of a bill of rights, and concerning the very need for, and the desirability of, an entrenched constitution. It is hard to believe that a Basic Law concerning vision, leaving most of these questions open, will significantly affect the completion of the constitutional project. Israeli society does not have at the moment enough agreement concerning a shared political framework within which these basic arrangements can be debated and agreed upon. Most parties prefer a relatively flexible and volatile reality, within which they can make gains through "ordinary politics." This is the reality that makes it hard to agree on either the completion of the constitution or on a credible process of enacting a Basic Law anchoring the vision of the state.

RECOMMENDATIONS CONCERNING CONSTITUTIONAL ANCHORING OF THE VISION OF THE STATE

A complete constitution, and possibly even an agreed-upon shared vision, may indeed help in effecting the distinction between the shared framework and political disagreements. The absence of these things does indeed hinder the ability to work together on the basis of the shared framework while conducting political struggles within it. In Israel such ability is very much present in situations of crisis, and it is understandable and right that people seek ways to make it available more regularly. However, the goal is not always within reach. When the political, social, and cultural reality is not amenable to the achievement of this goal, the decision whether to move on and legislate or act in other ways is complex. My assessment is that it is better to leave the fabric of social life in its ambiguities, and not force debates and disagreements concerning drafts and declarations. Such declarations rarely solve concrete problems, and they often generate hostility and distrust.

Against this background, strengthening the vision of the state, including the emphasis on the importance and centrality of its Jewish character, will be better achieved through other varied and focused activities.

Recommendations if Legislation is Undertaken

I have explained above why I do not support the constitutional anchoring of the vision of the state in general, and especially the enactment of a Jewish nation-state Basic Law which proposes a separate anchoring of the Jewish component in the vision.

Let me clarify: there is no principled reason not to anchor in a constitution the vision of a state. Many states anchor their visions in their constitutions, even when these include particular national, cultural, or social components. The EU endorsed some such constitutions. There are always tensions among components of the visions of states, and such tensions also exist within each of these components. An agreement on a shared vision never means an agreement to all specific arrangements. However, when states choose to anchor their vision, they do so by means of a declaratory preamble to a full constitution, as a part of explicit and deliberate constitutional politics, when the legislation enjoyed broad and cross-partisan support, and after all relevant sectors of the relevant society were invited to participate in the process of deliberation and drafting. Moreover, these vision statements always include strong particular commitments alongside civic, democratic, and universal commitments. This is not the case in Israel today, and this is not true of many of the proposals pending in the Knesset.

If it is decided to seek a separate constitutional anchoring of the vision of the state, it is important to do so in ways that might help it achieve its declared goals:

- Discussions of the proposals should be conducted in a broad framework, as would befit an attempt to enact constitutional provisions. These should not be limited to the coalition or even to the Knesset factions. It should be agreed to seek a formulation that most of the sectors could accept, and that would generate a broad – even if not full – agreement. The issues should also be raised with the leadership of Jewish communities abroad. The process should be designed to garner the highest legitimacy it can have. There should be no strict deadline, indicating that this is a law of great constitutional significance.

- The vision should include the principles that Israel is the state where Jews exercise their right to political self-determination in their homeland; that it is a democracy in which sovereignty is granted to all the citizens of the state without distinction of religion or ethnic origin on the basis of freedom and equality; and that it is committed to respect the human rights of all its residents.

- It is preferable that the formulations be "softer" than is usual in regular laws. This is quite common in preambles (and is also the case in the Declaration of the Establishment of the State). The law itself should clarify that its provisions do not have an independent legal power to generate rights or duties.

- The legislation should **not** be a part of the Basic Laws dealing with human rights, as if they expand on the expression "the values of Israel as a Jewish and democratic state." Similarly, it should not have a limitation clause. The law is not a part of the bill of rights, and it should not include the specific characteristics of such a bill of rights.

- The law should be enacted by means of a special procedure, and be passed at least with the majority required to change it. (This requirement does not at present apply to the legislation of Basic Laws, but a law anchoring the vision of the state is of prime importance, and it should not be vulnerable to claims challenging its legitimacy.)

STRENGTHENING THE VISION IN THE ABSENCE OF A BASIC LAW

Whether or not the vision of the state is constitutionally anchored, the state should seek to make it known and endorsed by the general population. A robust society, enjoying a healthy measure of civic patriotism and communal partnership, is an important ingredient in the success of a state. Identifying suitable ways to strengthen the vision in different social and institutional contexts is no easy matter. The reality in many realms is not optimal. Discussions concerning matters related to the components of the vision become charged, and it is hard to undertake them with judgment and restraint. In addition, a systemic and long-term engagement with these questions is often delayed because attention is directed at urgent crises. After some thought, I have decided not to present here my own ideas about how to strengthen the vision in our society. The right way of doing this is a subject that deserves ongoing thought and implementation in many relevant places. Some general ideas were included above.

The solidarity required for the success of the State of Israel consists of three separate circles: the civic circle, including all citizens; the Israeli Jewish circle; and the circle of all Jews in the world – "the Jewish people." All citizens and only citizens take part in the elections to the Knesset. They are the "civic nation" or the *demos* of the state. Each of them has one equal vote. At the same time, the Zionist Jewish public is the backbone of the state and society. If this group does not act effectively, the state will not be the nation-state of Jews. At the same time, Israel defines itself as the nation-state of the Jewish people; it relies on the Jewish communities abroad, and its activities affect their fate and life. This is why a measure of solidarity within all these circles is needed for the state to flourish. This insight should inspire and legitimate action in all three circles (rather than deal exclusively with any one of them). It also highlights the importance of making sure that whatever is in fact done is sensitive to the need to balance civic and communal solidarity with the plurality of identities and views.

Commitment to society, and to the state that facilitates it, must be grounded in a deep cultural foundation. For Jews, solidarity also means promoting the recognition of the importance and value of the culture to which they belong – alongside other moral and professional commitments. Yet it is also important that all cultural groups in Israel will have a measure of commitment to the state. The structuring of a meaningful shared citizenship requires also the recognition that besides their civic partnership all citizens may have important non-civic affiliations, and that these, too, deserve to be recognized and developed.

Seeking civic and Jewish solidarity, against the background of deep disagreements among the circles of solidarity and within them, is a matter of a social, ideological, and cultural quest. The law has an important task in the guiding and enforcement of the limits of freedom of expression and action, but the challenge is not legal, and the law in itself cannot deliver results.

The vision of the state is transmitted primarily through education, discourse, and socialization, but it must also rely on the convergence of rhetoric, social action, and social reality. This convergence should be exhibited in education, employment, housing, and actions to promote all civic dimensions of life in the state. These social and political activities, too, should be sensitive to the tension between seeking civic solidarity and the wish to maintain distinct and separate communities. They may include various combinations of inclusive civic activities and intra-community activities. This is true not only for the relations between Jews and Arabs, but also for all sub-groups with unique cultural characteristics.

The educational system in Israel provides a special challenge to efforts to increase solidarity, in both the civic and the Israeli-Jewish circle, due to the separation between institutions and "streams" in education. Insisting on teaching the vision of the state, including all its various components, in all parts of the educational system, is of special importance: in some of these parts, what students are taught stands in tension, or even in contradiction, with important (different) components of the vision of the state. In each of these sectors a special effort should be made to strengthen those components of the vision that the schools tend to neglect and challenge. All educational institutions in Israel should act to teach their students the vision of the state and its political and moral justification, and to develop civic, national, and cultural identities in the light of this vision. It is important to remember that education is more effective when it is a part of a rich and cohesive social and cultural system. The state should therefore enlist the help of the religious and cultural leaders of the various groups living in Israel. It is important that these leaders be seen as part of the effort to teach the vision, rather than as its enemies.

The vision of Israel has been the key to its achievements and its success from its inception to this very day. This is a vision which is still relevant and moving. The founders claimed that debates about a constitution would distract them from dealing with urgent practical matters and would generate a war of culture. Their insight is still valid today. Declarations and Basic Laws are not a good way to deal with disagreements. We should promote the vision of the state in other ways, which will help it continue to flourish.

DRAFT BILLS

A.

Proposal presented by Moshe Koppel to the Knesset Constitution, Law, and Justice Committee, July 11, 2004

Basic Law Proposal: The State of Israel as the State of the Jewish People

1. The State of Israel is a Jewish and democratic state and is the state of the Jewish People.

2. a. The State of Israel shall strive for the unity of the Jewish people and the well-being of members of the Jewish people wherever they are located.

   b. The State of Israel will act to preserve and to cultivate the heritage of Israel.

   c. The education system in the State of Israel will give special emphasis to bequeathing Jewish culture.

3. The State of Israel will enable non-Jews in Israel to act to preserve their identity, heritage, and language as they see fit and in accordance with the laws of the state.

4. a. The State of Israel will encourage the ingathering of exiles and Jewish settlement in the land.

   b. Every Jew has the right to immigrate to Israel, unless the interior minister deems that there is a high likelihood that he or she will endanger the health or safety of the public.

   c. Every Jew who immigrates to the land is entitled to Israeli citizenship, in accordance with the law.

   d. This clause does not prevent others from obtaining citizenship in accordance with conditions set by law.

5. a. Hebrew is the official language of the State of Israel.

   b. Arabic will be granted special legal status.

6. a. Designated days of rest in the State of Israel are the Sabbath and the holy days of Israel.

   b. The public character of these days of rest will be regulated by law. Any law legislated on the basis of this article shall not be interpreted or abolished by other Basic Laws.

7. Kashrut will be observed in all public institutions that fulfill a legally mandated function.

B.

Basic Law Proposal: Israel – The Nation-State of the Jewish People (2011, P/18/3541)

The 18th Knesset

Initiators: Members of Knesset

> Avraham Dichter
> Ze'ev Elkin
> David Rotem
> Einat Wilf
> Haim Katz
> Roni Bar-On
> Shaul Mofaz
> Ruhama Avraham-Balila
> Ze'ev Bielsky
> Yoel Hasson
> Gideon Ezra
> Arie Bibi
> Nahman Shay
> Moshe (Motz) Matalon
> Otniel Schneller
> Marina Solodkin
> Uri Orbach
> Zevulun Orlev
> Hamad Amar
> Robert Ilatov
> Eli Aflalo
> Zion Finian
> Julia Shmuelov-Berkovic
> Orli Levi-Abekasis
> Aryeh Eldad
> Ofir Akunis
> Ronit Tirosh
> Carmel Shama

Miri Regev

Anastasia Michaeli

Tzipi Hotovely

Israel Hasson

Shay Hermesh

Yaacov Edri

Meir Sheetrit

Uri Ariel

Yariv Levin

1. Jewish State

a. The State of Israel is the national home of the Jewish people, in which they realize their aspiration to self-determination in accordance with their cultural and historical heritage.

b. The right to exercise national self-determination in the State of Israel is uniquely that of the Jewish people.

c. The provisions of this Basic Law or any other legislation shall be interpreted in light of what is determined in this paragraph.

2. Democratic State

The State of Israel has a democratic regime.

3. State Symbols

a. The state anthem is Hatikvah.

b. The state flag is white with two blue stripes near the edges and a blue Star of David in the center.

c. The state emblem is a seven-branched menorah with olive leaves on both sides and the word "Israel" beneath it.

4. Language

a. Hebrew is the official state language.

b. The Arabic language has a special status, and its speakers have the right to access state services in their native language, as will be determined by the law.

5. Return

Every Jew has the right to immigrate to Israel and acquire citizenship of the State of Israel in accordance with the law.

6. Ingathering of the Exiles and Jewish Settlement

The state shall act to gather the exiles of Israel and to promote Jewish settlement on its territory and it shall allocate resources for these purposes.

7. The Connection to the Jewish People in the Diaspora

a. The state shall act to strengthen the connection between Israel and Jewish communities in the Diaspora.

b. The state shall assist members of the Jewish people in trouble or in captivity because they are Jewish.

8. Jewish Heritage

a. The state shall act to preserve the cultural and historical heritage of the Jewish people and to cultivate it in Israel and the Diaspora.

b. In all educational institutions serving the Jewish public in Israel, the history, heritage, and traditions of the Jewish people shall be taught.

9. The Right to Heritage Preservation

a. All residents of Israel, regardless of religion or nationality, are entitled to work to preserve their culture, heritage, language, and identity.

b. The state may allow a community that includes followers of a single religion or members of a single nation to establish a separate communal settlement.

10. Official Calendar

The Hebrew calendar is the official state calendar.

11. Independence Day and Memorial Days

a. Independence Day is the national holiday of the state.

b. Day of Remembrance for the Fallen Soldiers of Israel and Holocaust and Heroism Remembrance Day are official state memorial days.

12. Days of Rest

Designated days of rest in the State of Israel are the Sabbath and the holy days of Israel, on which no worker shall be employed except under conditions determined by law; members of communities recognized by law are entitled to rest during their holidays.

13. Hebrew Law[1]

a. Hebrew law shall serve as the source of inspiration for lawmakers.

b. Should the court encounter a legal question that demands a ruling and be unable to find an answer through the body of legislation, legal precedent, or clear analogy, it shall decide in light of the principles of freedom, justice, integrity, and peace associated with the heritage of Israel.

14. Protection of Holy Sites

Holy places shall be protected from desecration and all other harm, and from anything that may harm religious followers' free access to their sacred places or their feelings regarding these places.

15. Immutability

This Basic Law shall not be amended, unless by another Basic Law enacted by a majority of Knesset members.

Explanatory Notes

The First Zionist Congress adopted the Basel Program, according to

---

1 [SR: The term used, *mishpat ha-'Ivri,* is also properly translated as Jewish law, but it is important to note that the term used in the law is *not* halakha, which also means Jewish law.]

which the goal of Zionism is "to establish a national home for the Jewish people in the land of Israel"; in the Declaration of Independence it was proclaimed that the new state is a Jewish state and the national home of the Jewish people; in 2001 the Kinneret Covenant was published, signed by public figures across the political spectrum, in which it was established in the first paragraph that "the State of Israel is the national home of the Jewish people." Despite the broad consensus among the Israeli public on the definition of the State of Israel as a Jewish state, the characteristics of the State of Israel as the nation-state of the Jewish people have never been anchored in the Basic Laws of the state. The necessity of the Basic Law: Israel – The Nation-State of the Jewish People is particularly valid at a time when there are those who seek to abolish the right of the Jewish people to a national home in their land and the recognition of the State of Israel as the nation-state of the Jewish people. The anchoring of the Jewish character of the State of Israel in a Basic Law will make it possible to reach a broad agreement on the establishment of a complete and comprehensive constitution in the future.

The first paragraph stipulates that the provisions of state laws shall be interpreted in light of this paragraph. In this context, it is appropriate to cite the former President of the Supreme Court, Justice Aharon Barak: "The values of Israel as a Jewish state possess a constitutional, supra-legal status. They influence the interpretation of all Basic Laws, and thus affect the constitutionality of all statutes. They affect the interpretation of all legal texts, for they should be viewed as part of the fundamental values of the State of Israel, and as such they are also part of the general purpose underlying every legal text in Israel. Thus, for example, it is presumed that every law passed by the Knesset and every order issued by the government are meant to realize the values of the State of Israel as a Jewish state." [Aharon Barak, *Shofet be-khevra demokratit* (Jerusalem: Keter, 2004), 89]

Throughout the law are included practical aspects expressing the nature of the State of Israel as the nation-state of the Jewish people that are partially expressed in existing legislation: symbols of the state (anthem, flag, emblem), its language, the Law of Return, the ingathering of the exiles, Jewish settlement, the connection with the Jewish people in the Diaspora, Jewish heritage, Hebrew calendar, and holy places.

The determination that the State of Israel is a democratic state as well as a Jewish one is secured in paragraph 2 of the present bill and interwoven like a red thread throughout different paragraphs, including those on language, heritage preservation, community settlement, days of rest, and protection of holy places.

Presented to the Speaker and Deputy Speakers of the Knesset and brought before the Knesset on
August 3, 2011 – 3 Av, 5771[2]

---

2 An identical bill was later resubmitted by Aryeh Eldad in the 18th Knesset (P/18/4096) and Ze'ev Elkin in the 19th Knesset (P/19/2502).

C.

Basic Law Proposal: Israel – The Nation-State of the Jewish People (2013, P/19/1550)

The 19th Knesset

Initiators: Members of Knesset

Ayelet Shaked
Yariv Levin
Robert Ilatov

1. Jewish State

a. The State of Israel is the national home of the Jewish people in which they realize their aspiration to self-determination in accordance with their cultural and historical heritage.

b. The right to exercise national self-determination in the State of Israel is uniquely that of the Jewish people.

c. The land of Israel is the historic homeland of the Jewish people and the place where the State of Israel has been established.

2. Purpose

The purpose of this Basic Law is to define the identity of the State of Israel as the nation-state of the Jewish people in order to anchor these values in a Basic Law, in the spirit of the principles in the Declaration of the Establishment of the State of Israel.

3. Democratic State

a. The State of Israel shall have a democratic regime.

b. The State of Israel shall be based on the foundations of freedom, justice, and peace as envisioned by the prophets of Israel, and committed to the individual rights of all its citizens as detailed by all Basic Laws.

4. State Symbols

a. The state anthem is Hatikvah.

b. The state flag is white with two blue stripes near the edges and a blue Star of David at its center.

c. The state symbol is a seven-branched menorah with olive branches on both sides and the word "Israel" beneath it.

5. Return

Every Jew has the right to immigrate to Israel and acquire citizenship of the State of Israel in accordance with the law.

6. Ingathering of the Exiles and Strengthening the Connection with the Jewish People in the Diaspora

The state shall act to gather the exiles of Israel and strengthen the link between Israel and Jewish communities in the Diaspora.

7. Help to Members of the Jewish People in Trouble

The state shall act to provide help to members of the Jewish people in trouble or in captivity because they are Jewish.

8. Jewish Heritage

The state shall act to preserve and instill the cultural and historical heritage and tradition of the Jewish people and to cultivate it in Israel and the Diaspora.

9. The Right to Heritage Preservation

The state shall act to guarantee to all residents of Israel, regardless of religion or nationality, the opportunity to work to preserve their culture, heritage, language, and identity.

10. Official Calendar

The Hebrew calendar is the official state calendar.

11. Independence Day and Memorial Days

a. Independence Day is the national holiday of the state.

b. The Day of Remembrance for Fallen Soldiers of Israel and Holocaust and Heroism Remembrance Day are official state memorial days.

12. Days of Rest

Designated days of rest in the State of Israel are the Sabbath and the holy days of Israel, on which no worker shall be employed except under conditions determined by law; members of communities recognized by law are entitled to rest during their holidays.

13. Hebrew Law

a. Hebrew law shall serve as a source of inspiration for lawmakers and judges in Israel.

b. Should the court encounter a legal question that demands a ruling and be unable to find an answer through the body of legislation, legal precedent, or clear analogy, it shall decide in light of the principles of freedom, justice, integrity, and peace associated with the heritage of Israel.

14. Protection of Holy Places

Holy places shall be protected from desecration and all other harm, and from anything that may harm religious followers' free access to their sacred places or their feelings regarding these places.

15. Violation of Rights

Rights accorded by this Basic Law are not to be infringed upon except through law befitting the values of the State of Israel, designed with proper purpose, and to an extent no greater than required, or according to a law by virtue of explicit authorization stated within it.

16. Immutability

This Basic Law shall not be amended, unless by another Basic Law enacted by a majority of Knesset members.

Explanatory Notes

The First Zionist Congress adopted the Basel Program, according to which the goal of Zionism is "to establish a national home for the Jewish people in the land of Israel"; in the Declaration of Independence it was proclaimed that the new state is a Jewish state and the national home of the Jewish people; in 2001 the Kinneret Covenant was published, signed by public figures across the political spectrum, in which it was established in the first paragraph that "the State of Israel is the national home of the Jewish people." Despite the broad consensus among the Israeli public on the definition of the State of Israel as a Jewish state, the characteristics of the State of Israel as the nation-state of the Jewish people have never been anchored in the Basic Laws of the state.

This bill emphasizes the traditional and historical connection between the Jewish people and the land of Israel and the national rights vested in the Jewish people as expressed in the Declaration of Independence: "The land of Israel was the birthplace of the Jewish people. Here their spiritual, religious, and political identity was shaped... After being forcibly exiled from their land, the people kept faith with it throughout their Dispersion... Impelled by this historic and traditional attachment, Jews strove in every successive generation to re-establish themselves in their ancient homeland... This right was recognized in the Balfour Declaration of the 2nd November, 1917, and reaffirmed in the Mandate of the League of Nations which, in particular, gave international sanction to the historic connection between the Jewish people and the land of Israel and to the right of the Jewish people to rebuild its national home." The justice of the Jewish people's path in the land of Israel is based on political, national, and historical grounds, and the principled rules stemming from the right of the Jewish people to self-determination apply to them. The necessity of the Basic Law: Israel – The Nation-State of the Jewish People is particularly valid at a time when there are those who seek to abolish the right of the Jewish people to a national home in their land and the recognition of the State of Israel as the nation-state of the Jewish people. The anchoring of the Jewish character of the State of Israel in a Basic Law will make it possible to reach a broad agreement on the establishment of a complete and comprehensive constitution in the future.

The law includes throughout practical aspects expressing the nature of the State of Israel as the nation-state of the Jewish people that are partially expressed in the existing legislation: symbols of the state (anthem, flag, emblem), its language, the Law of Return, the ingathering of the exiles, Jewish settlement, the connection with Jewish people in the Diaspora, Jewish heritage, Hebrew calendar, and holy places. According to this law, Hebrew law and the principles of Jewish heritage serve as a source of inspiration for the legislature in establishing the body of legislation and for the court in interpreting it. As determined by the former Deputy President of the Supreme Court, Justice Menachem Elon (in Hendels v. Bank Kupat Am [Rehearing of Civil Appeal 13/80], vol. 35, section 2, p. 795): "Appealing to the system of Hebrew law [*mishpat ha-'Ivri*] as the first and foremost source of inspiration for the interpretation of Israeli law, when this appeal is made with care and necessary precautions, in accordance with the present needs and the concern of the law, will provide Israeli law with historical roots of its own and develop a synthesis between the system of Hebrew law and the legal system of the Jewish state."

The determination that the State of Israel is a democratic state as well as a Jewish one is secured in paragraph 3 of the present bill and interwoven like a red thread throughout different paragraphs, including those on language, heritage preservation, community settlement, days of rest, and protection of holy places.

Proposed laws similar in essence were tabled during the 18th Knesset by Members of Knesset Avraham Dichter and a group of other members of Knesset (P/18/3541) and by Member of Knesset Aryeh Eldad.

Submitted to the Speaker and Deputy Speakers of the Knesset and brought before the Knesset on
July 22, 2013 – 15 Av, 5773[1]

---

1 An identical bill was later resubmitted by Miri Regev (P/19/2530).

D.

Basic Law Proposal: The Declaration of Independence and the Jewish and Democratic State (2013, P/19/1539)

The 19th Knesset

Initiators: Members of Knesset

Ruth Calderon
Amram Mitzna
Rina Frenkel
Shimon Solomon
Elazar Stern
Ronen Hoffman
David Tzur
Boaz Toporovsky
Binyamin Ben-Eliezer

1. Purpose

This Basic Law aims to secure and protect the values of the State of Israel as a Jewish and democratic state by giving the force of law to the basic principles stated in the Declaration of Independence, which is annexed verbatim to this law.

2. Stability

Emergency stipulations shall not be able to alter this Basic Law or temporarily annul its validity or add any provisions to it.

3. Immutability

This Basic Law shall not be amended, unless by another Basic Law enacted by a majority of Knesset members.

APPENDIX

(Clause no. 1)

The Declaration of the Establishment of the State of Israel[1]

The land of Israel was the birthplace of the Jewish people. Here their spiritual, religious, and political identity was shaped. Here they first attained to statehood, created cultural values of national and universal significance, and gave to the world the eternal Book of Books.

After being forcibly exiled from their land, the people kept faith with it throughout their Dispersion and never ceased to pray and hope for their return to it and for the restoration in it of their political freedom.

Impelled by this historic and traditional attachment, Jews strove in every successive generation to re-establish themselves in their ancient homeland. In recent decades they returned in their masses. Pioneers, defiant returnees, and defenders, they made deserts bloom, revived the Hebrew language, built villages and towns, and created a thriving community controlling its own economy and culture, loving peace but knowing how to defend itself, bringing the blessings of progress to all the country's inhabitants, and aspiring towards independent nationhood.

In the year 5657 (1897), at the summons of the spiritual father of the Jewish state, Theodor Herzl, the First Zionist Congress convened and proclaimed the right of the Jewish people to national rebirth in its own country.

This right was recognized in the Balfour Declaration of the 2nd November, 1917, and re-affirmed in the Mandate of the League of Nations which, in particular, gave international sanction to the historic connection between the Jewish people and the land of Israel and to the right of the Jewish people to rebuild its national home.

The catastrophe which recently befell the Jewish people – the massacre of millions of Jews in Europe – was another clear demonstration of the urgency of solving the problem of its homelessness by re-establishing in the land of Israel the Jewish state, which would open the gates of the homeland wide to every Jew and confer upon the Jewish people the status of a fully privileged member of the community of nations.

---

1 [SR: Translation, with minor modifications for consistency, from the Knesset website: http://www.knesset.gov.il/docs/eng/megilat_eng.htm.]

Survivors of the Nazi holocaust in Europe, as well as Jews from other parts of the world, continued to migrate to the land of Israel, undaunted by difficulties, restrictions, and dangers, and never ceased to assert their right to a life of dignity, freedom, and honest toil in their national homeland.

In the Second World War, the Jewish community of this country contributed its full share to the struggle of the freedom- and peace-loving nations against the forces of Nazi wickedness and, by the blood of its soldiers and its war effort, gained the right to be reckoned among the peoples who founded the United Nations.

On the 29th November, 1947, the United Nations General Assembly passed a resolution calling for the establishment of a Jewish state in the land of Israel; the General Assembly required the inhabitants of the land of Israel to take such steps as were necessary on their part for the implementation of that resolution. This recognition by the United Nations of the right of the Jewish people to establish their state is irrevocable.

This right is the natural right of the Jewish people to be masters of their own fate, like all other nations, in their own sovereign state.

Accordingly, we, members of the People's Council, representatives of the Jewish community of the land of Israel and of the Zionist movement, are here assembled on the day of the termination of the British Mandate over the land of Israel and, by virtue of our natural and historic right and on the strength of the resolution of the United Nations General Assembly, hereby declare the establishment of a Jewish state in the land of Israel, to be known as the State of Israel.

We declare that, with effect from the moment of the termination of the Mandate being tonight, the eve of Sabbath, the 6th Iyar, 5708 (15th May, 1948), until the establishment of the elected, regular authorities of the state in accordance with the constitution which shall be adopted by the elected Constituent Assembly not later than the 1st October 1948, the People's Council shall act as a Provisional Council of State, and its executive organ, the People's Administration, shall be the Provisional Government of the Jewish state, to be called "Israel."

The State of Israel will be open for Jewish immigration and for the ingathering of the exiles; it will foster the development of the country for the benefit of all its inhabitants; it will be based on freedom, justice, and peace as envisaged by the prophets of Israel; it will ensure complete equality of social and political rights to all its inhabitants irrespective of religion, race, or sex; it will guarantee freedom of religion, conscience, language, education, and culture; it will safeguard the holy places of all religions; and it will be faithful to the principles of the Charter of the United Nations.

The State of Israel is prepared to cooperate with the agencies and representatives of the United Nations in implementing the resolution of the General Assembly of the 29th November, 1947, and will take steps to bring about the economic union of the whole of the land Israel.

We appeal to the United Nations to assist the Jewish people in the building-up of its state and to receive the State of Israel into the community of nations.

We appeal – in the very midst of the onslaught launched against us now for months – to the Arab inhabitants of the State of Israel to preserve peace and participate in the building-up of the state on the basis of full and equal citizenship and due representation in all its provisional and permanent institutions.

We extend our hand to all neighboring states and their peoples in an offer of peace and good neighborliness, and appeal to them to establish bonds of cooperation and mutual help with the sovereign Jewish people settled in its own land. The State of Israel is prepared to do its share in a common effort for the advancement of the entire Middle East.

We appeal to the Jewish people throughout the Diaspora to rally round the Jews of the land of Israel in the tasks of immigration and upbuilding and to stand by them in the great struggle for the realization of the age-old dream – the redemption of Israel.

Placing our trust in the Rock of Israel,[2] we affix our signatures to this proclamation at this session of the Provisional Council of State, on the soil of the homeland, in the city of Tel Aviv, on this Sabbath eve, the 5th day of Iyar, 5708 (14th May, 1948).

---

2 [SR: The Knesset translates "*tsur Yisrael*" as "the Almighty."]

Explanatory Notes

The Declaration of Independence is a renowned document which anchors the most basic and important fundamental principles regarding the State of Israel's identity. As a result, the court of law has been turning to this document for decades when ruling on a variety of issues. This Basic Law offers to anchor the Declaration of Independence, which expresses Israel's credo and the fundamental principles at its base, by giving it the force of a Basic Law. Anchoring the Declaration of Independence is necessary in order to secure and protect the values of the State of Israel as a Jewish and democratic state.

Since the State of Israel does not yet have a constitution, the Basic Laws are those that define its character and identity, and hence are the highest-ranked legal statutes. Today, laws are interpreted by the courts in light of the few already existing Basic Laws. That said, a Basic Law dealing with the state's identity has not been enacted to date. Therefore, there is a genuine need to enact a Basic Law which shall ratify the Declaration of Independence and shall provide this fundamental document with the force of a Basic Law.

This Basic Law, like those previously enacted, determines that the State of Israel is the homeland of the Jewish people. It is important to emphasize that the notion of a Jewish state does not refer to Judaism as a religion, but rather to the cultural character of the nation-state as the home of the Jewish people. That said, the State of Israel is committed to ensuring complete equality of social and political rights to all its inhabitants irrespective of religion, race, or gender. Within the Declaration itself, there is an inherent expression of the will and intention to establish a country that has a Jewish character on the one hand and is committed to equality on the other. This Basic Law aims to secure equal rights as well as Israel's democratic character.

Presented to the Speaker and Deputy Speakers of the Knesset and brought before the Knesset on

July 22, 2013 – 15 Av, 5773

E.

November 23, 2014: Announcement of the Cabinet Secretary at the End of the Cabinet Meeting

Today the Cabinet discussed the drafts for the Basic Law: Israel – The Nation-State of the Jewish People that had been submitted by Member of Knesset Ze'ev Elkin (P/19/2502 [which is the same as P/18/3541]) and Members of Knesset Ayelet Shaked, Yariv Levin, and Robert Ilatov (P/19/1550), and decided as follows:

To support the principles outlined by the prime minister as detailed in the resolution's appendix.

To support in the initial reading and in the framework of a preliminary discussion by the full Knesset the drafts of the Basic Law: Israel – The Nation-State of the Jewish People submitted by Member of Knesset Ze'ev Elkin (P/19/2502) and Members of Knesset Ayelet Shaked, Yariv Levin, and Robert Ilatov (P/19/1550). This is on condition that the proponents will agree that to all bills will be attached the government bill on the subject submitted by the prime minister, which shall be worded on the basis of the principles detailed in the appendix to this resolution and coordinated with it. The government bill will be prepared in coordination with the Attorney General.

APPENDIX

1. Purpose

To define the identity of the State of Israel as the nation-state of the Jewish people and to anchor the values of the State of Israel as a Jewish and democratic state, in the spirit of the principles in the Declaration of the Establishment of the State of Israel.

2. Fundamental Principles

a. The land of Israel is the historic homeland of the Jewish people and the place where the State of Israel has been established.

b. The State of Israel is the national home of the Jewish people in which they realize their right to self-determination in accordance with their cultural and historical heritage.

c. The right to exercise national self-determination in the State of Israel is uniquely that of the Jewish people.

d. The State of Israel is a democratic state, based on the foundations of freedom, justice, and peace as envisioned by the prophets of Israel, and it upholds the individual rights of all its citizens according to any law.

3. State Symbols

a. The state anthem is Hatikvah.

b. The state flag is white with two blue stripes near the edges and a blue Star of David in the center.

c. The state emblem is a seven-branched menorah with olive leaves on both sides and the word "Israel" beneath it.

4. Return

Every Jew has the right to immigrate to Israel and acquire citizenship of the State of Israel in accordance with the law.

5. Ingathering of the Exiles and Strengthening the Connection with the Jewish People in the Diaspora

The state shall act to gather the exiles and strengthen the link between Israel and Jewish communities in the Diaspora.

6. Help to Members of the Jewish People in Trouble

The state shall act to provide help to members of the Jewish people in trouble or in captivity because they are Jewish.

7. Heritage

a. The state shall act to preserve the cultural and historical heritage and tradition of the Jewish people, and to instill and cultivate it in Israel and the Diaspora.

b. In all educational institutions serving the Jewish public in Israel, the history, heritage, and traditions of the Jewish people shall be taught.

c. The state shall act to guarantee to all its residents, regardless of religion, race, or nationality, the opportunity to work to preserve their culture, heritage, language, and identity.

8. Official Calendar

The Hebrew calendar is the official state calendar.

9. Independence Day and Memorial Days

a. Independence Day is the national holiday of the State.

b. Day of Remembrance for the Fallen Soldiers of Israel and Holocaust and Heroism Remembrance Day are official state memorial days.

10. Days of Rest

Designated days of rest in the State of Israel are the Sabbath and the holy days of Israel, on which no worker shall be employed except under conditions determined by law; members of communities recognized by law are entitled to rest on their Sabbath and holidays.

11. Hebrew Law

a. Hebrew law shall serve as the source of inspiration for the Knesset.

b. Should the court encounter a legal question that demands a ruling and be unable to find an answer through the body of legislation, legal precedent, or clear analogy, it shall be decided in light of the principles of freedom, justice, integrity, and peace associated with the heritage of Israel.

12. Protection of Holy Places

Holy places shall be protected from desecration and all other harm, and from anything that may harm religious followers' free access to their sacred places or their feelings regarding these places.

13. Violation of Rights

Rights accorded by this Basic Law are not to be infringed upon except through law befitting the values of the State of Israel that is designed with proper purpose and to an extent no greater than required, or according to a law by virtue of explicit authorization stated within it.

14. Immutability

This Basic Law shall not be amended, unless by another Basic Law enacted by a majority of Knesset members.

General Background

In the 19th Knesset, two private bills on the subject of the Basic Law: Israel – The Nation-State of the Jewish People were submitted on behalf of Member of Knesset Ze'ev Elkin (P/19/2502) and Members of Knesset Ayelet Shaked, Yariv Levin, and Robert Ilatov (P/19/1550).

On June 8, 2014, decision no. HK 930 was passed by the Ministerial Committee for Legislation regarding the bill submitted on behalf of Members of Knesset Shaked, Levin, and Ilatov (P/19/1550), according to which it was decided to record the announcement by the minister of justice that, based on the idea of the prime minister, a committee chaired and attended by representatives of all factions comprising the coalition will be established in order to examine the bill and additional legislative proposals on this subject (the decision received the status of a government resolution on June 26, 2014, no. HK 1761/930). This committee did not submit a draft of a bill on the subject.

On November 16, 2014, the bill submitted by Member of Knesset Elkin (P/19/2502) was put on the agenda of the Ministerial Committee for Legislation. In accordance with her authority as the chairwoman of the Ministerial Committee for Legislation, the minister of justice decided to postpone the debate on the bill.

According to the present resolution, the government will support in the initial reading and in the framework of a preliminary discussion by the full Knesset the drafts of the Basic Law: Israel – The Nation-State of the Jewish People submitted by Member of Knesset

Ze'ev Elkin (P/19/2502) and Members of Knesset Ayelet Shaked, Yariv Levin, and Robert Ilatov (P/19/1550). This is on condition that the proponents will agree that to all bills will be attached the government bill submitted by the prime minister on the subject, which shall be worded on the basis of the principles detailed in the appendix to this resolution and coordinated with it. The government bill will be prepared in coordination with the Attorney General.

November 19, 2014 – 26 Heshvan, 5775

F.

Basic Law Proposal: The State of Israel (2014, P/19/2883)

The 19th Knesset

Initiators: Members of Knesset

> Elazar Stern
> Meir Sheetrit
> Amram Mitzna
> David Tzur
> Amir Peretz

1. The Essence of the State of Israel

a. The State of Israel is a Jewish and democratic state.

b. Israel is the nation-state of the Jewish people in which they realize their right to self-determination; a democracy founded on the principles of freedom, justice, and peace and providing equality to all its citizens, all as stated in the Declaration of the Establishment of the State.

2. Return

Every Jew has the right to immigrate to Israel.

3. Symbols of the State of Israel

The anthem, the flag, and the emblem of the State of Israel are as detailed in the State Flag, Emblem, and Anthem Law, 1949.

4. Immutability

This Law cannot be changed but by the majority of Knesset Members.

Explanatory Notes

The purpose of this law is to anchor in an immutable Basic Law the very essence of the State of Israel and its principal symbols in a way that strikes a balance between its being the Jewish nation-state and a democratic state. The definition of the essence of the State of Israel in the first paragraph of this law relies on "The Declaration of the Establishment of the State of Israel" (May 14, 1948), known as "The Declaration of Independence," in which the Establishment of the State of Israel was proclaimed and it was determined, inter alia, that:

> The State of Israel will be open for Jewish immigration and for the ingathering of the exiles; it will foster the development of the country for the benefit of all its inhabitants; it will be based on freedom, justice and peace as envisaged by the prophets of Israel; it will ensure complete equality of social and political rights to all its inhabitants irrespective of religion, race, or sex; it will guarantee freedom of religion, conscience, language, education, and culture; it will safeguard the holy places of all religions; and it will be faithful to the principles of the Charter of the United Nations.

Presented to the Speaker and Deputy Speakers of the Knesset and brought before the Knesset on
November 24, 2014 – 2 Kislev, 5775

G.

Basic Law Proposal: The State of Israel (2015, P/20/1587)

The 20th Knesset

Initiator: Member of Knesset

Ze'ev Binyamin Begin

1. Essence of the State

Israel is the nation-state of the Jewish people, based on the foundations of freedom, justice, and peace as envisioned by the prophets of Israel, and upholding equal rights for all its citizens.

2. Government of the State of Israel

The State of Israel is a democracy.

3. Symbols of the State of Israel

a. The state flag is white with blue stripes near the edges and a blue Star of David in the center.

b. The state symbol is a seven-branched menorah with olive leaves on both sides and the word "Israel" beneath it.

c. The state anthem is Hatikvah.

4. Immutability

This law shall not be amended, except by the passage of a Basic Law by a majority of eighty Knesset members.

Explanatory Notes

The purpose of the draft Basic Law is to enshrine in a Basic Law the permanence of the very essence of the State of Israel and its main symbols. The first article in this law defining the nature of the State of Israel is based on the Declaration of the Establishment of the

State of Israel, in light of Ordinance 1, known as the Independence Scroll, which states, inter alia:

> The State of Israel will be open for Jewish immigration and for the ingathering of the exiles; it will foster the development of the country for the benefit of all its inhabitants; it will be based on freedom, justice, and peace as envisioned by the prophets of Israel; it will ensure complete equality of social and political rights to all its inhabitants irrespective of religion, race, or sex; it will guarantee freedom of religion, conscience, language, education, and culture; it will safeguard the holy places of all religions; and it will be faithful to the principles of the Charter of the United Nations.

A principally similar bill was tabled in the 19th Knesset by Member of Knesset Elazar Stern and a group of Knesset members (P/19/2883). A principally similar bill was tabled in the 19th Knesset by Member of Knesset Ruth Calderon (P/19/2907) [P/19/1539].

Presented to the Speaker and Deputy Speakers of the Knesset and brought before the Knesset on
June 29, 2015 – 12 Tammuz, 5775

H.

Basic Law Proposal: Israel – The Nation-State of the Jewish People
(2015, P/20/1989)

The 20th Knesset

Initiators: Members of Knesset

Avraham Dichter
Avraham Neguise
Tali Ploskov
Mordhay Yogev
Yinon Magal
Yoav Kisch
Nava Boker
Bezalel Smotrich
Orly Levi-Abekasis
Robert Ilatov
Hamad Amar
David Amsalem
David Bitan
Eli Cohen

1. Basic Principles

a. The State of Israel is the national home of the Jewish people, in which they realize their aspiration to self-determination in accordance with their cultural and historical heritage.

b. The right to exercise national self-determination in the State of Israel is uniquely that of the Jewish people.

c. The provisions of this Basic Law or any other legislation shall be interpreted in light of what is determined in this paragraph.

2. Purpose

The purpose of this Basic Law is to protect Israel's status as the nation-state of the Jewish people, in order to anchor in a Basic Law the State of Israel's values as a Jewish and democratic state in the spirit of the principles in the Declaration of the Establishment of the State of Israel.

3. Anthem, Flag, and Symbol

a. The state anthem is Hatikvah.

b. The state flag is white with two blue stripes near the edges and a blue Star of David in the center.

c. The state emblem is a seven-branched menorah with olive leaves on both sides and the word "Israel" beneath it.

4. The Capital of the State

Jerusalem is the capital of the state.

5. Language

a. Hebrew is the state language.

b. The Arabic language has a special status in the state, and its speakers have the right to access state services in their native language, as will be determined by the law.

6. Return

Every Jew has the right to immigrate to Israel and acquire citizenship of the State of Israel in accordance with the law.

7. Ingathering of the Exiles

The state shall act to gather the exiles of Israel.

8. The Connection to the Jewish People in the Diaspora

a. The state shall act to strengthen the connection between Israel and Diaspora Jewry.

b. The state will act to preserve the cultural and historical heritage of the Jewish people among Diaspora Jewry.

c. The state shall assist members of the Jewish people in trouble or in captivity because they are Jewish.

9. Heritage Preservation

a. All residents of Israel, regardless of religion or nationality, are entitled to work to preserve their culture, heritage, language, and identity.

b. The state may allow a community that includes followers of a single religion or members of a single nation to establish a separate communal settlement.

10. Official Calendar

The Hebrew calendar is the official state calendar.

11. Independence Day and Memorial Days

a. Independence Day is the national holiday of the State.

b. Day of Remembrance for the Fallen Soldiers of Israel and Holocaust and Heroism Remembrance Day are official state memorial days.

12. Days of Rest

Designated days of rest in the State of Israel are the Sabbath and the holy days of Israel, on which no worker shall be employed except under conditions determined by law; members of communities recognized by law are entitled to rest during their holidays.

13. Hebrew Law

Should the court encounter a legal question that demands a ruling and be unable to find an answer through the body of legislation, legal precedent, or clear analogy, it shall decide in light of the principles of freedom, justice, integrity, and peace associated with the heritage of Israel.

14. Protection of Holy Sites

Holy places shall be protected from desecration and all other harm, and from anything that may harm religious followers' free access to their sacred places or their feelings regarding these places.

15. Immutability

This Basic Law shall not be amended, unless by another Basic Law enacted by a majority of Knesset members.

Explanatory Notes

The purpose of this Basic Law is to protect in basic legislation Israel's status as the nation-state of the Jewish people in equal status to Israel's Basic Laws protecting human rights and the democratic character of the state. This will complement the characteristic combination of values in Israel's Basic Laws in the way of Israel as a Jewish and democratic state in the spirit of the Declaration of Independence.

The State of Israel is a democratic state committed to human and civil rights. At the same time, the State of Israel has a unique mission as the nation-state of the Jewish people. The President of the Supreme Court, Shimon Agranat, expressed this well in the following remarks: "There can be no doubt about it – and so things would be clear it was declared at the time of the Declaration of the Establishment of the State – that not only is Israel a sovereign independent state, desiring freedom and characterized by a regime of popular rule, it was also established as "a Jewish state in the land if Israel," that the act of its establishment was done first and foremost by virtue of "the natural and historic right of the Jewish people to live like all nations as a nation standing as an independent nation in its own sovereign state, and in this act realized the aspiration of generations for the redemption of Israel… [This is] a basic constitutional premise which no state authority should subvert in its actions… Acting in such a way would completely contradict the history and aspirations of the Jewish people" (H.C. 1/65, Yaakov Yeridor v. Chairman of the Central Elections Committee to the 6th Knesset, 19[3] [1965], 365, 385). Since these remarks were made, the Knesset has anchored the protection of human rights and Israeli democracy in Basic Laws. Therefore, however, it is necessary that the undertaking of Basic Laws in Israel also anchor in its values, with the same status, that Israel is the nation-state of the Jewish people.

This Basic Law will also anchor Israel's deep moral commitment to Diaspora Jewry. Israel sees itself as a nation-state intended for all the Jews of the world who wish to immigrate and is committed to all the Jews of the world wherever they may be. In the previous generation, we sometimes heard complaints that this link was weakening. There is evidence showing a decline in the sense of connection between Israel and Diaspora Jewry, both among Israelis and among young Jews of the Diaspora. This Basic Law anchors the Zionist foundations of Israel as a state for all of the Jewish people, will renew the historic covenant among all of the world's Jews, will strengthen Diaspora Jews' connection to Israel and the connection of Israelis to Diaspora Jewry.

Beyond the legal aspect described, the necessity of the Basic Law: Israel – The Nation-State of the Jewish People, is particularly valid at a time when there are those who seek to abolish the right of the Jewish people to a national home in their land and the recognition of the State of Israel as the nation-state of the Jewish people. The State of Israel, which demands its opponents recognize it as the state of the Jewish people, and asks its supporters in the world to back this demand, should be able to declare in its highest legislative norm that she herself proudly carries this identity. Such a Basic Law will also have a great educational influence within the state.

The first article anchors in the Basic Law Israel's sole status as the nation-state of the Jewish people. This article further provides that the Israeli rule of law must be interpreted in light of this principle, just as the court has already determined that the Israeli rule of law must be interpreted in light of the principles of human rights set out in the Basic Law: Human Dignity and Liberty. (H.C. [Additional Criminal Hearing] 2316/95, Amiad Ghanimat v. The State of Israel, 49[4] [1995], 589). This article therefore does not intend to accord priority to this Basic Law in opposition to the Basic Laws dealing with human rights, but rather to ensure an equal status between this

Basic Law and those Basic Laws. This Basic Law specifies practical aspects expressing the nature of the State of Israel as the nation-state of the Jewish people that are partially expressed in existing legislation: Symbols of the State (anthem, flag, emblem), Jerusalem as its capital, its language, the Law of Return, the ingathering of the exiles, Jewish settlement, the connection with the Jewish people in the Diaspora, Hebrew calendar, and holy places.

A proposed law on a similar subject was tabled in the 19th Knesset by Member of Knesset Ayelet Shaked and a group of members of Knesset (P/19/1550) and by Member of Knesset Miri Regev (P/19/2530) and tabled in the 20th Knesset by Member of Knesset Sharon Gal and a group of members of Knesset (P/20/1320).

Bills similar in essence were tabled in the 18th Knesset by Member of Knesset Ze'ev Elkin and a group of members of Knesset (P/18/3541) and by Member of Knesset Aryeh Eldad (P/18/4096) and tabled in the 19th Knesset by Member of Knesset Ze'ev Elkin (P/19/2502).

Presented to the Speaker and Deputy Speakers of the Knesset and brought before the Knesset on
July 29, 2015 – 13 Av, 5772

I.

A bill by Knesset members on behalf of a joint-committee of the Knesset Constitutional Committee and the Knesset Committee on Law and Order, for discussion of the proposed Basic Law: Israel – The Nation-State of the Jewish People:

Basic Law Proposal: Israel – The Nation-State of the Jewish People (2018, P/20/1989)[1]

The 20th Knesset

Initiators: Members of Knesset

> Avraham Dichter
> Avraham Neguise
> Tali Ploskov
> Mordhay Yogev
> Yinon Magal
> Yoav Kisch
> Nava Boker
> Bezalel Smotrich
> Orly Levi-Abekasis
> Robert Ilatov
> David Amsalem
> David Bitan

1. Basic Principles

a. The land of Israel is the historic homeland of the Jewish people, in which the State of Israel was established.

b. The State of Israel is the nation-state of the Jewish people, in which it exercises its natural, cultural, and historical right to self-determination.

---

1 [SR: Passed first reading in the Knesset at 3:45 AM, May 1, 2018, by 64 votes to 50, but required second and third readings (which were deferred) in order to become law.]

c. The right to exercise national self-determination in the State of Israel is uniquely that of the Jewish people.

2. State Symbols

a. The name of the state is "Israel."

b. The state flag is white with two blue stripes near the edges and a blue Star of David in the center.

c. The state emblem is a seven-branched menorah with olive leaves on both sides and the word "Israel" beneath it.

d. The national anthem is Hatikvah.

e. Details regarding state symbols will be determined by law.

3. Capital of the State

Jerusalem, complete and united, is the capital of Israel.

4. Language

a. Hebrew is the state language.

b. The Arabic language has a special status in the state, and its speakers have the right to access state services in their native language; details regarding this will be determined by law.

c. Nothing in this section shall prejudice the status of the Arabic language as practiced before this Basic Law's enactment.

5. Ingathering of the Exiles

The state will be open to Jewish immigration and to the ingathering of the exiles.

6. The Connection to the Jewish People

a. The state shall work to ensure the safety of the Jewish people and of its citizens who are in trouble and in captivity because they are Jewish or due to their citizenship.

b. The state shall act to preserve the bond between the state and the Jewish people wherever they may be.

c. The state shall act to preserve the cultural, historical, and religious heritage of the Jewish people among the Jews of the Diaspora.

7. Heritage Preservation

a. Every resident of Israel, regardless of religion or nationality, is entitled to work to preserve their culture, heritage, language, and identity.

b. The state may allow a community composed of members of one religion or one nationality to maintain a separate residential community.

8. Official Calendar

The Hebrew calendar is the official state calendar, and beside it the foreign calendar will be used as an official calendar; the use of the Hebrew calendar and the foreign calendar will be determined by law.[2]

9. Independence Day and Memorial Days

a. Independence Day is the national holiday of the state.

b. Day of Remembrance for Fallen Soldiers of Israel and Holocaust Heroism and Remembrance Day are official state memorial days.

10. Days of Rest and Sabbath

Sabbath and the holy days of Israel are the regular days of rest in the state; those who are not Jewish have the right to observe days of rest on their Sabbath and holidays; details of this matter shall be determined by law.

11. Foundations of the Law

Should the court encounter a legal question that demands a ruling and be unable to find an answer through the body of legislation,

---

2 [SR: The mention of the use of the "foreign calendar" as an "official calendar" alongside the Hebrew one did not appear in earlier proposals.]

explicit judicial precedent, or by analogy, it shall be decided in light of the principles of freedom, justice, integrity, and peace associated with the heritage of Israel.

12. Immutability

This Basic Law shall not be amended, unless by another Basic Law enacted by a majority of Knesset members.

Explanatory Notes

The purpose of this proposed Basic Law is to anchor in basic legislation the State of Israel's identity as the nation-state of the Jewish people, and to add to the constitutional system a series of provisions which deal with the fundamental characteristics of the state, as a Jewish state. The proposed Basic Law will add to the existing Basic Laws anchoring additional characteristics of the State of Israel as a Jewish and democratic state in the spirit of the principles of the Declaration of the Establishment of the State of Israel.

Section 1. It is proposed to anchor the fundamental principles regarding the State of Israel being the nation-state of the Jewish people. It is proposed to determine that the land of Israel is the historical homeland of t3he Jewish people, in which the State of Israel was established, in which it exercises its right to self-determination in a nation-state, and in which the realization of the right to national self-determination in the State of Israel is uniquely that of the Jewish people.

Section 2. It is proposed to establish in the Basic Law the symbols of the state: the state name, the state flag, the state symbol, and the state anthem. Today these symbols are anchored in the 1949 Law on the Flag, Symbol, and Anthem of the State (hereafter, Flag Law). In particular the flag and symbol are not fixed in the Flag Law, but they are defined by way of reference to the declarations of the Provisional Council of State. The name of the state is also defined by way of reference to a Council declaration of the nation, and the wording of the national anthem appears in the appendix to the Flag Law. It is proposed to specify the content of the symbols to anchor in a Basic

Law a brief description of them and to designate that the remaining details be determined by law.

Section 3. In light of the special historical importance of Jerusalem to the Jewish people, it is proposed to anchor in a second Basic Law Section 1 from the Basic Law: Jerusalem is the Capital of Israel.

Section 4. It is proposed to anchor the status of the Hebrew language and the Arabic language in the State. Point 82 of the King's Council on Palestine, from 1922 to 1947, determines the current wording that Hebrew and Arabic are official state languages, however in practice, Hebrew is granted preferential status both in legislation and in case law. Therefore it is proposed to establish that Hebrew is the state language, thereby expressing the centrality of the language in the character of the state as the nation-state of the Jewish people and the importance attributed to the revival of spoken Hebrew from the beginning of the Zionist movement. Alongside this determination, it is proposed to anchor in the Basic Law the special status granted in the state to the Arabic language, and to emphasize that nothing in the Basic Law harms the status granted in practice to the Arabic language today. It is also proposed to grant speakers of the Arabic language the right to access state services [in Arabic], which is not anchored in an independent right in existing legislation.

Section 5. It is proposed to anchor declaratively in the Basic Law the state's commitment as the nation-state of the Jewish people to Jewish immigration and the ingathering of the exiles, as it is mentioned in the Declaration of the Establishment of the State. This basic principle comes first and foremost from that expressed in the Law of Return, 1950 (which establishes who is eligible to return), as well as Section 2 of the Law on Citizenship, 1952 (which establishes citizenship for all who immigrate under the Law of Return).

Section 6. It is proposed to anchor in the Basic Law the special connection between the state and the Jewish people throughout the world, and the state's obligation to ensure the safety of Jewish people who are in trouble because they are Jewish, as it is obligated to ensure the safety of the state's citizens who are in trouble because of their citizenship. It is also proposed to anchor the state's commitment to preserve the state's bond to the Jewish people everywhere in the world, and to preserve the cultural, historical, and religious heritage of the Jewish people. It is proposed as such to give expression to a central aspect of the state's Jewish character – to be the national home for all of the world's Jewish people, and not only of the Jews living in it.

Section 7. Subsection "a" proposes to legislate for the first time to grant to all of the state's residents the right to act to preserve their culture, their heritage, their language and their identity.

Subsection "b" proposes to authorize the state to allow a community, the majority of whose members are from a single religion or from a single nationality, to maintain a separate residential community. Such authorization does not exist in legislation today. When preparing the proposed law the second reading and the third reading will reexamine this provision for inclusion in the Basic Law.

Section 8. It is proposed to anchor the status of the Hebrew calendar as the official state calendar, as it is one of the expressions of the Jewish people's cultural uniqueness and historical heritage. It is also proposed that the foreign calendar be used alongside the Hebrew calendar as an official calendar, as the yearly calendar (Gregorian) is the world's accepted calendar and is used as the state's primary calendar.

Section 9. Currently, Independence Day and the state's memorial days are anchored in specific laws: Law of Independence Day, 1949, the Day of Remembrance for Fallen Soldiers of Israel, 1963, and Holocaust Heroism and Remembrance Day, 1959. It is proposed to anchor these laws in a Basic Law in view of their status as a fundamental principle of the state's identity as the nation-state of the Jewish people. It should be noted that it is proposed for the first time to name Independence Day the national holiday of the state, as Independence Day is so designated in other states.

Section 10. Sabbath and the holy days of Israel are of cultural and national importance in the state, and therefore it is proposed they be anchored in a Basic Law. The proposed formula is based on the provision of Section 18a of the Code of Law and Order, 1948, which determined that the Sabbath and the holy days of Israel are regular days of rest in the state, but that those who are not Jewish have the right to observe days of rest on their own days of rest. Details regarding the applicable arrangements for the days of rest, employing workers on days of rest, and so on, will be determined according to regular legislation as is currently being done.

Section 11. It is proposed to anchor by Basic Law the principle currently anchored in Section 1 of the Foundations of Law Act, 1980, according to which if there is a lacuna in a legal question, after the court has found no answer in the legislation, explicit legal precedent, or by analogy, it must turn to "the principles of freedom, justice, integrity, and peace associated with the heritage of Israel."

Section 12. It is proposed to establish a strict rule, according to which in order to amend the proposed Basic Law it will be necessary to pass a Knesset Basic Law by a majority of 61 Knesset members.

LAW

Basic Law:
Israel – The Nation-State
of the Jewish People*

1. Basic Principles

a. The land of Israel is the historic homeland of the Jewish people, in which the State of Israel was established.

b. The State of Israel is the nation-state of the Jewish people, in which it exercises its natural, cultural, religious, and historical right to self-determination.[1]

c. The right to exercise national self-determination in the State of Israel is uniquely that of the Jewish people.

2. State Symbols

a. The name of the state is "Israel."

b. The state flag is white with two blue stripes near the edges and a blue Star of David in the center.

c. The state emblem is a seven-branched menorah with olive leaves on both sides and the word "Israel" beneath it.

d. The national anthem is Hatikvah.

e. Details regarding state symbols will be determined by law.

3. Capital of the State

Jerusalem, complete and united, is the capital of Israel.

---

* Passed in the Knesset on 7 Av, 5778 (July 19, 2018) [at the meeting that began on 5 Av, 5778 (July 17, 2018)]; the bill and explanatory notes were published in Knesset Bills 768 (p. 134), from 26 Adar, 5778 (March 13, 2018).

1 [SR: The words *ha-datit,* "the religious," were added to clause 1 (b) between the first reading in March 2018 and the law's passage.]

4. Language

a. Hebrew is the state language.

b. The Arabic language has a special status in the state; regulating the use of the Arabic language in state institutions or by them will be set by law.[2]

c. Nothing in this section shall prejudice the status which was given in practice to the Arabic language before this Basic Law's enactment.[3]

5. Ingathering of the Exiles

The state will be open to Jewish immigration and the ingathering of the exiles.

6. The Connection to the Jewish People

a. The state shall work to ensure the safety of the Jewish people and of its citizens who are in trouble and in captivity because they are Jewish or due to their citizenship.

b. The state shall act in the Diaspora to preserve the bond between the state and the Jewish people.[4]

c. The state shall act to preserve the cultural, historical, and religious heritage of the Jewish people among the Jews of the Diaspora.

7. Jewish Settlement

The state views the development of Jewish settlement as a national value, and shall act to encourage and promote its establishment and foundation.[5]

---

2 [SR: Article 4 (b) in the bill's first reading stated that "speakers [of Arabic] have the right to access state services in their native language," but this specific right was replaced with the more ambiguous language in the law's passage.]

3 [SR: Minor changes in wording were made to article 4 (c) between the first reading and the law's passage, and the word *she-nitan*, "which was given," was added.]

4 [SR: Between the bill's first reading and its passage the word *ba-tfutsot*, "in the Diaspora," was added to article 6 (b) (indicating that the state shall act there, rather than in general) in place of "wherever they may be" that previously closed the article.]

5 [SR: Articles 7 (a) and 7 (b) on "Heritage Preservation" were removed between the

8. Official Calendar

The Hebrew calendar is the official state calendar, and beside it the foreign calendar will be used as an official calendar; the use of the Hebrew calendar and the foreign calendar will be determined by law.

9. Independence Day and Memorial Days

a. Independence Day is the official national holiday of the state.[6]

b. Day of Remembrance for Fallen Soldiers of Israel and Holocaust Heroism and Remembrance Day are official state memorial days.

10. Days of Rest and Sabbath

Sabbath and the holy days of Israel are the regular days of rest in the state; those who are not Jewish have the right to observe days of rest on their Sabbath and holidays; details of this matter shall be determined by law.

11. Immutability

This Basic Law shall not be amended, unless by another Basic Law enacted by a majority of Knesset members.[7]

Benjamin Netanyahu

Prime Minister

Reuven Rivlin   Yuli Yoel Edelstein

State President   Knesset Speaker

---

bill's first reading and its passage and replaced by a single article on "Jewish Settlement," based loosely on article 6 from the very first Dichter bill (2011, P/18/3541).]

6 [SR: The word *rishmi*, "official," was added to article 9 (a) between the first reading and the law's passage.]

7 [SR: Article 11 on "Foundations of the Law" from the bill's first reading was passed into law separately as an amendment to the 1980 Foundations of Law Act. Though the agreement in the coalition in March when the amendment passed was to reiterate the article on Foundations of Law in the nation-state law if and when it could be passed, the article was dropped from the final version.]

PART II:

REFLECTIONS

Lightness in Times of Darkness

Michael Marmur

The text of the Basic Law: Israel – The Nation-State of the Jewish People existed for a long time in a molten state, gestating, periodically hardened by populist polemics and softened by political compromise. At least eight versions of the bill were submitted to the Knesset since 2011, in addition to the one passed into law in July 2018. While the details vary, the key assertions remain constant: The State of Israel is to be understood primarily as the expression of the political will of the Jewish people. The Jewish nature of the state is to be expressed in its symbols, and in the interpretive tools to be employed by its judiciary. It is possible to reduce the law in its various iterations and final form to two essential components. The first is a foundational statement that Israel is to be understood as the nation-state of the Jewish people. The other component involves a number of attempts to underline this assertion, and to bolster attempts to give the state discernibly "Jewish" characteristics. Of these the most far-reaching is the notion that when "Jewish" and "democratic" priorities clash, the former is to take priority over the latter.

The law looks reasonable to many Israelis. After all, they say, it only underlines the same kind of claims to an indivisible link between a people, a language, and a land, which is to be found in the constitutions of Greece and France and several other nation-states.[1] Why, they ask, would we deny to the Jewish people that which is considered sacrosanct for other peoples?

The law is couched in ostensibly plausible and defensible terms.

---

[1] For a discussion of parallels between the Jewish nation-state and examples culled from Greece, Ireland, Scandinavia, Tibet, Italy and elsewhere, see Alexander Yakobson, "Jewish Peoplehood and the Jewish State, How Unique? – A Comparative Survey," *Israel Studies* 13, no. 2 (2008): 1–27.

If an official from the Israeli Foreign Ministry were composing debating points to brief emissaries or spokespersons, they would be able to mount a spirited defense of the law. If you disagree with it, so goes the argument, you must have a problem with the notion of Jewish sovereignty. The problem is with you, not the law.

The promulgators of this law present it as part of a noble legislative enterprise, offering the state a much-needed explicit constitutional infrastructure. An appreciation of the political and social backdrop against which the law came into being raises a less uplifting possibility. The law is in fact directed to opponents of Israeli policy at home and abroad: to Israel's Arab citizens; and to the Supreme Court of Israel. To all these and to others the law represents an unapologetic assertion of Jewish majority rights. Whatever its borders are finally to be, whether it is to dwell alongside a Palestinian state or in isolation, the State of Israel is to be a Jewish state, expressed by its symbols, guided by its values, driven by the national aspirations of the Jews.

Israel's Arab citizens are unlikely to interpret this legislation as an open-armed welcome into the shared project of a contemporary society. The Jews are saying, once again: this is *our* nation-state. You non-Jews may be eligible to enjoy some democratic privileges, but only once you have acknowledged the limits of your aspiration. The legislature is saying to the judiciary: your commitment to abstract and Western-influenced concepts of justice are to be limited and, if needs be, overruled by our assertion of the primacy of Jewish national interests and Jewish legal concepts. There is a degree of sophistry in the instruction to the courts to rule in the spirit of the freedom, justice, integrity, and peace of the Jewish heritage. That heritage certainly is redolent with these values, but it has other characteristics as well. This explicit instruction to the judiciary was removed from the final nation-state law only because it was passed first in a separate item. It seems clear that the hope of Israel's current minister of justice is that a new generation of Supreme Court judges in whose appointment she will have a hand will be able to use this new law as the basis for a far less "progressive" judicial agenda.

As for the international community (an increasingly tenuous

construct in the twenty-first century), the message is: your unwilling-ness to accept the reality of Jewish peoplehood has to be overcome. We are here to stay as a local powerhouse, a nation-state thrusting its way forward in the world. Those who support the law see it as embodying the essence of political Zionism. It serves as a litmus test. If the State of Israel is seen as a democratic expression of a resurgent Jewish people, then the other pieces of the Middle East puzzle may yet fall into place.

The law has indeed become an indicator of acidity, but not perhaps in the way intended by those who have had a hand in its formulation. Some (including me) see it less as an embodiment of all that is best in the Zionist enterprise, and more as evidence of that project's crisis. A raft of laws has recently been passed which, when seen together, provide evidence that liberal democracy is under attack in Israel. The motivation for many of these laws is a dangerous combination of political opportunism, ideological com-mitment, and an inability to distinguish between a debating point and a substantive concern. The Right is in the ascendant, and two parties, both of which are members of the coalition, are competing to portray themselves as the true promoters of a nationalist agenda. Initiating contentious legislation, much of it infected by the toxin of populism, is one way in which politicians can show themselves to be serving the will of the people.

Compared to some of the other laws recently passed or currently under consideration, this Basic Law in its final form may appear rel-atively mild. One such law makes it possible to bar entry to peaceful and law-abiding visitors to the country if they espouse support for BDS (the movement for boycott, divestment, and sanctions) and similarly unacceptable views. Another, the Law on the Regulation of Settlement in Judea and Samaria, states that the claim of Pales-tinians to land rights in the territories may in effect be trumped by a Jew without such a legal claim, by dint of the pre-eminent Jewish claim on all the territories. The first of these is ominous, and likely to drive a wedge between Israel and significant populations, Jewish and non-Jewish, around the world. (There is an irony here: just as the nation-state law asserts the indelible ties linking Israel and the

Diaspora, the current slide into populist exceptionalism will fray those ties, at least those linked to progressive Jews.) To anyone for whom the rule of law means something more than the right of the strong to trample on the weak, the Regulation Law is pernicious and indefensible.

Something of this spirit is to be found in the nation-state law. In some iterations, one clause intended that it would allow groups insisting that their community comprise members of only one ethnic group protection against the incursions of an activist Supreme Court. Now there is an abstract conversation one might have about the legitimacy of groups restricting access to their communities, assuming that society at large provides rich opportunities for various groups to express their cultural autonomy.[2] But in contemporary Israel there can be little doubt what this clause was intended to allow: for Jews to be able to keep non-Jews out of their communities with impunity. In the form proposed by Avraham Dichter in 2015 and taken up by the Knesset in 2017, this aspect of the law was almost erased. Rather, the proposal asserted the right of every citizen to act in furtherance of their group's culture, language, and identity. Taken by itself, such a statement may seem unobjectionable or even admirable. In the light of its evolution and the intention of its proposers, however, the clause bore dark overtones. Indeed, the version proposed in March 2018 included both clauses – protecting closed communities and the advancement of group culture – grouped together as articles of "Heritage Preservation."

In the end, to smooth the law's passage the clause on closed communities was ultimately replaced with a clause instead vaguely encouraging Jewish settlement, and the locus of advancing Jewish culture shifted to the Jews of the Diaspora. Nonetheless, any vaunting of universal democratic principles is liable to be trumped by chauvinism masquerading as particularism.

Opponents of the law dwell on its likely deleterious impact, and

---

2 Many of the key arguments surrounding the role of society in promoting cultural difference and survival are rehearsed in Charles Taylor, et al., *Multiculturalism: Examining the Politics of Recognition* (Princeton, NJ: Princeton University Press, 1994).

ask if there is any particular need to reap this whirlwind for the sake of a principle already enshrined in the Declaration of Independence. As for the comparison with other states, the signal lack of any mention of either democracy or equality in this Basic Law places us in a club in which we should have no interest in being a member.

The argument, then, is that this legislation manages to be both superfluous and harmful. Scant attention, however, has been paid to the conceptual underpinnings of the law, either by its proponents or its detractors. Some of the more overtly polemical and contentious aspects of the law were moderated before the law was finally adopted, but some core questions remain.

To my mind, the move to promulgate this foundational law raises a series of fundamental questions most Israelis would rather ignore. I want to focus on one of these perennial and insoluble questions, the Jewish nature of the State. My claim is that this new law epitomizes a turn away from *light* to *heavy*, from *thin* to *thick*, in the conception of Israel as a Jewish state. In today's Israel it is widely agreed within the majority that the state should embrace an unashamedly Jewish identity. Such a view is not restricted to the militant Right. Alexander Yakobson and Amnon Rubinstein have argued that "anyone who accepts the principle of partition and two states for two peoples cannot demand of Israel neutrality in terms of national identity. Such a demand finds no support in all the international norms and practice."[3] The argument here is that any notion of the State as a neutral shell, devoid of cultural characteristics, is untenable. Every state has some cultural identity or collection thereof. It is no surprise that a state born against a backdrop of conflict, and with the long-term arrangement of power relations in the region far from settled, should emphasize a specific national identity.

---

3 Alexander Yakobson and Amnon Rubinstein, *Israel and the Family of Nations: The Jewish Nation-State and Human Rights*, trans. Ruth Morris and Ruchie Avital (London; New York: Routledge, 2009), 191.

THE NEUTRAL STATE

In recent years, something has happened to the way in which the Jewishness of the Jewish state is understood. It has been noted that "the Ben-Gurion of the twenties and thirties, the Hans Kohn of the days of 'Brith Shalom,' and even the Jabotinsky of 1940 found great difficulty in imagining a state whose institutions would belong to a single ethno-national group."[4] In the years preceding and immediately following the establishment of the state, most theoreticians imagined an essentially secular state to which the Jews of the world have untrammeled access. This was a vision of a state with a "thin" Jewish character.

Ever since the Declaration of Independence, and at a rapidly increasing rate in recent decades, such an approach to the Jewishness of the state is being replaced by an activist agenda. According to this understanding, one aggressively espoused by a number of those in support of this new nation-state law, the state is to be more than a shell, a vehicle for the advancement of the legitimate national aspirations of a downtrodden people. Rather than being a shell, the state is to be a womb, offering nutrition to traditional expressions of Jewish identity. One expression of this vision is the state money channeled into a variety of Jewish institutions, typically at the instigation of those institutions' political patrons. Investment of state funds into the religious and cultural institutions of non-Jews is not at a comparable level. Another arena in which this struggle for the identity of the state is playing out is in the education system, for example in the way citizenship is taught.[5] The burden placed on the

---

4 Dimitry Shumsky, "Brith Shalom's Uniqueness Reconsidered: Hans Kohn and Autonomist Zionism," *Jewish History* 25 (2011): 349.

5 See Ayman Agbaria, "Ethnonational Politics of Citizenship Education in Israel and the Counterknowledge of Palestinian Teachers," in *Global Migration, Diversity and Civil Education*, ed. James A. Banks, Marcelo Suarez-Orozco, and Miriam Ben-Peretz (New York: Teachers College Press, 2016), 156–76; Zehavit Gross, "Civic Education in Israel: Between National-Ethnocentricity and Universalism," in *Citizenship Education Around the World – Local Contexts and Global Possibilities*, ed. John E. Petrovic and Aaron M. Kuntz (New York; London: Routledge, 2014): 150–64.

hyphen linking the words "Jewish" and "democratic" increasingly seems unbearable.

The position adopted by the late Yeshayahu Leibowitz, and more recently by such individuals as Avrum Burg, is at odds with the prevalent spirit reflected in the nation-state law.[6] Both of these men argue that imbuing the state with more and more Jewish characteristics is wrong-headed and likely to lead to disaster. Leibowitz stated categorically that this state, any state, is by definition a secular institution. Burg's journey from the heart of the Zionist consensus to the margins of contemporary discourse is evidence not only of the changes he has undergone, but also of the change of mood within Israel. Burg argues that Israel has fallen prey to an ideology lumping religion, territory, language, military might, and political sovereignty together into a volatile compound.[7] Expressions of racism and exclusivism are the inevitable result of this disastrous experiment. In his view, Israel has to reject these trends in order to return to its sanity. The Law of Return needs to be curtailed such that it refers only to Jews fleeing persecution, and the state needs to be understood as an instrument for furthering the interests of all its citizens.

Voices within Israel expressing this neutralist position are rare, and they are usually vilified in popular discourse. Such voices are also to be heard outside Israel. The late Tony Judt, for example, set out his position in stark terms. He regarded the approach of the Zionist movement as essentially anachronistic:

> Israel itself is a multicultural society in all but name; yet it remains distinctive among democratic states in its resort to ethnoreligious criteria with which to denominate and rank its citizens. It is an oddity among modern nations not – as its more paranoid supporters assert – because it is a *Jewish* state and no one wants the Jews to have a state; but because it is a Jewish *state* in which one

---

6 Yeshayahu Leibowitz, "The Religious Significance of the State of Israel," in *Judaism, Human Values and the Jewish State*, ed. and trans. Eliezer Goldman, et al. (Cambridge, MA: Harvard University Press, 1992 [1975]), 214–20.

7 Avrum Burg, "Medinat Yehudim, lo Medina Yehudit," *Haaretz*, September 10, 2016, http://www.haaretz.co.il/opinions/.premium-1.3062996.

community – Jews – is set above others, in an age when that sort of state has no place.[8]

The Leibowitz-Burg-Judt axis is one for which I have sympathy. It has the virtue of simplicity and certainty: if the Zionist ideal of a state with a distinctive Jewish character was ever justified, the decades which have elapsed since the establishment of the state have eroded that legitimacy. Any attempt to maintain the Jewishness of the Jewish state will end in a fiasco of chauvinism and separatism. The state must be decommissioned as an instrument of Jewish identity, and re-imagined as a framework for the promotion of the welfare of *all* its citizens.

Claims that espousal of this position is tantamount to self-hatred and incipient anti-Semitism are spurious. There has to be a way of conducting discourse about the most crucial questions confronting the Jewish people that avoids immediate recourse to accusations of disloyalty. If I had to choose between chauvinist maximalism on the one hand and this kind of non-romantic minimalism on the other, I would opt for the latter. If forced to decide between a Jewish and a democratic state, contrary to the furious insistence of the establishment here in Israel, I would privilege the democratic over the Jewish. I believe that the alternative would be profoundly damaging, not only to Jews, Arabs, and others who live here, but indeed to Judaism itself.

SPINOZA'S WHIMSICAL PREDICTION

It is worth dwelling briefly on the roots of the modern concept of the Jewish nation-state. In his *Tractatus Theologico-Politicus,* Baruch Spinoza asserted that "the law revealed by God to Moses was simply the laws of the Hebrew state alone."[9] Spinoza rejected the notion of uniquely ordained divine legislation. Rather, Jewish law is the law of

---

8 Tony Judt, "Israel: The Alternative," *New York Review of Books,* October 23, 2003, http://www.nybooks.com/articles/2003/10/23/israel-the-alternative/.

9 Baruch Spinoza, *Tractatus Theologico-Politicus,* trans. Samuel Shirley (Leiden: Brill, 1989), 54.

the Jewish state. He goes on to make a statement, read as a prophecy, a challenge, or an *ad absurdum* argument, which has reverberated across the centuries:

> Were it not that the fundamental principles of the religion discourage manliness, I would not hesitate to believe that they [the Hebrews] will one day, given the opportunity – such is the mutability of human affairs – establish once more their independent state, and that God will again choose them.[10]

For Spinoza, divine legislation, and for that matter divine election, is real insofar as the Jews have sovereignty. Thus the law is demystified. Its power is dependent precisely on its human provenance. Its efficacy is predicated on political power. The law of Sinai is no more intrinsically holy than the law of Givat Ram (the hill upon which the modern Knesset is situated).

Political Zionism represents a calling of Spinoza's bluff. The Jews have stepped back into history, and in so doing their claims to national identity and uniqueness are in some sense confirmed.[11] In Spinoza's model, then, the will of the reconstituted Jewish state is as "holy" as other human expressions of the Jewish social order, which is what he takes the Bible and Jewish law to be. The next chapter in Jewish political history is in fact the next chapter of the Hebrew Bible.

The political realities of seventeenth-century Holland are different from those in force in twenty-first-century Israel. Many in contemporary political discourse seem intent on re-mystifying Jewish sovereignty, seeing the state as the handiwork of the Divine. Nonetheless, an insight inherent in Spinoza's approach has not lost its validity. Jewish sovereignty represents a new chapter in the unfolding drama of Jewish creativity.

The neutralist position of Burg et al. would argue that any Jewish renaissance will have to make do without state sponsorship. Rather, voluntaristic communities will develop organically, without either obstruction or subsidy from the state.

---

10 Spinoza, *Tractatus*, 100.
11 This phrase has been particularly associated with the thought of Emil Fackenheim, who published a book on this subject in 1978.

I am inclined to believe that the reality is more complex than a simple binary proposition. The reality of a Jewish majority, and the necessity to grapple with the new challenges of sovereignty, offers not only the prospect of state sponsorship. It also should force Jewish thinkers from across the denominational spectrum to relate to new dilemmas, and in so doing to extend the Jewish vocabulary. The State of Israel is to educate its citizens, Jews and non-Jews, concerning the history of the country and of the people who bear a special affinity for it. Is it inevitable that such a history will be narrow-minded and triumphalist, or is it possible that it will show the breadth of perspective and generosity of spirit truly befitting of an *am olam*, a people of universal particularity?

In the rush to establish, defend, and promote the state, perilously little attention has been paid to the Jewish challenge of the Jewish state. Increasingly, the Jewishness of the state has been interpreted in simple ethnocentric terms – is a particular action good or bad for the Jews? It is in part as a response to this slide into chauvinism that some have argued for a neutral state.

Despite my sympathy for the moral motivation for the neutralist position, I am not convinced of its practical implications. Rather than give up on the notion that a state can bear any distinctive Jewish characteristics, I believe we are better served by fighting for the vision of Jewish life to which we are committed. All too often the contest for hearts and minds has been conceded before the contest has even begun. A version of Judaism which is male-dominated, halakhocentric, resistant to non-Jewish influences, often militaristic – such a version has been acknowledged de facto as the essence of Judaism. It is hardly surprising that, as a consequence, the nation-state of the Jews as reflected in the initial iterations of the law is at odds with liberal democracy.

Non-Orthodox iterations of Judaism have not fared well in the political establishment in Israel, but there is evidence that many Israelis are discovering their attraction. They offer the possibility of doing something other than simply succumbing to the populist surge or positing a post-Zionist neutral state. Like much in non-Orthodox Judaism, it is not clear that this third path can attract mass interest and generate intense enthusiasm, but I am not ready to give up on this possibility.

I am not upbeat about the immediate prospects for such a progressive Zionist approach, one in which the state will have a "thin" Jewish identity and a thick commitment to universal democratic values. Such ideologies are in retreat all over the world at present. An approach of deconstructionism on the one hand and a surge of reactionary nationalism on the other leave little space for progressive, moderate, humanist nationalism. I fear that Israel's political system may have to undergo many upheavals, some of them severe, before an approach such as this comes back into vogue.

In the meantime, it is worth searching for areas in which a "thin" approach to the Jewishness of Israel might prevail. One example was provided in 2014 by the doyen of Israeli Jewish thought, Eliezer Schweid, who published an analysis of the Basic Law: Human Dignity and Liberty, promulgated by the Knesset in 1992 and revised in 1994. He styled his analysis a reading of the law "in the light of the Torah of Moses."

Schweid's argument is that the conception of human freedom at the basis of the Basic Law is at odds with, or falls short of, what he presents as a normative or dominant understanding of freedom to be found in the prophetic tradition, or for that matter in its Western humanist counterpart. In Schweid's reading, the law fails to live up to the high ideals both of Rabbi Akiva and of Immanuel Kant. He describes it as "a law framed in the constitutional model of American liberalism, based on a neo-capitalist materialist competitive ideology, which is the source of its inspiration and its limitation."[12]

Schweid's article offers trenchant opposition to trends he regards as antithetical to the core values inherent in the prophetic and wider Jewish tradition. His is not an argument from Jewish law, but rather from Jewish values. The 1990s law, and the American neo-liberal capitalist worldview it represents, presents its citizens with no real obligations, as Schweid understands that term. To be sure, by neces-

---

12 Eliezer Schweid, *Ra'ayon ha-'am ha-nivkhar ve-ha-liberaliyut ha-khadasha* (Jerusalem: Hakibbutz Hameuchad, 2016), 35.

sity each citizen is forced to cooperate, or perhaps collaborate, with the system so that their rights may be made available. Such necessity, however, is hardly compatible with Schweid's understanding of social responsibility and solidarity. He believes that the unfolding process of privatization, the surrender of the State of Israel to capitalist forces and to the internal logic of neo-liberalism, is morally reprehensible and based on falsehood. To posit equality of rights while ignoring the inherent inequality of the human condition is to indulge in a dangerous fiction.

Moses, in Schweid's reading, did not base his legislative project on the flimsy and self-serving assumption of "rights," but rather on the basis of "mitsvot," which he understands to be responsibilities taken on by the individual in an act of free will. Freedom is not understood in the Mosaic system in terms of rights, but in terms of justice. Schweid's Moses assumes that "if all the children of Israel fulfil the system of Shabbat out of their own will, they will live in a system of just self-rule in which the positive meaning of freedom is embodied."[13]

In my reading of Schweid, he is railing against the neo-liberal turn in Israeli society, which seems to him to have thrown Israel off course. The arrival of Israel's own particular form of "vulture capitalism" has provoked both his outrage and his deep concern. Israel is in danger of losing its putative identity as a Jewish state not as a result of a demographic threat, but rather in terms of its core values. Schweid is channeling the Zionist publicist of a former era, Ahad Ha'am, and crying: *Lo Zu Ha-derekh*, this is not the way.

There is much in Schweid's critique of this piece of 1990s legislation, not least its unashamed essentialism, according to which the Torah of Moses stands for a state based on social democratic principles, which can be challenged. It should also be noted that compared to more recent attempts to legislate Basic Laws, the one protecting human rights looks like the least of our problems. Indeed, it serves as a bulwark against some of the worst incursions the institutions of state may yet face. Nonetheless, what is important about Schweid's

---

13 Schweid, *Ra'ayon ha-'am ha-nivkhar*, 40.

critique is that it acknowledges the notion that Israel should act as a Jewish state, but refuses to understand this simply in terms of military security, ethnic support, and hollow patriotism. This is an ethical reading of the Jewish enterprise, and the state which Schweid is working towards is to be founded on such a basis. Schweid is fully committed to the insights of the founders of Israel, so much so that he offers a Jewish critique of the most recent addition to Israel's constitutional canon. He is not arguing for a neutral state, but rather a Jewish state in his passionate understanding of that term.

WHAT SHOULD BE JEWISH ABOUT THE JEWISH STATE?

Jewish tradition offers a range of potential political approaches. An early example of Jewish political philosophy is to be found in the Mishnah, in the fourth chapter of tractate Avot. In the seventeenth mishnah of that chapter Rabbi Simeon teaches that there are three crowns – the crown of Torah, the crown of priesthood, the crown of sovereignty – and the crown of a good name which surpasses them all.[14]

In its original context this teaching can be seen as offering advice to the individual to avoid the seductions of power if integrity has to be sacrificed in the process. But the ancient saying also offers a framework for considering contemporary political realities. The rabbinic image of the four crowns offers a matrix for understanding the challenge of Jewish statehood in our own time. Just as it is possible to offer a small and specific reading of these categories (in which Torah denotes funding yeshivas, the Chief Rabbis are the High Priests, the army and the tax authorities symbolize sovereignty, and the advancement of our good name is handled by diplomats and advertisers), there is also an expansive version. This would include

---

14 For an elaboration on these categories in terms of Jewish political philosophy, see Daniel J. Elazar and Stuart A. Cohen, *The Jewish Polity* (Bloomington: Indiana University Press, 1985).

secular and sacred learning, culture and creativity, security (both military and economic), vigorous democratic institutions, and robust civil society. Israel's good name would not be a function of public relations, but an expression of an ancient nation embracing the paradigm of a modern open state.

The kind of Jewish state to which we should aspire will not only glorify the memory of the Maccabee warriors, but also the legacy of Israel's prophets, many of whom made uncompromising calls to rein in realpolitik in the name of higher principles. Just as in the prophets' own time, the claim will be made that to indulge in such moral abstractions is a luxury we cannot afford. It may yet prove to be the case that the insistent call of the prophet is an imperative we cannot afford to ignore.

Specific examples of the prophetic call are dangerous, since by their nature they ask for contentious acts of interpretation - another profound Jewish characteristic. I will take the risk. Isaiah 42:6-7 reads:

> I, the LORD, have called you in righteousness;
>> I will take hold of your hand.
> I will keep you and will make you
>> to be a covenant for the people
>> and a light for the Gentiles,
> to open eyes that are blind,
>> to free captives from prison
>> and to release from the dungeon those who sit in darkness.

In May 2017 Israel's Coordinator of Government Activities in the Territories reported that the supply of electricity to the Gaza strip was to be reduced by some 50 megawatts, leaving Gaza's two million inhabitants with even less access to electricity, and on the verge of a humanitarian crisis.[15] If scoring debating points were all that mattered, Israel had a case to make. The initiative for this action appeared to come at least in part from the leadership of the

---

15 See the report by Gisha - Legal Center for Freedom of Movement, "Hand on the Switch (2017)," http://gisha.org/UserFiles/File/publications/infrastructure/Hand _on_the_Switch-EN.pdf.

Palestinian Authority on the West Bank, and it was part of an internecine dispute within the Palestinian community. Our spokespeople argued: the leaders of Hamas abuse the electricity they receive. It is up to them to change their priorities.

According to my understanding of a Jewish discourse equal to the moral challenges of the hour, such an approach should have been, and should be, rejected *on Jewish grounds*. The provision of electricity to citizens for a few hours a day is not at the expense of Israel's security interests, unless it is understood that any potential harm to any Israeli outweighs palpable harm caused to our neighbors. The words of Isaiah should be ringing in our ears, enjoining us to free captives from darkness, rather than plunging them into further gloom.

Sadly, such a Jewish conversation about the state, one that would extend to social policies, economic philosophy, and more, is hard to find in contemporary Israel. Rather, our politicians concoct laws designed to bolster the Jewish character of the state – which is sullied and undermined with every unnoticed injustice, every casual application of our superiority. The power at our disposal should be exercised with the greatest restraint. It is my belief that in many cases this is what we do, but in some cases we simply do not; and then declarations that ours is the most moral army in the world ring hollow. Some Israelis are engaged in a search for Jewish voices offering different understandings of the essence of Judaism. In May 2017 a booklet on the political implications of the thought of Abraham Joshua Heschel by Dror Bondi appeared in Hebrew, published by the Israel Democracy Institute.[16] Bondi's reading of Heschel calls for an approach to the Jewish state which is remarkably close to that discussed in this article: a Jewish state in which Jewish racism would be a contradiction in terms, in which every non-Jewish citizen would be entitled to real equality, a state in which humanity could respond more keenly to the divine call. Such a political philosophy does not divorce the Jewish from the democratic part of the equation, but it calls for a radical re-understanding of what it means to be Jewish.

---

16 Dror Bondi, *Elohim, humanizm ve-demokratia be-mishnato shel Avraham Yehoshua Heschel* (Jerusalem: Israel Democracy Institute, 2017). See especially p. 27.

Heschel never lived in Israel and most of his social commentary related to the United States. Recent interest in Heschel on the part of Israelis previously cool to Diaspora thought suggests that some are searching for a different currency of Jewish commitment. Heschel, in 1955, in a chapter close to the end of *God in Search of Man* entitled "The Spirit of Judaism" wrote:

> We must not regard any human institution or object as being an end in itself. Man's achievements in this world are but attempts, and a temple that comes to mean more than a reminder of the living God is an abomination.
>
> What is an idol? A thing, a force, a person, a group, an institution or an ideal, regarded as supreme. God alone is supreme...
>
> Even the laws of the Torah are not absolutes. Nothing is deified: neither power nor wisdom, neither heroes nor institutions.[17]

According to this understanding of the spirit of Judaism, a Jewish nation-state cannot regard itself as an absolute value. For Israel to be a Jewish nation-state, it will not be enough to defend the interests of Jews alone. And for those interests to be truly served, Israel will need to come closer to Isaiah's vision. At stake is not only the "crown of a good name," the reputation of Israel within the family of nations. At stake are all the crowns together. By telling ourselves and persuading our children that we are a nation who dwells alone, by abusing Jewish education to engender separatist and supremacist views, by failing to allocate resources in an equitable manner, we are undermining one of the most remarkable political adventures of modern times.

Israel is a patchwork, and among its Jewish majority there are many different understandings of the essence of "the Torah of Moses." Schweid's social reading, for example, is contradicted by some and ignored by most. One response to this wide range of opinions is to privatize the debate, to take the state out of the equation. While appealing, the prospect of a neutral state may prove a chimera. The state I wish to live in will espouse causes, and it will take a stand.

---

17 Abraham Joshua Heschel, *God in Search of Man* (New York: Farrar, Straus and Giroux, 1955), 415.

Is gender equality to be striven for? Are the rights of LGBTQ people to be upheld? Can religious and cultural expression blossom?

States do have values. They are not neutral. It may be that the State of Israel will choose to replace its emphasis on Jewish values with avowedly Israeli values, but they are bound to have profound links to Jewish culture. Hebrew will long remain a dominant language (and would have done so even without the nation-state law), and for as long as it does the nuances and cadences of Jewish life will be embedded in the story of Israel, just as the Jewish calendar would have in any case continued to play an influential role in the rhythm of Israeli life. My own hope is that contrary to their own rhetoric the political leaders of Israel will take steps to ensure that a Jewish majority can hold sway in the nation-state of the Jews. Should they fail to do so, the prospect of a Jewish minority imposing its will on an unwilling majority is so gruesome as to render moot any meaningful discussion of such a state's Jewish identity.

The state for which I strive is one blessed with a "light" Jewish identity and a "heavy" commitment to pluralism and equality; one with a "thin" sense of Jewishness coupled with a "thick" sense of solidarity and community. The thicker and heavier the Jewish identifiers of the state become, the more likely we all are, Jew and non-Jew alike, to be plunged into darkness. In finding a light touch in understanding the Jewish character of Israel – a touch not to be found in the nation-state law – Israel may yet move toward the light.

The Current Crisis in Israel's Constitution

Yoram Hazony

Israel's political constitution has been in a condition of crisis since the 1990s – a crisis that the proposed and recently passed Basic Law reaffirming Israel's character as the Jewish state is intended to resolve. In what follows, I examine some key issues in general and Zionist political theory in order to understand the nature of the present crisis in Israel's constitution. I will suggest that in light of these considerations, a Basic Law reaffirming Israel's character as a Jewish state is in fact much needed at this time – not only in order to stabilize the Israeli constitution, but also as a basis for approaching the broader problem of state legitimacy that has in recent years crippled the state system in the Middle East.

I. THE TRADITION OF ISRAEL AS A JEWISH STATE

On the face of it, Israel should not need new legislation reaffirming its constitutional character as a Jewish state. Both Zionist political tradition and international diplomatic history amply confirm Israel's character as such. The expression "Jewish State" was coined by Theodor Herzl himself with reference to Jewish national independence, and became the title of his 1896 tract seeking to establish the political theory that would underpin such a state. In proposals submitted to the British government, Herzl went on to ask for the empire's assistance in establishing a territory "which shall be Jewish in character," "founded under laws and regulations adopted for the well-being of the Jewish people," with a Jewish name and a Jewish flag.

From here, the concept of a Jewish state developed in countless exacting debates between the Zionists and their Jewish detractors: in British diplomatic documents such as the Peel Commission report of 1937, which called for the establishment of a "Jewish State"; in the United Nations partition plan of 1947 supporting the establishment of a "Jewish State"; and in Israel's Declaration of Independence, which refers to Herzl's theory of the Jewish state explicitly and uses this term repeatedly. Much Israeli legislation, including the Law of Return offering automatic citizenship to Jews of all lands, was based on Herzl's view of Israel's purpose, which was embraced alongside a firm commitment to civil equality for non-Jewish citizens. And this tradition was upheld and confirmed in Israeli Supreme Court rulings for decades.[1]

Moreover, Israel's standing as the national state of the Jewish people rests on a broader body of political theory, which recognizes the principle of the self-determination of peoples as the best organizing principle for the international system.[2] Movements for national self-determination had been known in Europe at least since Dutch independence from imperial Spain in 1581, and had gradually led to the independence of additional conquered peoples from Greece to Poland and from India to Ethiopia. In *On Representative Government* (1861), John Stuart Mill urged national self-determination as the best organizing principle for the international order, arguing that only states with a high degree of linguistic and cultural homogeneity share sufficient common interests to become democracies: multi-ethnic states would necessarily be tyrannies, he wrote, because only oppression can keep the radically conflicting interests of the different peoples of the state at bay. Woodrow Wilson placed this principle at the center of his proposals for reconstruction after World War I.[3]

This does not, of course, mean that every people necessarily

---

1 I recount this history in detail in Yoram Hazony, *The Jewish State: The Struggle for Israel's Soul* (New York: Basic Books, 2000).

2 I have avoided the term "nation-state," which is often understood to mean that the nation consists of those individuals living in a given state.

3 John Stuart Mill, "On Representative Government," in *Utilitarianism, On Liberty, and Considerations on Representative Government*, ed. H.B. Acton (London: Everyman, 1984

wants or needs political independence. For example, it may be that today there are no compelling reasons for the Scots to be politically independent from the larger and more powerful English polity after several centuries of successful alliance within the framework of the United Kingdom. But where a people is repeatedly persecuted and massacred over centuries for its distinct traditions and loyalties, political independence is often the best option. This is the case right now with respect to the Kurds and the Assyrian Christians in Syria-Iraq, two peoples for whom only political self-determination and independence is at this point an appropriate response to the horrors they have experienced – and are still experiencing.

II. BUT IS A JEWISH STATE LEGITIMATE?

If Israel's political and legal standing as the national state of the Jewish people is so firmly supported in Israeli political tradition, international diplomatic history, and general political theory, why should this status require renewed affirmation now in the form of a Basic Law?

The reason is this: for the past half century, we have witnessed a fundamental shift in the political doctrines many in the West accept as providing the theoretical foundations for the state. And this shift, unjustified and undesirable though it would appear to be, has nevertheless raised pressing questions about the legitimacy of Israel as the state of the Jewish people.

This is not a new issue. It is fundamental to modern political theory and can be characterized as stemming from a disagreement between Montesquieu and Rousseau: for Montesquieu, different nations will necessarily have very different constitutions, since their design must be in keeping with the historical needs of different peoples, and must respond to the actual circumstances in which each state is established and maintained. Providing for such differences

---

[1861]), 391–98. See also Yoram Hazony, *The Virtue of Nationalism* (New York: Basic Books, 2018).

is, in fact, what is meant when we speak of the right of a nation to "self-determination." Rousseau, on the other hand, claimed that there is only one legitimate constitution, which derives from abstract reasoning and applies universally to all nations at all times and places. Any government that does not conform to Rousseau's universal constitution is, on this view, illegitimate.[4]

The form of constitution proposed by Rousseau is one that is known in Israeli political parlance as a "state of its citizens." Such a constitution assumes that all individuals in the territory of the state enter into an agreement to give up on any other historical political commitments that may have once bound them (e.g., commitments to tribes, peoples, religions) in order to become equal citizens of the state. This universal political model was adopted by Kant and became an integral part of the German Enlightenment. Arrayed against this concept of a universal social-contract state has been a long line of thinkers in the tradition of Montesquieu, including Hume, Ferguson, Hegel, Constant, Burke, and Mill, who, in different ways, argued that the insistence that there is only one politically correct constitution must necessarily lead to oppression and bloodshed – as the attempted homogenization of mankind under a single form of regime comes into conflict with the historical, national, and religious ties that bind actual peoples to one another in real life.

It is not surprising, then, that in the debate over the universal constitution, Herzl and the Zionists were from the outset, in principle, on the side of Montesquieu. Indeed, in *The Jewish State* and in other writings, Herzl repeatedly rejects Rousseau's social contract as the basis for the state, just as he rejects the French government's claim that the Jews are no longer a people because they have tacitly signed on to the social contract that supposedly established the French Republic. Instead, Herzl argues that large numbers of Jews all over the world retain their political attachment to the Jewish

---

4 This argument between empiricist and rationalist theories of government appears in England as a disagreement between John Selden and John Locke. See Ofir Haivry and Yoram Hazony, "What Is Conservatism?" *American Affairs* 1, no. 2 (Summer 2017), https://americanaffairsjournal.org/2017/05/what-is-conservatism/.

people, and that they have the political and moral right to act as a people in order to establish a national home in which Jews can be safe from persecution and live in accordance with laws that they will determine themselves.

Among Jews, the question of the universal constitution was decisively settled in favor of the view of Montesquieu and Herzl during the Holocaust, when the policies of the United States and Britain allowed (and in the case of the British blockade of Palestine, actively contributed to) the deaths of countless Jews whose lives might have been saved. A Jewish state that was constitutionally mandated to prioritize the defense of Jewish lives and Jewish civilization would certainly have operated differently than America or Britain. By the time of Harry Truman's Yom Kippur Eve address in 1946 indicating America's possible support for a Jewish state in Palestine, nearly all of organized Jewry had reached the conclusion that Jewish self-determination in the form of a national state of the Jewish people was both justified and necessary.

But as is well known, history has not been kind to the idea of national self-determination. The end of World War II brought a tidal shift, first in Europe and later in the United States, in the direction of Rousseau's universal constitution as the sole legitimate constitution. By the 1960s, Western elites had begun to turn against national particularism of any kind, pointing to Nazi Germany as proof that drawing national and religious distinctions is the root of all political evil. In Europe, the result has been the attempt to dismantle the system of independent national states and replace it with a European Union. In the United States, as well, an accelerating aversion to drawing distinctions based on religion or nationality was felt across a variety of issues, from immigration to national security. (The British vote to leave the EU in 2016, followed months later by the election of an avowedly nationalist president in the United States, are dramatic attempts to reverse these trends. It is too early to say whether these attempts will prove successful.)

That Nazi Germany should be cited as an excuse for delegitimizing the institution of the national state is ridiculous: Hitler was a fanatical opponent of the Western institution of the national state, which he saw as an effete construction of Western liberalism. His plan for world empire left no room for the principle of the self-determination of peoples. His goal was rather to put an end to the self-determination of peoples once and for all.

Nevertheless, one cannot deny that for increasing numbers of educated people today, the very idea of the self-determination of the Jews in their own national state is to be regarded as akin to racism and Nazism.[5] Both in America and Europe, the movement to brand Zionism as a form of racism continues to gather steam. In Israel, too, "post-Zionism" became the buzzword of fashionable opinion in the 1990s, indicating a preference for setting aside the Jewish-national aspects of Israel's constitution and public culture. Today, this term is less popular than it once was. But among Israeli academics and jurists, there has been a profound shift in political values in step with the change that we see throughout the West. Rousseau's concept of the universal constitution has made deep inroads in Israel. And with it the suspicion that the Israeli regime is not a "true democracy" and will not be legitimate until it is reshaped into a "state of its citizens."

In this, Israel's intellectual trends are out of step with the vast majority of the Israeli public. But that does not make the present situation any less dangerous.

III. THE THREAT TO THE ISRAELI CONSTITUTION

If we read the minutes of the meeting of the National Assembly that adopted Israel's Declaration of Independence and its first constitutional provisions on May 14, 1948, we read a debate overtly concerned with a series of issues in democratic theory, including civil liberties and the separation of powers. The representatives of all parties supported the establishment of a democratic form of government

---

5 On European hatred of Israel and its parallels in the United States, see my essay, "Anti-Nationalism and Hate" in *The Virtue of Nationalism*, 190–234. See also "Israel Through European Eyes," *Jerusalem Letters* (July 2010) and "More on Kuhn, Kant and the Nation-State," *Jerusalem Letters* (August 2010), http://jerusalemletters.com/.

and were concerned to safeguard it. Nevertheless, it is striking that in tens of pages of debate, there is not a single reference to the possibility that the term "Jewish State" (used by all the participants) or the right of the Jewish people to an independent state of its own, is in any way in conflict with a democratic form of government. The representative of the Communist party proposed that the term "Jewish State" be amended to refer to an "Independent Jewish State" or to an "Independent and Sovereign Jewish State" – proposals that Ben-Gurion rejected. But neither he nor anyone else saw a need to alter the traditional Zionist concept of a "Jewish State" to make it somehow more democratic, because they already believed the Jewish state would be governed democratically in the fullest sense.[6]

This same situation is reflected in Israeli legislation and Supreme Court decisions for the first forty years of the existence of the new nation. Yet beginning in the 1970s, prominent Israeli academics and jurists, in keeping with the support for the concept of a universal constitution then sweeping Europe, began advancing the claim that the state established by the Zionists was a Jewish state instead of being a properly constituted democracy. Such arguments began making headway among Israeli political leaders – some of whom, like former Education Minister Shulamit Aloni, were willing explicitly to argue that the idea of Israel as the state of the Jewish people is "anti-democratic, if not racist."[7] At that time, we were introduced to a series of alternative concepts ("State of the Jews,"[8] "Jewish and Democratic State," "State of the Jews and of Its Citizens") whose aim was to obscure, attenuate, or displace the traditional concept of Israel as the national state of the Jewish people in order to bring the country into conformity with the theory of the universal constitution.

When the decisive moment came in 1992, the Knesset of Israel

---

6 Minutes of the National Assembly and the Temporary State Assembly (Jerusalem: The State of Israel, 1948), vol. 1.

7 Shulamit Aloni, "Medinat gutnik ve-Moskovich," *Maariv*, November 30, 1998. See also *idem*, "Khok yesod: Kevod ha-adam ve-kheruto," *Te'oriya ve-bikoret* 12–13 (1999): 367–75.

8 Contrary to what is often said, the expression "State of the Jews" does not originate with Herzl. Herzl coined the term "Jewish State" and used it throughout his career. See Yoram Hazony, "Did Herzl Want a Jewish State?" *Azure* 9 (2000), 37–73.

passed two constitutional Basic Laws declaring Israel to be a "Jewish and Democratic State." While both laws declare themselves, in their preambles, to have been legislated "to establish ... the values of the State of Israel as a Jewish and Democratic state," the fact is that the rights enumerated in them are concerned exclusively with protecting values derived from the supposed universal constitution – values such as freedom of speech, privacy, and so on. This means that neither law addresses the possibility that the Jewish state may have the right or the duty to enact specialized, non-universal provisions in some of these areas that would differ from the laws of other nations. For example, Israeli law restricts freedom of speech and religion by restricting missionary activities aimed at converting Jews to other faiths; and it similarly restricts freedom of occupation by regulating the sale of certain food products during Passover, and by limiting the operation of places of entertainment on Holocaust Memorial Day. By explicitly enumerating only universal rights and saying nothing about the Jewish state as expressing the right to self-determination of the Jewish people, the new Basic Laws make it difficult for even a balanced Supreme Court to protect Israel's historical identity and purpose.

When passed, little significance was attached to this legislation, a fact reflected in the absurdly small number of legislators who even bothered to vote on these bills: the new laws passed by votes of 21–32 and 0–23, respectively, out of 120 members of Knesset. But the consequences were immediately felt in Israeli constitutional law, which has been thrown into a state of confusion from which it has not recovered, as Supreme Court justices and law professors rushed to try to offer new interpretive constructions to fill the theoretical vacuum surrounding the term "Jewish and Democratic State." The result has been a profusion of competing, superficial, and ad hoc theories, virtually none of which makes significant reference to the relevant political theory or intellectual history of the concept of a Jewish state.[9] It is in this context that Israel's then-President of the Supreme Court, Aharon Barak, shamed the Zionist and Israeli

---

9 For discussion, see Yoram Hazony, *The Jewish State*, 48–52.

political tradition by declaring the country's Jewish character to be "in tension" with democracy, and embarked on a series of decisions aimed at gradually eroding Israel's legal status as a Jewish state.[10] This process reached a climax in the 2000 Ka'adan decision, in which the Supreme Court declared that "the general purpose of all legislation is to secure equality among human beings without discrimination on the basis of religion or nationality," and asserted that policies by the Israeli government and the Jewish Agency are on their face illegal if not in conformity with the principle of equality.[11]

Like the 1992 Basic Laws that recklessly sidelined the concept of Israel as the Jewish state, the importance of the Ka'adan opinion appears to be greatly underestimated even now. A Supreme Court ruling stating explicitly that equality (and not also security, liberty, the well-being of the Jewish people, and other values) is the general purpose of Israeli law, and explicitly invoking American cases such as Brown vs. Board of Education to rule inequality illegal in Israel, is an announcement of a new constitutional order. For example, in the US, Brown vs. Board of Education rules out state institutions that are "separate but equal," and the Ka'adan decision likewise rules that "separate but equal" institutions are not permissible in Israel. Of course, there should be no legitimate parallel between the American case, which deals with segregation on the basis of race, and the conditions that we find in Israel, in which Jews and Arabs are not different races at all, but are rather ancient civilizations with highly developed national, linguistic, and religious traditions that they are concerned to preserve and pass on to their children. Unfortunately, the court did draw this parallel, inserting it into Israeli constitutional law. If taken seriously, this would mean, for example, that Israel's present educational system – in which Jews and Arabs for the most part send their children to different school systems – is unconstitutional. So is Israel's Law of Return, which offers automatic citizenship to Jews who wish to immigrate. So are Israeli security policies aimed

---

10 Aharon Barak, *Iyunei Mishpat* 24 (September 2000): 11.
11 H.C. 6698/95, Aadel Ka'adan v. Israel Lands Administration, 5(1) P.D. 258 (2000), https://www.escr-net.org/node/365464.

at protecting Jews around the world. And the same can be said for other Israeli laws and policies as well.

The fact that all the implications of the universal constitution declared in the Ka'adan decision have not yet been unfolded at this time is irrelevant. So long as it stands without clarification in the form of new constitutional law, this ruling is a ticking time-bomb whose consequences are yet to come.

The disappearance of Jewish national self-determination from the court's list of the legitimate aims of Israeli policy is what stands behind the present crisis of Israel's constitution. It is what stands behind the need for a Basic Law reaffirming Israel as the national state of the Jewish people – a law whose purpose is to re-establish the previous status quo in conformity with the Herzlian political traditions upon which the State of Israel was founded, and from which it was, until recently, understood to draw its legitimacy.

IV. THE ISRAELI CONSTITUTION AND THE FUTURE OF THE MIDDLE EAST

The Herzlian political model has been dramatically successful. As the Jewish state, Israel has absorbed millions of destitute Jewish refugees from Arab lands, Iran, the former Soviet Union, and elsewhere, offering them freedom from persecution, economic opportunity, and public schools where their children can be introduced to the heritage of their people by learning Hebrew, Jewish history, and Bible (something available in the United States only to Jews who can afford private school tuition due to the current interpretation of the US Constitution). Far from creating a xenophobic and racist regime, the Jewish state has blossomed into a powerful example of a successful democracy – the only country in the Middle East in which Christians, Druze, and other minorities enjoy free worship and need not fear for their lives.

This success has not been in spite of Israel's character as the state of the Jewish people, but because of it. To see this, one need only compare Israel's trajectory to that of other states established in the region at around the same time but based on a "multi-national" model: Syria (independent 1946) was assembled by the French by forcing together Alawite, Druze, Kurd, Assyrian Christian, and Sunni Arab peoples – willfully ignoring national and religious boundaries, and vocal demands by some of these peoples to be granted independent states of their own. Iraq (independent 1932) was a similar British construct, imposing a single state on radically disparate Kurdish, Assyrian, Sunni Arab, and Shia Arab peoples, among others. Most states in the Middle East – "Pan-Arab" in name only – were built by the Western powers in just this way.

The results of these experiments in constructing multi-national states have been just as Mill predicted: Israel, built around a cohesive and overwhelming Jewish majority, was able to establish internal stability without repression, and quickly developed into a fully-functioning democracy. In contrast, the other states of the region have been able to retain their integrity only through brutality and state terror. The destruction of the Sunni city of Hama by the Alawites in Syria in 1982, and the gassing of Kurds in Halabja by the Sunnis in Iraq in 1988, are only the best-known examples of what has in fact been a chronic dilemma for these regimes: either greater repression, or collapse.

There can be no freedom and peace in Syria-Iraq until the borders are redrawn along ethnic and religious lines. In the end, Kurds, Alawites, Christians, Druze, Sunni Arabs, and Shiite Arabs must each have their own national state, each devoted to the well-being and interests of one people only. And each must have its own "Law of Return," offering a place of refuge and automatic citizenship to the scattered and persecuted members of this one people.

In a sense, this is a distinctly Israeli vision, emerging from the Jews' experience of suffering and redemption in the last century. But it is also a humane and universal vision – the only one that can offer genuine hope to the devastated peoples of the region. This vision receives concrete reaffirmation in the proposed Basic Law confirming Israel as a Jewish state, which reinforces a vision of the Middle East as advancing (much as Europe did after emerging from the Thirty Years' War in the seventeenth century) in the direction of an order of independent nations based on the principle of religious and national self-determination.

V. DO WE BELIEVE THERE IS ONE POLITICALLY CORRECT CONSTITUTION?

The universal constitution of Rousseau and Kant is the one "politically correct" constitution permitted by a certain strand of radical Western political thought that has currently become fashionable in the West. The fact that this political theory is widely accepted does not, however, make it moral or prudent. Of course, equality before the law is a crucial political and legal principle that is (as Aharon Barak correctly emphasizes) already expressed in the laws of Moses: if individuals come before a judge in a murder case or in suit over property rights, for example, then we must demand that the law be applied equally to all without distinguishing between individuals on the basis of wealth or gender or national identity. We rightly consider this to be a fundamental principle distinguishing civilized nations from those of barbarians.

However, the moral necessity of such "equality before the law" does not mean that everyone in the world has to be equal in all things and at all times. Indeed, as the Soviets, the Chinese, and the Khmer Rouge amply demonstrated, it is just as easy to conduct a murderous persecution in the name of equality as it is to conduct one in the name of inequality. Jews must never forget that it was in the name of a Rousseau-style "state of its citizens" that Napoleon in 1807 forced French Jews to renounce their historical identity as a people with political aspirations of its own, and to revise Jewish law on all matters that the French government saw as dividing Jews from the broader French public (e.g., marriage and divorce). This is perhaps ironic, given recent events in France, but it is nonetheless a fact: the French concept of a "state of its citizens," in which Jews were given equal citizenship, was imposed on the Jews by force. It was a persecution in which the Jews were made to give up their traditional identity and law under explicit threat of being expelled from the country.

Nor is this the exception. It is the rule. In Europe today, sporadic efforts to render Judaism illegal – through bans on circumcision, on kosher slaughter, and so forth – are all ultimately based on the claims of the universal constitution, which insists that "reason" can determine a single proper framework of rights that is correct for all humanity. Because of this conceit, persecutions of minority peoples will always take place in the name of Rousseau's homogenizing political theory. In the name of making everyone "equal," the majority can and will continue to persecute the minority until everyone comes out the same.

Like every nation, Israel has a political and constitutional tradition that is its own, and that differs from those of other peoples. This has perhaps been forgotten by some. But this forgetfulness will not go on forever. Long after the current constitutional fashions have passed from the world, there will be an Israel "which shall be Jewish in character," and which will be "founded under laws and regulations adopted for the well-being of the Jewish people." It will be a nation that cherishes its non-Jewish citizens who have chosen to make their lives in the Jewish state and to contribute to its upbuilding, defense, and flourishing, and it will work diligently to ensure that they enjoy equality before the law. But this will not be because of any supposed universal constitution – a fiction, with no reality to it. It will be because the Jewish political tradition demands this of us.

The Hegemony of Neo-Zionism and the Nationalizing State in Israel – The Meaning and Implications of the Nation-State Law

Amal Jamal

Israel has been undergoing major changes in the last few decades. One of these major changes is the rise of a very conservative and even messianic ultra-nationalistic political block that is dominating center stage in the political system, and turning its ideology into the official policy of the state. This development, which started decades ago and reached a hegemonic position in the last few years, reflects a process according to which Israel has moved into a Neo-Zionist era, characterized by an intensive "nationalizing" process, manifested in the legal, judicial, and cultural fields.[1] The process of nationalizing, as described by Rogers Brubaker, "is the tendency to see the state as an 'unrealised' nation-state, as a state destined to be a nation-state, the state of and for a particular nation, but not yet in fact a nation-state (at least not to a significant degree); and the concomitant disposition to remedy this perceived defect, to make the state what it is properly and legitimately destined to be, by promoting the language, culture, demographic position, economic flourishing, or political hegemony of the nominally state-bearing nation."[2] Since this process of nationalizing is rather too complex to be reflected upon in one short paper, the following pages address it at the legislative level,

---

1 Uri Ram, *Israeli Nationalism: Social Conflicts and the Politics of Knowledge* (London: Routledge, 2010).
2 Rogers Brubaker, "Nationalizing States in the Old 'New Europe' – and the New," *Ethnic and Racial Studies*, 19, no. 2 (1996): 412–37.

focusing on the Jewish nation-state bill. Examining the promotion of this bill can form a window through which one is able to delve into the deeper causes of the nationalizing process and reflect upon the hidden agenda of the hegemonic Neo-Zionist block.

THE EMERGENCE OF THE NEO-ZIONIST HEGEMONY

It is hard to dispute Anthony Smith's claim that every nationalism contains civic and ethnic elements in varying degrees and different forms.[3] Nonetheless, it is also hard to escape the coming to power of a deeply exclusive and hegemonic ethnic nationalistic block in Israel that praises and justifies inequality based on citizens' national or cultural affiliation. This trend speaks out against a common and shared civic public good in Israel. It insists that "general well-being" and "public interest" in Israel have to be exclusively determined and should be maintained in the hands of not only the Jewish majority, but actually the entire Jewish people. The hegemonic power of this ideological block makes it difficult to speak about the Rousseauian concept of "civic religion" or the Habermasian concept of "constitutional patriotism" as a minimal characteristic common to all Israeli citizens.[4] It stands for an ethnic sovereignty that transcends citizenry and worships the bond between people, land, and state.

One may argue, as the sociologist Sammy Smooha has, that this trend isn't new, and that the Israeli regime is defined by ethnic nationalism.[5] Notwithstanding Smooha's argument, the current Neo-Zionist era is characterized by the abandonment of central veiling mechanisms, such as the liberal academic and judicial discourses that assisted in framing Israel as an open, vibrant democratic

---

3 Anthony Smith, *The Ethnic Origins of Nations* (Oxford: Blackwell, 1986).

4 See Jean-Jacques Rousseau, *The Social Contract* (many editions), and Jürgen Habermas, *Struggles for Recognition in the Democratic Constitutional State* (Princeton, NJ: Princeton University Press, 1994).

5 Sammy Smooha, *Arabs and Jews in Israel*. Volume 1, *Conflicting and Shared Attitudes in a Divided Society* (Boulder and London: Westview Press, 1989).

system, despite institutionalized discrimination by the state against non-Jews. What is being argued here is that the Neo-Zionist block is today much more blunt and daring in its discourse and policies. The hegemonic ultra-nationalistic block is willing to trample whichever central traditional institutions, such as academic institutions and the High Court of Justice, that seek to protect liberal values and decent democratic procedures. The hegemonic ultra-nationalistic block utilizes ethno-majoritarianism as a despotic "democratic" mechanism in order to promote its worldviews and turn them into practical policies. The demographic weight of the conservative segments of the Jewish majority is exploited, and those segments are mobilized to establish the institutional and material privileges of Jewish citizens through majoritarian decision. This policy, which is not completely new, is reaching new peaks in the Neo-Zionist age, as more than forty bills and several laws enacted by the Knesset in the last decade demonstrate.[6]

The manifestations of the abovementioned trends are various and can be found in the political system, in civil society, and in the intersection between them.[7] The following pages demonstrate how the cooperation between what has been called in the literature "bad civil society"[8] and the political system nourishes Neo-Zionist trends, which gradually erode civil values and democratic procedures. Many nationalist civil society organizations are deeply involved in lobbying for more radical legislation that aims to either criminalize or delegitimize liberal civil activism and target the funding sources of liberal civil society organizations.[9] A unique manifestation of this dangerous trend is embodied by one of the most influential civic organizations identified with Neo-Zionist thought; namely "The

---

6 See Adalah's website for the list of bills: https://www.adalah.org/en/content/view/7771.
7 Amal Jamal, "The Rise of 'Bad Civil Society' in Israel," in *Stiftung Wissenschaft und Politik* (Berlin: German Institute for International and Security Affairs, 2018), https://www.swp-berlin.org/fileadmin/contents/products/comments/2018C02_jamal.pdf.
8 S. Chambers and J. Kopstein, "Bad Civil Society," *Political Theory* 29, no. 6 (2001): 837–65.
9 Jamal, "The Rise of 'Bad Civil Society' in Israel," ibid.

Institute for Zionist Strategies." In one of the Institute's 2009 publications, Dubi Helman and Adi Arbel best expressed the principle of exclusivity as a legitimate characteristic of the state and asserted the exclusive relationship between the Jewishness of the State of Israel and the principle of equality. They claimed:

> In the past, the State's status as National Home for the Jewish People was never questioned: it was obvious to the public and to the authorities, including the Judiciary. Practical manifestation of the Jewish status of the state can be seen in the very name of the State and from a multitude of laws such as the Flag, Symbol and Anthem Law 1949–5709; the Independence Law 1949–5709; the Law of Return 1950–5710 (which grants each Jew with the right to immigrate to Israel); the Work and Rest Hours Law 1951–5711 (which adopts the Sabbath and Jewish Holidays as days of rest); laws that institutionalise the cooperation between the State of Israel and the National Institutions of the Jewish People, and many more. Additionally, the State of Israel initiated programs and invested resources for the welfare of the Jewish people in the Diaspora, including: the promoting of *aliya* to the land of Israel, programmes to bring Jews to the Galilee, assisting in the *aliya* of Ethiopian Jewry, supporting Jewish Zionist education, memorialising the Holocaust, and others.[10]

Helman and Arbel complain that the principle of equality has become central in Israeli judicial discourse and has been posed as a legitimate demand by non-Jewish citizens of the State of Israel. They demonstrate that the principle of equality has become an internal danger which must be cured by legislation. In their view, equality contradicts the fundamental right of the Jewish people to have exclusive privileges in its own state, despite the fact that 20 percent of the population is not Jewish.

---

10 Dubi Helman and Adi Arbel, "The State of Israel as the National Home of the Jewish People," The Institute for Zionist Strategies, http://izs.org.il/2015/12/jewish-national-home/.

In recent years, a back-peddling trend has developed, which weakens the position of the State of Israel as the National Home of the Jewish People. The State of Israel, which was established as a Jewish state with a democratic form of government, would be turned into a liberal-democratic country with Jewish characteristics only to the extent that these characteristics do not contradict the principle of absolute equality among all groups. This radical liberal approach regards strict and absolute adherence to rigid and ubiquitous equality as the exclusive supreme value in a democratic society.[11]

According to Helman and Arbel, adopting the principle of equality as a "supreme value in Israel would deny the Jewish people its right to self-determination, seriously distorts democratic principles, violates the intention of the founders, and thwarts legitimate majority rule." Based on this internal danger – and in order to face it – they make clear that "it is imperative that Israel enact a Basic Law setting forth clearly that Israel is a Jewish state and the National Homeland of the Jewish people, and defining explicitly its Jewish character and mission."[12]

Such clear statements would not be of practical value and importance if not for the fact that a Basic Law proposal, similar to the one proposed by Helman and Arbel, was introduced to the Knesset by Avraham Dichter, who is currently a member of Knesset, was a minister in the Israeli government, and led the Israeli internal intelligence service (known as the Shin Bet, or Shabak) a few years earlier. Furthermore, the position of Helman and Arbel would have remained private if not for the clear process taking place in Israel in the last decade, when new laws were promoted which aimed to anchor Jewish hegemony and its privileges in the constitutional structure and in culture. One of the best examples of this trend is the 2003 amendment to the Citizenship and Entry into Israel Law, which made it almost impossible for Palestinian citizens of Israel to obtain permits for their Palestinian spouses and children from

---

11 Ibid.
12 Ibid.

the occupied Palestinian territories to enter and reside in Israel for purposes of family unification.[13] In 2007, the law was amended again to prohibit spouses from "enemy states" – Syria, Lebanon, Iran, and Iraq – to enter Israel as part of family unification, in order to avoid charges that the law was racist, being formerly directed solely and specifically against Palestinians.[14] These racist amendments, which were declared by the Israeli High Court as constitutional, complement the Israeli Law of Return of the early 1950s – viewed by Ben-Gurion as a foundational law of Israel – which provides automatic and rapid Israeli citizenship to any person of Jewish descent.

Another example which illustrates this point is the recent Nakba law, which allows the finance minister to withhold funds from official organizations which decide to commemorate the Palestinian Nakba of 1948.[15] This law is part and parcel of the grand policy of epistemic violence against Palestinian history, memory, and consciousness, as manifested in school books, literary and art policies, and even gastronomy.[16]

The immediate meaning of the discriminatory nationalistic legislation promoted by the Neo-Zionist camp is that it enjoys a convenient automatic majority to support its views, especially when these are combined with the protection of the rights of the entire Jewish people and the reiteration of its right for a sovereign state in its contested historical land. The bond between the State of Israel and the entire Jewish people is elevated into the major principle of the Neo-Zionist ideology, redefining the territory of the nation and membership in it. Neo-Zionists omit the difference between Israel and the occupied Palestinian territories from 1967, and view these as one entity, emphasising the right of the Jewish people over its entire

---

13 D. Barak-Erez, "Israel: Citizenship and Immigration Law in the Vise of Security, Nationality, and Human Rights," *I•CON* 6, no. 1 (2008): 184–92.

14 Amos Schocken, "Citizenship Law Makes Israel an Apartheid State," June 27, 2008, http://www.haaretz.com/citizenship-law-makes-israel-an-apartheid-state-1.248635.

15 A. Jamal, "Constitutionalizing Sophisticated Racism: Israel's Proposed Nationality Law," *Journal of Palestine Studies* 45, no. 2 (2016): 40–51.

16 D. Bar-Tal and Y. Teichman, *Stereotypes and Prejudice in Conflict: Representatives of Arabs in Israeli–Jewish Society* (Cambridge, UK: Cambridge University Press, 2005).

homeland. When speaking about the state they make clear that the sovereign agent to determine the future of the state is not the citizens of the state, but rather the entire Jewish people. Accordingly, the State of Israel expresses the aspirations of all Jews, including those living in the US, Canada, Australia, Russia, the UK, etc., emptying civic sovereignty from any meaning and replacing it with ethnonationalistic sovereignty that goes beyond the state. This trans-ethnic sovereignty depletes citizenship of any substantial meaning and replaces it with kinship as the main logic of sovereign power.

THE JEWISH NATION-STATE LAW AS SYMPTOM OF A NEO-ZIONIST HEGEMONIAL PROJECT

The nation-state law is of utmost importance for a number of reasons, the most important of which can be summarized as follows: (1) it reveals the aggressive racist proclivities of Israeli institutions; (2) it aims to entrench the national and religious Jewish ideology of the state; (3) it limits the ability of political and legal institutions to support democratic and civic interpretations of its constitutional precepts; and (4) it dispenses with non-Jewish citizens as a politically significant class.[17]

Since 2011 the nation-state bill has gone through many versions, but three basic iterations. Avraham Dichter, as a member of the Kadima Party at the time, proposed the first formulation of the bill in August 2011, based on a proposal by the aforementioned Institute for Zionist Strategies.[18] The second formulation was put forward by Ayelet Shaked of the Jewish Home Party and Yariv Levin of the Likud Party during the 19th Knesset in 2013.[19] Despite superficial

---

17 Tova Zimoki, "Akharey shana: Se'arat khok ha-le'om she-ba la-Kneset," *Yedioth Ahronoth*, October 21, 2015, https://www.ynet.co.il/articles/0,7340,L-4714531,00.html.

18 "Constitution of the State of Israel," Institute for Zionist Strategies, http://www.izs.org.il/userfiles/izs/file/Constitution.pdf.

19 Ayelet Shaked was appointed as minister of justice in Prime Minister Netanyahu's fourth government after the March 2015 elections. She recently proposed a new bill according to which representatives of human rights organizations would have to

differences, both proposals emphasize Israel as the state of the Jewish people in which self-determination belongs solely to Jews and where the Jewish character of the state overrules the democratic arrangement.

The proposed bill was presented to the Ministerial Committee for Legislation in November 2014.[20] The then-head of the committee, Tzipi Livni, who was also justice minister at the time, had raised political and ideological objections to the proposal all along, arguing that it contradicted the Declaration of Independence. Livni's objections led Netanyahu to propose a revised version of the bill in order to surmount Livni's objections. The proposal that eventually won the approval of the Cabinet did not make it through the legislative process as a result of the collapse of the ruling coalition in autumn 2014, which precipitated early elections.[21] Netanyahu's proposed compromise included fourteen principles, which were translated into the bill proposed by Dichter and brought to legislation as the third venture in the 20th Knesset after the 2015 elections. Since then the negotiations between the coalition parties led to many changes in the draft bill, but a proposal that maintained the basic principles from the earlier bills passed its first reading in the Knesset on May 1, 2018 by sixty-four votes to fifty, and was approved by the Knesset on July 19, 2018 with the support of 62 members of Knesset, 55 opposed, and 3 abstentions.

The first part of the law, which was approved by the Knesset on July 19, 2018 with the support of 62 MKs, 55 opposed and 3 absten-

---

wear a tag with a statement that their organization received funding from a foreign country. See Jonathan Lis, "Justice Ministry to Introduce Bill Demanding Foreign Funded NGOs to Wear Special Tag in Knesset," *Haaretz*, November 1, 2015, https://www.haaretz.com/israel-news/.premium-new-bill-calls-for-left-wing-ngos-to-wear-special-tag-in-knesset-1.5415863.

20 Hazki Ezra, "Khok ha-le'om osher ba-memshala," *Arutz Sheva*, November 23, 2014, http://www.inn.co.il/News/News.aspx/287869.

21 "Basic Law Proposal: Israel as the Nation-State of the Jewish People," Inter-Agency Task Force on Israeli Arab Issues, Legislative Update (November 2014), http://web.law.columbia.edu/sites/default/files/microsites/gender-sexuality/nationality_law_summary.pdf. See also Barak Ravid, Jonathan Lis, and Jack Khoury, "Netanyahu Pushing Basic Law Defining Israel as Jewish State," *Haaretz*, May 1, 2014, http://www.haaretz.com/israel-news/1.588478.

tions (2018, P/20/1989), includes three basic principles. The first states that "The land of Israel is the historic homeland of the Jewish people, in which the State of Israel was established." The two most important points to be noted in this formulation are first, the clear attempt to establish a continuous historical bond between the Jewish people and the land of Israel, and second, that the State of Israel has been established in part of the historical land, not in all of it. The second principle defines the State of Israel as "the nation-state of the Jewish people, in which it exercises its natural, cultural, religious and historical right to self-determination." This formulation makes clear that no other cultural and historical tradition, namely that of the Palestinian citizens, can be translated into the identity of the state. The national home of the Jewish people cannot also be the national home of the citizens who are not of Jewish descent. The third basic principle of the bill determines that the "right to exercise national self-determination in the State of Israel is uniquely that of the Jewish people." It is important to note that none of these principles define the borders of either the land of Israel or the State of Israel, which is the expression of the right for self-determination.[22] If this last principle maintains that the right to self-determination is *exclusive* to the Jewish people, it means that no other people(s) may argue for self-determination within the territory of the state. And since that territory is not clearly defined, it could include everything within the Green Line (so-called Israel proper) as well as the Palestinian territories occupied in 1967. The policy of applying the Israeli law in Palestinian areas occupied in 1967 means that the other side of the coin of the exclusive principle of self-determination is the blocking of the right of any other people for self-determination in areas considered by the government to be part of the State of Israel, but also the criminalizing of any demand to compromise the sovereignty of the Jewish people over the land of Israel. This stipulation effectively means that civic sovereignty is not possible, since any demand to transform Israel into a state of all its citizens,

---

22 Israel's official boundaries have not been delineated since the 1949 armistice agreement that ended the 1948 war when the state was established.

all of whom would be considered sovereign and could express their right to self-determination, is not only declared illegal, but is also substantially impossible.

One of the central changes introduced in the 2018 version of the bill is the omission of the clause relating to the goal of the bill. In previous drafts this clause asserted the bill's purpose as "to define the identity of the State of Israel as the nation-state of the Jewish people and to anchor the values of the State of Israel as a Jewish and democratic state, in the spirit of the principles of the Declaration of the Establishment of the State of Israel." Based on this formulation, the revised bill – in what it omits – assumes two issues worth noting. The first is that there is a need to protect the identity and character of the state, as the state of the Jewish people. Presumably the spirit of the text introduced above – according to which establishing equality, as a basic principle in Israel, would turn the state into a state of all its citizens and thereby weaken the state's Jewish identity – would also weaken the text as an expression of the exclusive right of Jews for self-determination. The second is the absence of any encoding of the values of the State of Israel as a Jewish and democratic state in accordance with the principles of the Declaration of Independence in a Basic Law. The omission of this goal in the version confirmed in the first reading means that the balance between the Jewish and democratic character of the state, as institutionalized in previous basic laws, is not anymore valid. This step has been a clear indication that the ruling coalition is seeking to subordinate the democratic character of the state to its Jewish one. The democratic regime becomes therefore secondary to the Jewishness of the state, a step heavily criticized by leading constitutional experts in Israel, among whom are veteran justices of the High Court.

In comparing the citizenship rights of Jews and Palestinians in the approved law in relation to former versions we find that whereas Jews are granted collective and individual rights that complement each other, the civic status of Palestinian citizens is restricted and cannot contradict or challenge the exclusive priority of collective rights given to Jews. The fact that every Jew around the world has the individual right to immigrate to Israel and automatically receive citizenship exemplifies how the state defines itself as exclusively Jewish. By establishing the superiority of the Jewish people in and over the state, the bill creates a despotic majoritarian regime under the guise of majoritarian democracy, but also blocks the way for civic equality, establishing thereby what could be called "essential apartheid."

This interpretation of the law is supported by several clauses which are especially important for this context. The first important clause is the one concerning language. This clause establishes a new hierarchy between Hebrew, which is the "state language," and Arabic, which is downgraded from an official language into a language of "special status in the state." Despite the fact that the approved law declares that the clause relating to the Arabic language "does not harm the status given to the Arabic language before this law came into effect," it still mirrors the real intentions of the bill-drafters, who view the official status of the Arabic language as a violation of the identity of the state as Jewish. The targeting of the constitutional status of the Arabic language, which on practical terms is not translated into a serious burden on the state, reflects the hostility towards what the language symbolizes, namely the historical and cultural roots of the Palestinian citizens, which contradict the exclusive Neo-Zionist narrative promoted by the law.

The other important clauses are those regarding the relationship between the state and the Jewish Diaspora. These clauses define the nature of the bond between Israel and the Jewish people living outside its borders. The first clause declares that "The state will strive to ensure the safety of the members of the Jewish people in trouble or in captivity due to the fact of their Jewishness or their citizenship." The second clause states that "The state shall act within the Diaspora to strengthen the affinity between the state and members of the Jewish people." Further to that, the third clause declares that "The state shall act to preserve the cultural, historical and religious heritage of the Jewish people among Jews in the Diaspora." These clauses would not have drawn particular attention if not for the fact that they ignore that 20 percent of the state is made up of non-Jews, who also have relatives living outside the state. This differentiation establishes clear discrimination between different citizens of the state, something that could be seen even more clearly in a clause that had been part of the bill, but which was omitted from the final draft. In the draft that preceded the approved version of the law, this clause stated that "Every resident of Israel, regardless of religion or nationality, is entitled to work to preserve their culture, heritage, language, and identity." Thus the state has an active role vis-à-vis its Jewish citizens and the promotion of their culture, but a passive one toward its other citizens, whom it expects to take that responsibility upon themselves. According to this principle, the state is not committed to supporting and developing the culture, tradition, language, and identity of non-Jews, namely the Palestinian citizens of the state. Therefore, not only does the state discriminate against non-Jews in terms of its identity and symbols, but it is also entitled to exclude them from the allocation of public resources to develop and maintain their cultural identity. Even though this clause has not been included in the last version of the law, it reveals the actual policies of the state and reflects its malicious intentions and practical policies towards non-Jewish citizens. These policies declare the state's commitment to protect Jews no matter where they live. They also express the state's pledge to protect, develop, and provide education about Jewish historical and cultural traditions to Jews in the Diaspora.

The principle of the right to protect one's tradition includes another clause that is worth noting. This clause declares that "The state views the development of Jewish settlement as a national value and will act to encourage and promote its establishment and consolidation." This means that the state does not view the development of Arab settlements to meet the growing needs of the Palestinian citizens as a national value and will not act to promote their establishment and consolidation. Knowing that the former version of the law included a clause stating that "the state may allow a community composed of one religion or one nationality to maintain a separate residential community" reveals the real intention of the approved version of the clause. The former version of the clause has been omitted since it has been heavily criticized, for it establishes segregation as a constitutional principle and has clear racial implications. It intended to clearly and bluntly grant Jewish communal settlements the right to establish themselves on state land and to be supported by state funds and, simultaneously, the power to block Palestinian citizens from being able to build or buy houses in these areas, something that has, on several occasions, already occurred.[23] Changing the wording of the clause does not hide the real intentions behind it, despite the "sophisticated" discriminatory language used in the approved law.

Other principles of the law deal with the official calendar of the state and its symbols, which are fully and exclusively Jewish. One of the important clauses that adorned the former version of the law proposed Jewish jurisprudence as a source of inspiration for the Knesset when it creates laws. This idea, which mirrors the growing influence of religious ideology in state affairs and in Israel's legal and judicial systems, has been omitted, as a result of intense debate within the ruling coalition. Notwithstanding the omission of this clause, one notes that religion has been added to the second basic principle of the law, which states that "The State of Israel is the nation-state of the Jewish people, in which it exercises its natural, cultural, *religious* and historical right to self-determination" (italics added).

While the approved law may be less extreme and directly hostile than the original version that was drafted in 2011, it still includes the same conceptual values and excludes the principle of equality. It also further demotes the democratic character of the state to the advantage of its Jewish identity. The amended proposal formally secures the divorce between the national rights of the Jewish people and the civil rights of the citizens of the state, practically resulting in ongoing duress and coercion in terms of the civil and national status of the Palestinian citizens of Israel. The law makes the Jewish people the sole custodians of the State of Israel. It does not only characterize Palestinian citizens as a group of individuals who are not guaranteed any national or collective expression, but also views

---

23 See more on the topic on the website of the Association for Citizens Rights in Israel, https://www.acri.org.il/he/97.

any effort by them to call for such rights as a violation of the law. This reading is supported by the declaration made by the custodian of the law, Avi Dichter, on the eve of its approval, that "We are approving this important law today in order to prevent the slightest thought, let alone an attempt, to transform Israel into the state of all its citizens."[24] Put simply, the law states that the entirety of the world's Jews have sovereignty over the state, even those who do not reside in Israel and are citizens of other countries, while Palestinian citizens – natives of the land – are not included in Israel's civil sovereignty. Such a law closes the door on Palestinian civil struggle for equality, criminalizing any efforts to grant a common civic horizon for a shared and tolerant plural society.

Given that the Declaration of Independence – which has special constitutional standing in the Israeli juridical tradition – defined Israel as a Jewish state ever since its establishment, questions must be raised about the justification for the nation-state law. Israel has fully exercised its Jewishness in all areas of politics. It has established a moral and material system that favors the Jewish historical narrative throughout the entirety of Israel's jurisdiction, including the lands occupied in 1967. But it maintains a democratic veneer via institutions that are administered according to democratic principles. For example, Israel has a transfer of power by elections, a separation of powers, and a wide arena for freedom of expression in matters relating to the Jewish community's social, economic, and cultural life. These practices allow the Jewish majority to exercise ethnically-oriented and blatantly discriminatory policies while simultaneously framing them as expressions of democratic majorities, and thereby to present Israel as a hallmark of modern democratic states.

The nation-state law, however, exposes the intentions of the Israeli political system, which no longer feels the need to justify its racist policies and exploits international opinion, and the situation of Arab states since the popular upheavals that started in 2011 (the so-called

---

24 Moran Azoulai, "The Nationality Law Approved: The Coalition Cheered, the Opposition Shouted Apartheid." *Yedioth Ahronoth*, July 29, 2017, https://www.ynet.co.il/articles/0,7340,L-5312599,00.html

Arab Spring), in order to enact policies in the name of "defensive democracy."[25] These policies exploit the subordinate status of the Palestinian minority and fly in the face of democracy's very essence. The bill proposals were drawn up against a background of major constitutional changes that had been taking place in Israel for over a decade, including the 2003 amendment to the citizenship act.[26]

EXTERNAL AND INTERNAL FACTORS BEHIND THE NATION-STATE LAW

A number of external and internal factors account for the prominence of the Jewish nation-state law in the Israeli political arena. The first external factor relates to the Palestinians and the question of an agreement leading to Palestinian independence in accordance with international law and UN resolutions. Prime Minister Netanyahu has now made recognizing Israel as a Jewish state a demand in negotiations with the Palestinians. The Palestinian leadership emphatically objects to this request, stating that while they may be willing to concede the point that Israel is a sovereign state, they would not go into details about its identity.[27]

Were Palestinians to recognize Israel as the state of the Jewish people, they would in fact be recognizing that the only people who have a "right of return" there are Jews. Such an acknowledgment on the part of the Palestinians would achieve two goals: first, it would

---

25 Naomi Heiman-Rish, "Demokratiya mitgonenet be-Yisrael," The Israel Democracy Institute, September 2008, https://www.idi.org.il/parliaments/5478/8552.

26 "The Citizenship and Entry into Israel Law (temporary provision) 5763 – 2003," The Knesset, last modified 2003, http://www.knesset.gov.il/laws/special/eng/citizenship_law.htm. See also Amal Jamal, "The Contradictions of State-Minority Relations: The Search for Clarification," *Constellations* 16, no. 3 (2009): 493–508; and Guy Davidov, Jonathan Yuval, Ilan Saban, and Amnon Reichman, "Medina o mishpakha? Khok ha-ezrakhot ve-ha-knisa le-Yisrael (hora'at sha'a)" *Mishpat u-mimshal* 8 (2005): 643–99.

27 Daoud Kuttab, "Abbas Delivers Message of Peace to Israeli Students," *Al-Monitor*, February 20, 2014, http://www.daoudkuttab.com/articles/3478/; "We Recognize Israel, They Should Recognize Palestine," *Jerusalem Post*, June 30, 2011, http://www.jpost.com/Diplomacy-and-Politics/We-recognize-Israel-they-should-recognize-Palestine.

provide retroactive recognition legitimizing Israel's past treatment of the Palestinians and its establishment as a state of the Jewish people, even when its policies violated the basic rights of Palestinians in general and of the Palestinian citizens in particular. Second, it would prevent the return of any Palestinians to territories defined as Israeli, limiting the practice of the internationally-recognized Palestinian refugees' right of return to a future Palestinian state, if such a state were established.

In this regard, it is important to note that, as proposed by the Netanyahu Cabinet, the Jewish nation-state law would obstruct any solution of the Israeli-Palestinian conflict in the near future as it makes future Israeli concessions contingent upon the recognition of the state's exclusive identity. It is important to note that all members of Knesset who drafted the original bill clearly and explicitly object to any Israeli withdrawal from occupied Palestinian territories. Their proposal is part of a larger effort to compel moderate legislators into either supporting the bill, thereby promoting their right-wing agenda, or being exposed as traitors, given the narrowly-defined national character of the state.

The second external factor relates to the international legitimacy of Israel and the state's need to assert itself as the expression of the state envisaged by the 1947 UN Partition Plan and its subsequent recognition by the UN in 1949. This comes at a time when Israel's international standing is being steadily eroded as boycotts of the state are gradually taking root in a variety of cultural sectors in different parts of the world.[28] This change in public opinion overwhelmingly reflects growing recognition of the State of Palestine despite Israel's best efforts to block such a development (Israel, for its part, claims that such recognition sabotages direct peace negotiations between the two sides). It is these kinds of changes in the international climate that have led Israeli right-wing politicians, Netanyahu among them, to support the legislation of the nation-state law. In its attempt to

---

28 See Omar Barghouti, "Why Israel Fears the Boycott," *The New York Times*, January 31, 2014, http://www.nytimes.com/2014/02/01/opinion/sunday/why-the-boycott -movement-scares-israel.html.

strengthen Israel's legitimacy and to ground the Jewishness of the state in international law, the bill advocates the dominant Israeli interpretation of the Partition Plan's call for establishing two states in Palestine, one Jewish and one Arab.[29]

The third external factor involves redefining the relationship between the Israeli state and Jewish communities abroad, especially as liberals from those communities have expressed increasing exasperation with official Israeli government policies in the last decade.[30] Thus, the law seeks to address younger generations of Jews across the world by re-characterizing Jewish identity politics as transcending the various civic affiliations of Diaspora Jews, with Israel at their center. The redefinition of Israel as the state of the Jewish people serves to remind the global Jewish community that not only is Israel their home, but that, even in the presence of ideological differences, the premise remains unshakeable. Thus, the law promotes a definition of the state that requires a clear commitment on the part of Jewish communities not only to accept the state as their own but also to defend it at any cost, since it is the embodiment of their identity and safety. This type of expression manifests a tribal aspect of Jewish nationality, according to which Jewish ethnic affiliation is an essential indication of political loyalty, regardless of one's residence or citizenship. Netanyahu's call for French Jews, after the January 2015 terrorist attacks in Paris, to "come home," for instance, falls within this perception of Israel as an organic entity and a safe haven for the entirety of the Jewish people worldwide.

The ideological viewpoint just described reflects Israel's concern to counter the effects of the Boycott, Divestment, and Sanctions (BDS) movement and its efforts to recruit Jewish communities everywhere to join in that effort. Netanyahu's June 2015 statement that, "attacks against Jews have always been preceded by the slander of

---

29 "UN General Assembly Resolution 181 (II). Future Government of Palestine," United Nations, November 29, 1947, https://unispal.un.org/DPA/DPR/unispal.nsf/0/7F0AF2BD897689B785256C330061D253.

30 See "Us and Them," *The Economist*, August 2, 2014, http://www.economist.com/news/briefing/21610312-pummelling-gaza-has-cost-israel-sympathy-not-just-europe-also-among-americans.

Jews," attempts to equate BDS with Nazi and other anti-Semitic rhetoric and to preempt any discussion of BDS and its relationship to official government policies.[31] In other words, the official discourse depicts BDS as aiming to delegitimize Israel as the state of the Jewish people rather than to liberate Palestinians from Israeli occupation. Accordingly, Israeli legislators expect Jewish communities in Europe, the United States, Australia, and beyond to commit to helping Israel, regardless of its conduct.

In addition to the above external factors, there are two major internal factors that inform the law. The first deals with the current institutional struggle within the Israeli political system between the legislative and the judicial authorities. The legislative authority, embodied in the Knesset, represents the "will of the people" and is responsible for passing laws. Today, most legislators are either nationalists, religious, or conservative, or a combination of the three political actors whose view of Israel tends to be messianic and absolutist. Most MKs of the ruling block view the moral and ideological values of the state in absolute terms, arguing that it is legislative authority that determines the character of the state and its policies.[32] These legislators claim that the civil and liberal political figures that make up the judicial authority, represented by the High Court of Justice, consider Israel to be a state with a Jewish majority – without committing to national or cultural values.

This tension between the legislative and judicial authorities stems from what Menachem Mautner, a prominent scholar of Israeli constitutional law, identifies as the decline of formalism and the rise of values in the Israeli judicial system.[33] Right-wing legislators argue that judicial authority, which is constitutionally responsible for interpreting the law according to the spirit in which it was intended,

---

31 "Netanyahu on BDS: Attacks on Jews always preceded by slander of Jews," *Yedioth Ahronoth*, June 15, 2015, http://www.ynetnews.com/articles/0,7340, L-4668771,00.html.

32 Shai Bermanis, Daphna Canetti-Nisim, and Ami Pedahzur, "Religious Fundamentalism and the Extreme Right-Wing Camp in Israel," *Patterns of Prejudice* 38, no. 2 (2004): 159–76.

33 Menachem Mautner, *Law and the Culture of Israel* (Oxford: Oxford University Press, 2011). See especially chapter 4, "The Decline of Formalism and the Rise of Values."

is encroaching on the authority of the legislator by promoting liberal interpretations of the law.[34] Thus, in their view, by positioning itself above the elected representatives of the people, who happen to be conservative nationalists, judicial authority is usurping its role.

In light of the intensification of this conflict between the two sides in recent years, the nation-state law is an attempt by legislators to impose a new constitutional formula that would in their view represent the will of the majority and its support for a conservative ideology as expressed at the ballot-box. This formula would thus limit the manoeuvring room of the High Court of Justice to defy the will of the people either by interpreting nationalistic laws liberally or by striking down legislation that does not meet what the judiciary considers to be the minimum threshold of rights. This institutional conflict has been reflected in right-wing promotion of certain types of legislation, and in allegations against the judiciary system in general, and against the High Court in particular, with the nationalist and religious right both threatening to and attempting to pass laws that limit the ability of the High Court to "exploit" legal ambiguities. Thus, the Jewish nation-state law seeks to settle the ambiguity that the Declaration of Independence allows, which Israel's highest court has thus far considered the primary document determining the state's liberal values, especially those of equality and freedom. By enforcing the Jewish identity of the state, the law would restore

---

34 Recently, a Knesset member from the Jewish Home (Bayit Yehudi) party, Motti Yogev, accused the High Court of Justice of betrayal for delaying a decision made by the army to demolish Palestinian houses in retaliation for the killing of four Israelis (Danny Gonen, Malaachi Rosenfeld, and the couple Naama and Eitam Hanken). Members of the families who own the houses are accused of the killing. See Sharon Folber, "Baga"ts hakipi harisut batei kama mekhabelim ba-tsav arai," *Haaretz*, October 22, 2015, http://www.haaretz.co.il/news/law/1.2758489. In response to the accusation, which reflects the tension between the dominant right-wing political forces in the Knesset and the judicial system, the Vice President of the Supreme Court, Elyakim Rubinstein, argued in a lecture that the accusation of the Supreme Court as betraying national loyalty is empty of meaning. His argument was based on the fact that the High Court has not prevented the demolition of Palestinian houses when the correct judicial procedures have been followed. For more details on this dispute, see Eitan Kalinski, "Ha-shofet Rubinstein ha-ya'ad ha-ba shel Yogev?" *News1*, November 4, 2015, http://www.news1.co.il/Archive/003-D-00-107124.html.

authority to the legislature. This understanding is reiterated in the new Basic Law on Legislation introduced by Justice Minister Ayelet Shaked and Education Minister Naftali Bennett, which, according to them, comes to "restore the balance" between the legislator and the high court.[35] The proposed bill would actually allow the Knesset to circumvent the High Court of Justice and the Supreme Court in the event Justices disqualify Knesset legislation.

The second internal factor that led legislators to propose the nation-state law concerns Israel's Palestinian citizens and their repeated challenges to the political and judiciary systems in recent decades. In its effort to establish "loyalty" and "allegiance" as determinant factors in Israeli political culture (and thereby define citizenship according to the fulfilment of certain duties such as army service or civic service), rather than through the exercise of equal civic rights, the law is part of a strategy to impose new rules of the political game on Israel's Palestinian citizens. If successful, it would subject the community to absolute Jewish hegemony, hollowing their political struggle for collective rights of any substantive meaning.

In the early 1990s, the National Democratic Assembly (NDA or Balad), led by Azmi Bishara and Jamal Zahalka, proposed "a state of all its citizens" as an alternative constitutional formula. The proposal called on the state to respect basic democratic principles despite the demographic asymmetry between the Jewish majority and the Palestinian minority. This alternative challenged Israel's hegemonic, exclusive, and antagonistic political model and introduced a more inclusive political vision that upheld genuine democratic values – especially equality, dignity, and freedom. Moreover, the NDA proposal demonstrated that the Jewish-and-democratic formula was incompatible with a genuine democratic polity that consists in openness, diversity, and magnanimity. The NDA's proposal further demonstrated that the Jewish-and-democratic formula entails internal contradictions since the definition of the privileged national

---

35 Marissa Newman, "Shaked, Bennet Propose Constitutional Law to Circumvent Supreme Court," *The Times of Israel*, September 15, 2017, https://www.timesofisrael.com/shaked-bennett-propose-constitutional-law-to-circumvent-supreme-court/.

group in exclusive ethnic terms renders meaningless any political aspiration to civility and equality between the minority and majority groups.[36] Finally, the NDA-proposed alternative formulation exposed legislators' purported democratic procedures as counteracting basic democratic principles.

More than a decade after the NDA presented its state-of-all-its-citizens vision, in three separate but related initiatives Palestinian intellectuals, academics, and activists in Israel issued another set of documents demanding total civil and national equality. Appearing in 2006–7, the three documents – Mada al-Carmel's Haifa Declaration; Future Vision, developed under the auspices of the Committee of Arab Mayors in Israel; and the Democratic Constitution, issued by Adalah – The Legal Center for Arab Minority Rights in Israel – challenged the Jewish hegemony of the state once again and demanded full democratization based on liberal and collective rights embedded in international law.[37] By calling for the transformation of Israel into a fully democratic state which would effectively establish a difference between Jewish citizens' right to self-determination and Israel as the state of the Jewish people everywhere, these initiatives dealt an additional blow to the Jewish-and-democratic constitutional equation. These documents make the point that Israel's existence as the expression of the Jewish right to self-determination does not necessarily entitle all Jews everywhere to immediate rights in the state or make them the only stake-holders in such a state, arguing that such a policy effectively degrades the status of the Palestinian citizens to second-class citizenship. In the eyes of many Israelis, the formulation of such demands was tantamount to a declaration of war against the Jewish state, and some have consequently regarded Arab citizens as enemies of the state.[38] The approval of the nation-state law has led Palestinian academics, as they face the possible ramifications of

---

36 Amal Jamal, *Arab Minority Nationalism in Israel: The Politics of Indigeneity* (London; New York: Routledge, 2011).

37 "The Haifa Declaration," Mada al-Carmel, published May 15, 2007, http://mada -research.org/en/files/2007/09/haifaenglish.pdf.

38 Amal Jamal, "The Political Ethos of Palestinian Citizens of Israel: Critical Reading in the Future Vision Documents," *Israel Studies Forum* 23, no. 2 (2008): 3–28.

the new law, to call for a reformulation of the earlier visionary documents. This call is deeply related to the vision documents having been based on the two-state formula as the institutional solution to the Israeli-Palestinian conflict. Assuming that the new law blocks implementing this option in any future negotiations between the two sides, it is argued that there is a need to envision a new political and legal reality that challenges the law and grants equal status to all Palestinians, including those living in the West Bank and Gaza, as well as refugees in exile.

In his presentation of the Jewish nation-state bill in the Knesset on November 26, 2014, Netanyahu asserted, "Israel will always preserve full equal rights, both personal and civil, of all citizens of the State of Israel, Jews and non-Jews as one, in the Jewish and democratic state.... Indeed, in Israel, individual rights and civil rights are guaranteed to all – something which makes us unique in the Middle East and beyond it."[39] Thus, the Jewish nation-state law reiterates that Palestinians have to be satisfied with only individual rights in the Jewish state. Emphasizing individual and civil rights and comparing Israel with other Middle Eastern countries is a way of stressing that the Palestinian citizens of Israel have no better alternatives and should be content with their status; after all, citizens of Arab states do not even enjoy civil democratic rights. This argument maintains the traditional Israeli position that Israel is a so-called "democratic villa in the jungle," and that as the sole "moral" state in the region it is entitled to determine the measure and character of the rights accruing to its Palestinian citizens.[40] Those who do not like it or are unwilling to act accordingly will be either outlawed or crushed, as evinced in the recent declaration of the northern wing of the Islamic Movement as an "unauthorized assembly."[41]

---

39 Moran Azolai, "Netanyahu hatsig le-rishona: ele 'ikronot khok ha-le'om sheli," *Yedioth Ahronoth*, November 26, 2016, http://www.ynet.co.il/articles/0,7340,L-4596506 ,00.html.

40 Aluf Benn, "The Jewish Majority in Israel Still See their Country as 'a Villa in the Jungle,'" *The Guardian*, August 20, 2013, http://www.theguardian.com/commentisfree /2013/aug/20/jewish-majority-israel-villa-in-the-jungle.

41 Barak Ravid, "Israel Outlaws Islamic Movement's Northern Branch," *Haaretz*,

CONCLUSION

The results of the March 2015 Israeli elections and the Knesset majority that approved the nation-state law in 2018 leave open the possibility that the nation-state law, as well as other bills proposed by nationalist members of Knesset, will remain a fixture of the political agenda in Israel. While one of the central parties in the current coalition, Kulanu, has had reservations over certain clauses of the bill and managed to change parts of it, nationalist legislators continue to promote policies that differentiate between those who belong to the majority and accept their nationalistic values and those who do not. The ruling coalition managed to revitalize the legislation process on the nationality law on May 7, 2017, when the Ministerial Committee for Legislation decided to promote the legislation of a new version of the bill.[42] This decision opened the door to a governmental bill that is agreed upon by all coalition members, something that guaranteed a supportive majority in the Knesset. That a majority of sixty-four Knesset members supported the first reading of the 2018 bill made possible the approval of the law with a majority of sixty-two MKs. That certain clauses of the bill were either amended or omitted reflects the differences between the various components of the ruling coalition. It also reflects the disagreement with the President of the High Court, Esther Hayut. Hayut opposed the bill for several reasons, central of which is the imbalance it engenders between the Jewish and democratic character of the state and the proposed law's ramifications on the liberal character of the Israeli constitutional tradition. The changes that took place in the final draft were intended to facilitate the approval of the High Court, something that we still have to wait for, since appeals against the law have been just filed. One of these appeals

---

November 17, 2015, https://www.haaretz.com/israel-news/israel-outlaws-islamic
-movement-s-northern-branch-1.5422760.

42 Jonathan Lis, "Israeli Ministers Green-light Nation-state Bill: Arabic Isn't an Official State Language," *Haaretz*, May 7, 2017, https://www.haaretz.com/israel-news
/ministers-okay-nation-state-bill-arabic-not-an-official-language-1.5469065.

has been introduced by three Druze Knesset members, who argue that the law has major ramifications on non-Jews, who mandatorily serve in the Israeli army. Defining the state as the state of the Jewish people means that serving in the Israeli army is serving in the army of the Jewish people, not the army of the Israeli state that guarantees equality to all citizens, as stated in the Declaration of Independence. According to this appeal and the public debate taking place among Druze citizens, the law turns Druze soldiers into mercenaries, whose life and loyalty is subordinated to the will of the Jewish people in exchange not for full citizenship, but rather for symbolic recognition and material privileges. The unwillingness of the prime minister to consider any change in the approved law, and in a meeting with leaders of the community his proposal to facilitate a development plan for the Druze villages, made the tension with the Druze community even worse. Many in the community interpreted the proposal made by the prime minister as an insulting attempt to buy its conscience and silence it with money.

Should the trend of radical right-wing politics continue to shape the state's constitutional and legal climate, the assumption that the Jewish-and-democratic equation is a tenable one may finally come undone. The legislative trend may finally expose one of the central veiling mechanisms enabling the state to promote exclusive ethnic and discriminatory policies while at the same time maintaining its image as democratic. Now that the Knesset has approved the law, the discrepancy between the reality of the Jewish state and its image will become glaring. The nationalizing process in the Neo-Zionist era put Israel in a new place, in which democratic values are abandoned and the gatekeepers of democracy are weakened. The dwindling power of liberal forces and the domination of the political system by conservative ultra-nationalist forces demand re-evaluation of Israeli political culture, especially its common classification in comparative political science literature as mostly democratic. The approval of the nationality law and the continuation of nationalizing legislative trends make Israel more vulnerable to critique and makes the life of those seeking to stigmatize the Jewish state as an apartheid state much easier.

The Triumph of Majoritarianism, and the Decline of Democracy

David N. Myers

At the end of March 1919, Jewish leaders from Europe and the United States assembled in Paris in advance of the peace talks that would bring a formal end to the First World War. Gathered together as the Comité des Délégations Juives (Committee of Jewish Delegations), this group sought to gain assurances from the Allied Powers for the protection of the rights of Jews, as individuals and as a collective. The collapse of the old imperial order had placed Jews in eastern Europe in a profoundly vulnerable condition; many were threatened, displaced, and murdered in the midst of the Great War and immediately after. Along with the Allies and other representative groups, the Comité sought to ensure that the new nation-states taking rise out of the ashes of empire guarantee the linguistic, cultural, educational, and physical well-being of large minorities in their midst, including the Jews.

The resulting Minorities Treaties that accompanied the establishment of these new states did indeed contain clauses protecting the right of national minorities to use their own language, create their own educational institutions, and preserve their own religious traditions. But enforcement of these clauses fell by the wayside soon after the creation of the new states, rendering the "Versailles system," as it was known, largely impotent. What might have been an hour of grand triumph for the principle of collective rights for national, ethnic, and religious minority groups instead became a missed opportunity with stark consequences for the future.

Notwithstanding the failed implementation of the Minorities Treaties, it is helpful to juxtapose that moment of possibility with the current moment in which we again find Jews seeking to enshrine their linguistic, cultural, and educational rights, this time in the new spate of nationality, or nation-state, bills, one version of which finally passed in the Israeli Knesset in July 2018. The major difference, of course, is that a century ago, Jews were a tattered minority attempting to gain protection from European powers, whereas those seeking such rights today belong to a national majority in their own sovereign state. It is easy to understand why Jewish representatives were so concerned to memorialize protections for their co-religionists in 1919. It is a bit more difficult to understand why Israeli Jews seek it today.

I

The intense flurry of legislative activity around a new nationality bill began in 2011 with a proposal by thirty-seven right-wing parliamentarians to draft a Basic Law that defined Israel as "the Nation-State of the Jewish People."[1] Many regard Basic Laws, or at least some of them, as building blocks of an Israeli constitution that has not yet been written, in no small part because of the fractious divisions in that country's political culture. The proposed 2011 Basic Law declared, among other provisions, that Israel was "the national home of the Jewish people," that Hebrew was the sole official state language, that the state should "preserve the cultural and historical heritage of the Jewish People," and that this heritage should be taught in Jewish schools. The draft also proposed that Israel be recognized as "a democratic state" and that all its residents "are entitled to the right to work to preserve their culture, heritage, language, and identity." The versions of the bill that finally passed in the Knesset seven years later eliminated any reference to democracy or a democratic state and added a clause calling for the promotion of Jewish settlement in the state. There can be little doubt that the sponsors of the various drafts, especially the final version that passed, aimed to codify the

---

1 See document B. (2011, P/18/3541).

supremacy of Jewish law, norms, and values over all others, including democracy.

Why such widespread insecurity from a usually – in fact, unusually – self-confident, technologically advanced, and militarily powerful state? The declared reason, as the drafters have argued, is that there are forces in the world seeking to deny the right of the Jews to their homeland and to a state. Among them, one might surmise, are advocates of global BDS (boycott, divestment, and sanctions), who have argued for the right of return of Palestinian refugees – an act that many Israelis fear would spell the demise of Israel as a Jewish state.

In fact, as important as those supposedly sinister, albeit unnamed, forces are, deep internal divides have riven Israel for decades. The nation-state bills are the latest iteration of Israel's *Kulturkampf.* I refer not to the simmering tensions between Israel's Jewish majority and Palestinian Arab minority, but rather to competing camps and visions within the Israeli Jewish population. For nearly a quarter century, there has been a swing of the pendulum back and forth between the poles of democracy and Judaism as the guiding light of the Israeli polity. In 1992, the Knesset passed the Basic Law whose opening clause declared the law's aim "to protect human dignity and liberty." An amendment to this law two years later displaced the earlier opening clause with: "Fundamental human rights in Israel are founded upon recognition of the value of the human being, the sanctity of human life, and the principle that all persons are free." It was in this sense that Israel could be, as former Supreme Court Chief Justice Aharon Barak – a key architect of this language – imagined, both Jewish and democratic. That vision of an Israel at peace with itself held sway, at least briefly, in the 1990s, the era of the Oslo peace process when it seemed possible for the century-long enmity between Jews and Arabs in historic Palestine to come to an end.

With the collapse of that vision – commencing with the assassination of Prime Minister Yitzhak Rabin in 1995 and leading up to the outbreak of the Second Intifada in 2000 – the pendulum swung away from the pole of a self-declared democratic Israel toward a more insular, fearful, and insecure Israel intent on foregrounding its

Jewish identity. The effort to legislate the primacy of Jewish values over democratic values is evident in the negligible mention of the latter in the various draft bills.

These bills read like a defensive response – as if Jews and their identity are beleaguered in their own state. Efforts to protect their language, heritage, and education would make more sense if the Jews were a minority in a state controlled by a non-Jewish majority. But in fact, they represent 80 percent of the population and are in control of all levels of governance. And the effect – and a key intent – of these laws is not merely to shift the balance of power away from democracy as part of the ongoing culture war, but, even more grimly, to signal to the Palestinian Arab population of Israel that it is and will remain practically and legally subordinate to the Jews in the State of Israel.

The scourge of majoritarianism has reared its head before. This motif was somewhat muted in Israel's founding Declaration of Independence from May 14, 1948, which described Palestine "as the birthplace of the Jewish people," but also included powerful language promising "complete equality of social and political rights to all inhabitants irrespective of religion, race or sex." Some of the first legislative steps by the Knesset, however, gave pause to this ecumenical promise. For example, the first Nationality Law (also known as the Citizenship Law) passed by the Knesset in 1952 set out differential paths for Jews and Arabs to acquire citizenship, privileging the former over the latter (and setting up obstacles for Arabs who had been displaced from their homes to return to them). An Israeli legal scholar writing at the time, Yehoshua Freudenheim, affirmed that "those who claim that the law remands the minority to the mercy of the authorities and does not grant it any rights are correct."[2] This law operationalized the majoritarian logic of mainstream Zionism and of incipient Israeli statehood. Now, more than six decades later, the Knesset has passed a new "nationality" law that provides definitional cover to Jewish majoritarianism with little regard for the substantial ethnic and national minority within the state's borders.

---

2 Yehoshua Freudenheim, *Ha-shilton bi-medinat Yisrael* (Jerusalem: Rubin Mass, 1950), 190.

II

The question of why Israeli politicians would feel compelled to draft these recent laws – laws that issue from a majority acting like an oppressed minority – is, at one level, vexing, but at another, understandable. As noted above, there is a palpable fear that enemies from within and without are trying to strip away Israel's Jewish character. That fear produces, in turn, a profound and paralyzing blindness with a set of glaring symptoms.

The first symptom of this blindness is the persistent neglect of Palestinian citizens within Israel's borders. One might have expected that with the passage of time, as Israel has grown in strength and confidence, it would choose to devote more attention to the interests of its economically disadvantaged and politically disaffected minority population. Despite the promising language of the Declaration of Independence and repeated statements of an intent to do so, Israel has not devoted much attention or resources to its Palestinian citizens, prompting the state-appointed Or Commission to proclaim in 2003 that "government handling of the Arab sector has been primarily neglectful and discriminatory."[3] Now, the new nation-state bill passed in 2018 came along to shore up the language, symbols, heritage, holidays and day of rest, and religious law of the *Jewish majority*. In the final version, all of the eleven clauses perform that task. By contrast, only two clauses make mention of the rights of minorities. One of them refers vaguely to the "special status" of Arabic, though only when Hebrew is declared to be the single "state language" of Israel. The other refers to the right of non-Jews to "maintain days of rest on their Sabbaths and festivals," the details of which will be further determined by law.

When reading the bill, one recalls the probing mid-century Jewish thinker, Simon Rawidowicz, who expressed concern in the 1950s that the new Israeli state was ignoring the historical, political, and moral

---

3 "Israeli Arabs: The Official Summation of the Or Commission Report," Jewish Virtual Library, http://www.jewishvirtuallibrary.org/jsource/Society_&_Culture /OrCommissionReport.html.

lessons of centuries of Diaspora life, during which time Jews were a small minority attempting to preserve their culture in the midst of often hostile hosts. Rather than apply those lessons to the new minority in their midst, they were replicating, Rawidowicz warned, the patterns of their erstwhile oppressors.[4] His admonition remains apposite today.

A second symptom of the blindness at work in the nation-state bills is the refusal to acknowledge that the gravest threat to Israel's existence as a Jewish state is the ongoing occupation of the West Bank since 1967. This is not even a matter of the legality of Israeli settlements, though most of the world seems convinced that settlements are in violation of the 49th article of the Fourth Geneva Convention that prohibits an occupying power from "transfer[ing] parts of its own civilian population into the territory it occupies."[5] It is simply a matter of demography. Should Israel retain control over large parts of the West Bank (Areas B and C under the Oslo plan), and should the Palestinian Authority collapse as a result of failed negotiations, then Israel will be faced with the prospect of controlling the entire West Bank, whose Arab population is estimated as more than 2.5 million people. At that point, Israel will either have to extend full rights to this population, an act that, as a result of demographic change, will likely spell the demise of Israel as a Jewish state. Or it will *not* extend full rights to Palestinians in the West Bank, in which case it can lay no claim whatsoever to being a democracy. The new nation-state law, which reinforces the Jewish symbols and self-definition of the state, will not save Israel from the suicidal consequences of the occupation. On the contrary, it will make return from the brink even more difficult.

A third and final symptom of the blindness is the apparent belief that Israel can get away with this kind of definitional act and still call itself a democracy. Amnon Rubinstein and Alexander Yakobson have

---

4 See David N. Myers, *Between Jew and Arab: The Lost Voice of Simon Rawidowicz* (Waltham, MA: Brandeis University Press, 2008).

5 "Convention (IV) Relative to the Protection of Civilian Persons in Time of War: Article 49," International Committee of the Red Cross, Geneva 1949, https://www.icrc.org/ihl/WebART/380-600056.

argued in *Israel and the Family of Nations* that Israel's self-definition as a Jewish and democratic state is not exceptional among nation-states.[6] Whether or not one accepts that claim, it seems clear that the current proposals move Israel well beyond a sustainable balance and accepted constitutional practice. Let us recall the recurrent language in the bills that the State of Israel is "the nation-state of the Jewish people" and "the national home of the Jewish people" in which it and it alone "exercise[s] national self-determination."

A good source of comparison is India, created a year before Israel as part of a partition carved out of territory that had been under British control. India's constitution, drafted in 1949, defined the new country as a "Sovereign Socialist Secular Democratic Republic" that rests on four pillars: justice, liberty, equality, and fraternity. It went on in article 29 to assure the protection of minorities by guaranteeing them the right to their own language and culture and freedom from discrimination.[7]

Perhaps a more suitable comparison is the constitution of the Republic of Armenia, which was approved in 1995. Insofar as the Armenians are a group with a large diaspora community that had sought to return to its ancestral homeland, this example bears resemblance to the Zionist movement. And insofar as the Armenians experienced a genocide during the years 1915 to 1923, they felt a similar need to create a place of refuge where their physical and cultural well-being could be preserved. In fact, Armenians looked quite consciously to Zionism and the State of Israel as models from which to learn in transforming a dispersed people into a sovereign state. Interestingly though, the Armenian constitution begins quite differently from the Israeli Declaration of Independence; there is no lengthy historical preamble narrating the passage from exile to homeland. Nor is there any attempt to trumpet the Armenian-ness of the Republic, as in the Israeli nation-state bills. It commences in

6 Amnon Rubinstein and Alexander Yakobson, *Israel and the Family of Nations: The Jewish Nation-State and Human Rights*, trans. Ruth Morris and Ruchie Avital (London; New York: Routledge, 2009).

7 "The Constitution of India," https://india.gov.in/my-government/constitution-india/constitution-india-full-text.

Article 1 simply by referring to the new polity as a "sovereign, democratic, social state governed by rule of law."[8] The constitution of the Armenian Republic goes on to state in article 3 that "the human being, his/her dignity and the fundamental human rights and freedoms are an ultimate value." This language is much closer in letter and spirit to Israel's Basic Law on Human Dignity and Justice from 1992, against which the nation-state law is directed.

A final source of comparison is the constitution of a nearby country to Israel's north, Turkey. Similar to Israel, Turkey is in the throes of rethinking and recalibrating the balance between its democratic roots and cultural-religious sensibilities, as its authoritarian president, Recep Erdoğan, moves the country away from the secularist orientation introduced by the modern state's founder, Mustafa Kemal Atatürk, in 1923. Erdoğan has taken steps to alter the old constitutional system, engineering an April 2017 referendum that transformed Turkey's government from a parliamentary system with a prime minister to a strong presidential system. And yet, despite all his threatening gestures, Erdoğan has not yet discarded wholesale the 1982 constitution that defines the country as "a democratic, secular and social state governed by rule of law, within the notions of public peace, national solidarity and justice, respecting human rights, (and) loyal to the nationalism of Atatürk" (Article 2). To be sure, the text is replete with expressions of Turkish nationalist fervor and pride, but it does not privilege one ethnic group over another in legal terms. In fact, an amendment to the constitution in 2010 (Article 10) clarified that "all individuals are equal without any discrimination before the law, irrespective of language, race, color, sex, political opinion, philosophical belief, religion and sect, or any such considerations."[9] (That said, it must be noted that the Preamble to the Constitution strips away protection from anyone who impugns "Turkishness," as does the notorious clause 301 of the Turkish Penal

---

8 "The Constitution of the Armenian Republic," National Assembly of the Republic of Armenia, http://www.parliament.am/parliament.php?id=constitution&lang=eng#1.

9 "Constitution of the Republic of Turkey," https://global.tbmm.gov.tr/docs/constitution_en.pdf.

Code from 2005 that makes punishable by imprisonment anyone who "publicly denigrates Turkishness, the Republic or the Grand National Assembly of Turkey." It was under that clause that Nobel laureate Orhan Pamuk was charged in 2005 for his references to the Armenian genocide and the murder of 30,000 Kurds.)[10]

What does this comparative glance offer us? First, while hardly exhaustive, it suggests that the nation-state law that Israeli parliamentarians drafted and eventually passed places Israel beyond the pale of countries with similar or less robust democratic cultures. The Knesset bill places overwhelming weight on assuring the supremacy of Jewish identity and culture while making only fleeting reference to the presence or rights of the large Arab minority. Second, the comparison reminds us of the troubling absence of a constitution in Israel that could build on the Declaration of Independence from 1948. And yet, the use of Basic Laws to fill the constitutional void not only risks memorializing the political sentiment du jour; it has the potential, as the nation-state law surely does, to erode further the democratic foundations of Israel, whose stability ought to be measured not by defense of the majority, but rather of the minority.

The protection of the minority is one of the key lessons to be learned from Jewish history, of which the Israel of today is proving, ironically enough, to be an indifferent student. Sadly, Israel's embrace of an unabashed majoritarianism belongs to a wider retreat from democracy afflicting much of the world in 2018. At both local and global levels, urgent action is needed to prevent democratic values from being further eroded – and perhaps even consigned to the dustbin of history.

10 "Article 301 of Turkish Penal Code," World Law Direct, http://www.worldlawdirect .com/forum/law-wiki/13828-article-301-turkish-penal-code.html.

Mind the Gap: The Cost of Overlooking Gender in the Jewish Nation-State Question

Tanya Zion-Waldoks

BEYOND JEWISH AND/OR DEMOCRATIC

I am an Orthodox Jew and a feminist,[1] a proud Zionist whose children intentionally attend a Jewish-Arab school, a middle-class, educated, light-skinned Jew of Ashkenazi origins living in the Negev, Israel's southern region – an ethnically and socio-economically marginalized periphery. These seemingly divergent elements intertwine to shape my identity, affording me different forms and degrees of social capital and grounding my multiple belongings. Yet in Israel's increasingly polarized politics such complexities are often denied. I am frustrated daily by how rarely non-binary identities are represented and articulated in mainstream media. Israeli public discourse rarely recognizes intersectionality – how social experiences, opportunities and relationships are constructed by the multi-faceted intersection of axes of power and identity (ethnicity, race, gender, religion, class, nationality, sexuality, being able-bodied, etc.). Collective identities and institutions are also crafted by the power dynamics

---

1 Though feminism and religion were once considered antithetical and religious feminism is still often belittled as an inauthentic paradox, gender relations are being critiqued, challenged, and renegotiated in most major religious traditions. Over the last fifty years Jewish feminism as an idea and as a social movement has taken root and is currently transforming Jewish life even in conservative Orthodox circles. Increasingly, women, and notions of gender equality, are being incorporated in Jewish theology, law (halakha), and commentary, as well as cultural beliefs and social norms, communal structures and leadership, religious rituals, identities and more.

193

of these intersections, affecting perceptions and interactions on an inter- and intra-group level. However, when it comes to discussions of Israel's collective identity and attempts to codify it or embody its essence in Israeli institutions, recognition of such complexities and power differentials is ignored, and tensions are either oversimplified or dismissed as a threat to "Israeli unity." I believe it is these attempts to reduce Israel and Israeliness to limited monolithic identities that threaten to undermine our social bonds, deplete our cultural resources, and weaken our resilience.

In this essay, I wish to highlight intersectional analysis, particularly the important role gender plays in constructing collective identity, and explain why this is crucial to any discussion of the nation-state law (as proposed in its various forms and as passed). By gender I refer to the hierarchical structuring of power relations between actual men and women as well as the construction of masculinities and femininities, including the assumption that these categories are fixed, contradictory, and salient to determining the social order. By no means do I claim that gender is the only important perspective that must be added to the mix, nor that it is a stand-alone concept (unrelated to race, ethnicity, class, etc.). I do believe, however, that it is crucial for conversations, such as the one taking place between the pages of this book, to take gender – and more specifically the intersection of gender, religion, and state – into account.

GENDERING THE "JEWISH STATE"

Being Jewish has meant multiple things in different periods and in diverse locales, but Jewishness has rarely been reduced to the private sphere alone (e.g., personal belief, lifestyle preferences, or individual praxis). On the contrary, Jewish identity seems to be consistently and inherently enmeshed in the political. Judaism is tied to collective identity and the public sphere in multiple ways: human bodies and their interactions give rise to Jewish life and knowledge, by which they are, in turn, regulated. Jewish rituals are at their fullest when practiced in communal contexts. Many Jewish values and norms aim to shape and regulate public institutions and articulate a moral order through which to manage social relations. Jewish tradition establishes guidelines for the allocation of resources and assigning authority, and Jewish institutions accrue political and economic assets. Jewishness writ large formulates bodies of knowledge, including the development of language, meanings, discursive rules, and traditions of exegesis. It demarcates cyclical time and produces the rhythms of a life-span, as well as differentiating spaces and imbuing them with meaning. Overall, Judaism is political in that it is normative and seeks to propagate a certain social order (though what that entails is often debated). Thus, any discussion of Judaism and Jewish life must be examined in light of the gender question and its role in constructing power dynamics, specifically in shaping symbolic and material boundaries.

It is crucial to remember that historically, and in many ways to this day, being Jewish has meant different things for women and men. Not only does "Jewishness" encompass distinct experiences which follow gendered fault lines, these distinctions are also hierarchically ranked. Full-fledged Jewish citizenship is overwhelmingly based upon an ideal (heterosexual) male model. Jewish women are, by definition, a secondary, subservient, or flawed version – a less-than or "other" Jewish subject. Moreover, hierarchical gendered belonging to the Jewish collective is deeply embedded in cultural norms and social structures. Several institutions shape, and reflect, the normative and narrative gendered meanings of being a Jew on both a personal and political level: these "houses" ("*bayit*"/"*beit*") are home to the Jewish collective – the *beit knesset* (synagogue, house of communal gathering and prayer), *beit midrash* (study hall), *beit din* (courthouse) and the *bayit ha-Yehudi/ha-Le'umi* (Jewish domicile/national homeland). Women have traditionally been excluded from, or held in a subsidiary position in relation to, each of these houses. This manifests itself in kinship structures, legal rights, cultural literacy, ritual practices, public quorums, interpretive and legislative processes, communal decision-making, public leadership, and more. Thus, despite Judaism's many radical transformations throughout history, highly gendered images of "who is a (good) Jew" have endured.

These gendered belongings continue to carry many real-life consequences for Jews (and non-Jews) in modern Israel as well, since Jewish-Israeli gendered identities and power relations remain rooted in these cultural structures. Scholars have pointed to many prominent examples of this. They show how Israeli militarism and patriotism is tied to the Zionist imagining of the "new Jew" who embodies a specific masculine ideal. Others show how Jewish womanhood and matrilineal decent produce Israeli policies promoting familism and pronatalism, thereby establishing motherhood as women's central route to citizenship. As a result, attempts to define Israel as a Jewish state in general, or to attribute and codify a specific Jewish character for Israel, cannot be fully understood without adopting a gendered lens. Building upon this, I contend that *gender inequality is problematically used as a marker identifying the state – and its people – as Jewish*. Gender relations are an arena in which many of Israel's identity battles are fought, as is apparent in several recent controversies over and within the public sphere. But this is also why it is one of the arenas most resistant to deep-seated change.

For me, the social and cultural challenge of shaping a modern-day Israeli nation-state, and identifying a collective common ground, seems daunting but desirable. I am excited by the rigorous debate about what the content, character, and extent of this nation-state's public sphere and institutions should be, and how such institutions may interpret and implement Jewish, democratic, and human rights commitments. Yet it bothers me deeply that current formulations of this debate about defining Israel's character – which came to the fore surrounding attempts to institute a nation-state law – often neglect taking gender into account. I warn against positions that – far worse than overlooking gender – suggest compromises or political "solutions" that tolerate or even embrace highly specific and restrictive interpretations of *Jewishness as grounded upon gender inequality*. In fact, I posit that such arrangements (existing and newly proposed) endanger the very continuity and viability of the Jewish identity and peoplehood they purport to safeguard.

ANCHORING ISRAEL'S CHARACTER BY ANCHORING ITS WOMEN?

In her illuminating report, "Constitutional Anchoring of Israel's Vision," Ruth Gavison asserts that Israel adopts three core commitments. Each component – to be Jewish, democratic, and uphold human rights – is equally salient to Israel's identity. She defines "Jewishness" as the Jews' right to national self-determination, "democracy" as majority rule and the rule of law, and protecting "human rights" as derived from a universalist moral belief in human dignity (whether rooted in God's image or in a secular humanist perspective). Gavison argues that when this vision is defined in broad terms, like those outlined in Israel's Declaration of Independence, there is widespread support for it amongst Israelis (particularly within the Jewish majority). However, when it comes to diverging interpretations, practical implications, and the internal balance between these elements, Israelis engage in heated debates which often devolve into divisive struggles. Therefore, Gavison's report supports limiting both direct legislative action and any declarative or judiciary action by the courts aimed at embellishing upon and codifying these core values. This is because she considers the legal field a problematic arena for hashing out highly contentious questions of collective identity and their real-life consequences. Complex moral and social issues are better left open for cultural deliberation. Only by purposely maintaining vague language, she posits, will Israel's divided society manage to sustain its fragile sense of cohesion while also developing a fruitful public discourse about shared values and meanings.

Israel's political arena and public discourse are currently rich in derision and extremism and lacking in depth and solidarity. The weakening consensus is also evidenced by an undermining of trust in national institutions and symbols. Thus, coercing collective identity top-down risks leading to further rifts and disengagement from the collective. I agree with Gavison on principal that any such legislation should reflect a social and cultural common ground that grew bottom-up and was negotiated within less rigid discursive structures than that which a legal framework affords. Nonetheless, Gavison's argument must be taken one step further, since, in the current Israeli reality, top-down legislation enforcing a limited definition of Israel's character *already exists,* and any hope of encouraging an open and fruitful public debate about who and what Israel should stand for is contingent on creating the space to have such a conversation in the first place.

Gavison's hope is that maintaining a certain degree of ambiguity in the state's official self-declarations (by minimizing its expression and codification in legal terminology) will increase civic cohesion and encourage debate. Yet, for the first seventy years of its existence, the reality in Israel has been far from Gavison's idealized image of a vague space that enables open dialogue in which multiple players interact and deliberate, nurturing and crafting a shared vision of the common good. In reality, most political, social, and cultural Israeli leaders seem generally uninterested in taking up the daunting task of shaping Israel's character via serious debate, and the public seems to lack the motivation necessary to push these issues to the forefront of the electoral agenda. Although consensus-building discourse is lagging, specific piecemeal legislation, contradictory judicial rulings, and attempts to one-sidedly affix the character of Israel are thriving. When attempts to lock in certain meanings (and thereby also exert and seize power) raise too many red flags, the whole system seems to fall back to its *default* position. In many cases this means various arrangements that fall under the overarching title of the "status quo regarding religion and state," which is far from a consensus-based common ground. The "status-quo" is a historic arrangement considered highly problematic, partial, offensive, and unjust by most Israelis, on opposite sides of the political spectrum. In fact, even David Ben-Gurion, Israel's first prime minister, who was responsible for establishing this arrangement, seemingly later came to regret it.[2] Yet not only is this arrangement allowed to survive out of inertia, it is continuously maintained by governments both right and left, for

2 David Ben-Gurion to Shulamit Aloni, July 26, 1970, in the Ben-Gurion Archives at the Ben-Gurion Research Institute for the Study of Israel and Zionism, Sde Boker, Israel. My thanks to David Barak-Gorodetsky for bringing this document to my attention.

either narrow political and electoral interests or ideological causes. It can also be shown that far from stasis, the title "status quo" has disguised many changes that have been allowed to occur over the years, most often leading to more extremist policies, enlarging religious authorities' reach, and affecting more areas of public life. Consequently, the State of Israel *is* taking a stand on the very sensitive question of what "Jewish," "democratic," and "human rights" mean – separately and together. And, contrary to Gavison's position, the status-quo, when it comes to religion and state, is *un*ambiguous and *non*-consensual.

By calling attention to the gap between Israel's image and its actual practices (and how these relate to one another) I follow Joel Migdal's warning against viewing the state as a centralized, unified, coherent goal-oriented organization.[3] Migdal's "state-in-society" model distinguishes between the projected *image* of the state and its *actual diverse practices*, and highlights the relations between these mutually constitutive elements. Not only is it important to mind this gap (as taking gender into account allows us to do), it must also be noted that ignoring this gap has a cost. Take for example the specific issue of marriage and divorce, and the *aguna* plight in particular. Though some view this issue as an outlier, it is in fact a case-study worthy of scrutiny because it lies at the intersection of national, religious, cultural, and gendered power relations and reveals the importance of gendering questions of belonging and collective identity. Israel empowers religious national institutions such as the Rabbinate and Rabbinic courts, imbuing them with the full force of the state and fiercely protecting their autonomous and singular status as monopolies. Put briefly, Israel does not allow for civil marriage or divorce, instead according sole authority over matters of personal status to religious institutions. The democratic so-called secular state thus categorizes citizens according to their religious affiliation, regardless of their personal belief, observance,

---

3 Joel S. Migdal, *Through the Lens of Israel: Explorations in State and Society* (Albany: State University of New York Press, 2001), and *idem, State in Society: Studying How States and Societies Transform and Constitute One Another* (Cambridge; New York: Cambridge University Press, 2001).

or preference. Many citizens' access to marriage and/or divorce is thereby limited or even non-existent. All Jewish women, for example, are subject to halakhic family law as interpreted and meted out by the rulings of the mostly Haredi-controlled Rabbinic courts. As a result, all Jewish women become potentially vulnerable to various degrees of gender injustice – namely get[4] refusal, emotional abuse, and financial extortion.

Israel's Rabbinic courts are often heavily criticized for their administrative inefficiency, legal stringency, political wheeling and dealing, and lack of accountability to the varied citizenry they supposedly serve or to the civil state that appointed them. Their personnel, policies, outlook, and outcomes seem to represent *none* of the "core values" Gavison mentions: they do not represent a broad Jewish consensus and enhance solidarity, nor do they exhibit diverse views on the meaning of Jewish identity. They do not express the desire of the democratic majority (as evidenced by recent studies affirming that most Jewish Israelis reject state-run religious coercion even if their personal choice is to participate in Jewish life-ceremonies to maintain their cultural and religious traditions).[5] These institutions certainly do not advance or protect human rights. In fact, the opposite of each of these statements seems true. Thus, far from the state nurturing an inspiring ambiguity, Israel seems to be enabling a coercive extremist gendered regime on one hand, and a discursive, cultural, and moral vacuum on the other. This lack of ambiguity achieves the exact opposite of what Gavison strives for. Furthermore, in the immediate and long term, there is another acute cost to this arrangement: lives of real Jewish-Israeli women and children are being irreparably damaged every day by the "status-quo" of religion and state in Israel.

It is crucial to realize that the current arrangement is not one in which people can be left to their own social and cultural devices to work out the common good and reach a shared interpretation regarding Israel's desired collective identity. To paraphrase a feminist

---

4 A Jewish writ of divorce which, by Orthodox halakha, can only be given by the husband to the wife (not vice versa) and must be awarded of his own free will.
5 See the surveys conducted by Hiddush, such as http://hiddush.org/article-0-17055 -The_majority_of_Jewish_and_Arab_Israelis_support_marriage_freedom.aspx.

saying – Jewish women (and many others as well) cannot openly articulate their view of Israel's identity as long as the state forcibly keeps its foot on their necks. In fact, I would suggest this argument could be taken further. There is a case to be made that the current de facto sanctification of the status quo is covering up a more sinister set of interests. Why is it that the State of Israel, far from a unified entity, seems in this case to exhibit a surprisingly uniform position that it is crucial (or at least acceptable) that extremist religious authorities control matters of personal status? Why has this arrangement endured despite its overwhelming lack of popularity in the public eye, including critiques and solutions from "within" religious traditions? How is it consistently upheld by politicians across the political board and over so many decades? Perhaps the answer lies in the fact that the hierarchical structuring of gender relations (despite the abuses of power it entails) serves as a central means for anchoring the state's core "Jewishness" – precisely when more complex (and morally defensible) solutions seem politically unattainable and socially unimaginable. In other words – when the overarching vision, boundaries, and ideological identity of the state are unclear and contested, the system falls back on its existing practices. Yet the longer the state's problematic actual practices endure, the more they get reinforced, naturalized, and legitimized, thereby shaping the collective imagination and shared understandings of the state's *image*. Thus, subjugating women becomes the naturalized price of an (illusory) sense of security in our Jewish collective identity.

Nira Yuval-Davis argues that it is in times of crisis, when belonging is threatened, that it becomes articulated and affixed.[6] I posit that Israel's core sense of instability is "remedied" to some extent via, and at the expense of, women's lives. Israel suffers from chronic security concerns which threaten to undermine its core narrative and resilience. This goes far beyond military issues: the geographic borders and political boundaries of Israel remain in flux and their legitimacy – as well as Israel's very right to exist – is disputed both

---

6 Nira Yuval-Davis, *The Politics of Belonging: Intersectional Contestations* (Los Angeles; London: Sage, 2011).

within and without Israel. The resultant "demographic struggle" discourse places the onus of Israel's existence as a Jewish-majority state squarely on women's wombs. The notion of Israel as a democracy *and* as a Jewish state join forces in regulating women's sexuality and reproduction, since a Jewish majority is required to sustain this basic premise of Israel's core character. The discourse over Israel's right to national self-determination has become increasingly mixed with religious legitimizations linking the Jewish people to the holy land and promoting an ethno-national model of citizenship. Socially, there is a rise in the politicization of collective identities, often overtly shaped by negating a stigmatized "other," while elements like ethnicity and class which play a key role in the stratification of Israeli society are silenced. Furthermore, Israel's Arab citizens (and, I would argue, the existence of Arab-Jews and the construction of a "Mizrahi" identity) blur national and ethnic boundaries which could potentially impose order on the tumultuous relations between Israel and its neighbors.[7] Thus, Israel's insecurity manifests in many ways: its undecided physical borders and ambiguous symbolic boundaries, its multiple and contested collective identities, and its challenging social and cultural makeup.

Given the lack of consensus amongst Jews regarding the nature of Jewishness, its boundaries and meanings are often demarcated via Jewish women's embodied lives and constructions of femininity and motherhood. Israel is no exception. Feminist scholars have often shown how the burden of publicly performing collective identity (culturally, ethnically, religiously, or nationally) falls upon the women of the group (or by *othering* other women). Groups' boundaries and traditions are marked via regulation of women's dress codes, sexuality, reproduction, modesty, etc., and women carry this symbolic weight on their bodies. Indeed, even though Israeli women's rights in other areas are relatively progressive, Israel's ongoing use of women to anchor its Jewishness seems to become more explicit and urgent in direct relation to rising levels of insecurity. Thus, a diverse web of otherwise often conflicting interests and ideologies all end up supporting the

---

7 See Yehouda A. Shenhav, *The Arab Jews: A Postcolonial Reading of Nationalism, Religion, and Ethnicity* (Stanford, CA: Stanford University Press, 2006).

enforcement of highly patriarchal solutions. Today, the woman thus anchored lies injured at the collision site of ethno-nationalism and religious conservatism, of the majority's fear of losing its democratic rule and nationalist interests. This confluence encourages Israel to cede authority to extremist elements who use severe monitoring and stringent standards to ensure that the supposed "basic standard" of religious belonging and of "traditional" Jewish identity are sustained. Even among those who are uncomfortable with this arrangement, it becomes explicitly or implicitly justified as a necessary evil currently symbolically serving the greater good of upholding the Jewish family, the Jewish people, and/or the Jewish state.

The current arrangement, however, is detrimental and even destructive when seen from the perspective of those who wish to develop Israel's Jewish, democratic, and human rights commitments. Relying on the coercion of marriage and divorce in its extremely limited and misogynistic religious format in the name of ensuring Israel's continuity, cohesion, moral character, and legitimacy is – in my mind – morally flawed and socially faltering. The current arrangement does not protect human rights, does not promote democratic values or decision making, nor does it create a vibrant Jewish cultural connectedness or a deepened national connection. It merely strengthens the false and problematic linkage between Israel's Jewishness and ethno-national theocracy. The more Israel's Jewishness becomes synonymous with religionization and gender inequality, the more Israelis become either increasingly disillusioned, disinterested, and disgusted by the notion of a Jewish state or more convinced that national self-determination for Jews requires stringent religious anchoring (at the expense of women's rights, minority rights, and Jewish pluralism).

WANTED: THE FREEDOM TO CO-CREATE A VISION

By nationalizing, centralizing, politicizing, and monopolizing halakhic authority, and appointing extremist gatekeepers, modern Israel has created a terrible religious crisis. The state depreciates civic status and coerces religious belonging (one can no longer opt out as in the Ottoman *millet* system), standardizes cultural meanings (determining which cultural interpretations are legitimate), flattens multiple intersectional identities (moving from internally differentiated but interconnected local communities to a unified national collective lacking in solidarity) and lends the power of the state to oppressive hegemonic minority forces (undemocratically imbuing certain powerholders with the ability to determine who belongs and what belonging entails). In such a situation, Gavison's hope seems like a fantasy at best. Israel's collective identity is currently neither a reflection of citizens' individual choices nor a result of their joint deliberation. Lacking the basic freedom to determine one's own identity or personal status (whether anchored by a recalcitrant husband or the state), how can one fight for self-determination as a nation? Why should one believe in democratic principles or trust the state's interest in protecting basic human rights?

The majority of Israelis view the current State Rabbinate and Rabbinic courts as a political and religious anomaly that stringently enforces an aberrant form of what it means to be Jewish, democratic, and committed to human rights. This not only creates acute injustices for specific citizens, it also severely limits the development of a rich and complex national identity. Given the current linkage between the state's Jewish identity, these religious institutions, and hierarchical gendered arrangements of "the Jewish family," Israeli society is pushed into taking up dichotomous and divisive positions: some people uphold and protect these institutions and arrangements at all cost as the ultimate emblem and final safeguard of Israel's Jewish character. Others reject these institutions and seek to disassociate with everything they symbolize. Still others resign themselves to the fact that the status-quo is a price that must be paid for Jews' basic cohesion, continuity, and right to self-determination in this land. De facto, civic cohesion and the sense of cultural continuity and national solidarity are dangerously weakened by this arrangement. This situation weakens citizens' sense of belonging and connectedness and stifles attempts to engage in cultural explorations and public debates about what a Jewish, democratic, and human rights-based state might look like.

In sum, Gavison asserts that "maintaining Jewish solidarity, in Israel and abroad, requires a sense of all-Jewish kinship aimed at defending the rights of Jews to protect their lives, welfare, and identity, and an agreement that the existence of Israel as a Jewish state is a central form of that right." Yet I urge us to ask which Jews – and which Judaism – are currently being protected, and at whose expense? How did the denial of human rights to women become a condition for Jewish national identity? National solidarity and a sense of collective "kinship" is not morally defensible when built upon forcibly denying the right to self-determination and kinship of members within that collective. Providing basic civil liberties for all citizens, particularly around issues of marriage, divorce, and reproduction, does not *necessarily* pose a threat to Israel's Jewish character. It is in fact the current linkage between the state's "Jewishness," ethno-nationalism, gender inequality, religion, and theocratic monopolies which is harmful and detrimental to cultural and social resilience and cohesion. This framing generates a survivalist mode of discourse, a danger-obsessed emotional climate, polarized social relations, and an increasingly monolithic and extremist culture. Such an environment deteriorates the empathic capacities required for a strong social fabric. It structures the political imagination along narrow us/them, either/or, or all-or-nothing scenarios. Righting this terrible wrong – by dismantling the ultra-Orthodox monopoly and enabling civil marriage and divorce alongside voluntary religious community-based unions – will not lead to the destruction of the Jewish family, community, or people. It will not undermine Israel's identity as the Jewish state in a cultural sense nor will it undercut the legitimacy of Jews' self-determination. On the contrary, I believe untying this Gordian knot and removing its throttlehold on our lives and imaginations will actually free up Israeli society to develop varied modes of belonging. It will enable the kind of public conversation which gives rise to the creation of multiple meanings and interactions between Israel as Jewish, democratic, and a defender of human rights. And perhaps, from this, a better nation-state law will one day be conceivable.

Was it Right to Pass a Nation-State Law?

Gideon Sapir

In 2014, like in 2018, the media exposed the Israeli public to a barrage of spin regarding the Basic Law: Israel – The Nation-State of the Jewish People. Like all spin, both rounds spawned shallow and superficial debates. In 2015, when the issue was shelved, as part of *Marginalia's* Defining Israel Forum I laid out the primary arguments **against** the Basic Law and evaluated them on their merits or lack thereof. At the time my hope was to preempt the inevitable handwringing when the issue inevitably returned to the public agenda and perhaps raise the level of discussion on the topic. The arguments I made then have turned out to be no less applicable with the law's passage in July 2018.

ARGUMENT 1: THE NATION-STATE ITSELF IS A BAD IDEA

This claim is backed by historical and moral arguments. On the historical level, the argument is that the nation-state can easily descend into fascism, repressing its citizens and threatening its neighbors. On the moral level, the argument is that the nation-state **by definition** discriminates between citizens and turns those citizens who are not members of the nation into second-class citizens, which is a clear violation of the principle of equality.

This argument is easily refuted. First, even the most virulent opponents of Israel as a Jewish nation-state strongly support the right of the Palestinians to a nation-state of their own, and thus do not actually object to the principle as such. Second, at least on the legal and factual level, the debate regarding the nation-state has long since been decided. The right to self-determination in a nation-state is recognized and anchored in international human rights documents. Most Western states are nation-states, and their number has only increased with the collapse of many multi-national states since the end of the Cold War.

Third, a state cannot maintain neutrality on matters of culture and nation, and therefore the real choice is between a nation-state that acknowledges itself as such and a nation-state that denies it is one. More than that, and somewhat paradoxically, the condition of minorities in a nation-state that denies the reality of its nature is actually likely to be **worse**. While a nation-state openly defining itself as such can also openly commit to respecting the rights of minorities, a nation-state that denies its true nature effectively pressures its minorities to assimilate into the host majority nation. A classic example is France, which refuses to officially recognize any language other than French, as well as bans donning culturally and religiously unique symbols of minority groups in its public schools and in some cases in public places.

However, even if a state could shed the national dimension, it certainly is not clear that this is necessary. After being identified for many years with a conservative worldview, the national camp has recently been joined by not a few liberal writers, such as the political theorist David Miller, who propose liberal justifications for the nation-state.[1] These authors do not deny the danger of extreme nationalism to world peace, but in their opinion, coping with this danger does not require forfeiting nationalism altogether. And if we're already dealing with the dangers of ideologies and political structures, many thinkers and statesmen such as Angela Merkel and David Cameron have recently stressed the danger in adopting the multi-cultural political framework, the antithesis of the nation-state. It would seem that even among liberals (of whom the present author

---

1 David Miller, *On Nationality* (Oxford: Oxford University Press, 1995).

is one) John Lennon's dream of the abolition of states and nations as expressed in his song "Imagine" has ceased to be a desired goal.

ARGUMENT 2: THE JEWISH PEOPLE HAVE NO RIGHT TO A NATION-STATE

This argument comes in two versions. The first is that Judaism is not a national identity, and therefore the Jews have no right to a nation-state. According to the second, even if the Jews are a nation, they have no claim to the land of Israel and have no right to self-determination within its borders.

The former was argued some twenty years ago by Azmi Bishara, the founder of the Balad party, who has since fled the country and is suspected of aiding Hezbollah during the Second Lebanon War. The argument caused an uproar when it was made, but a look at its sources may dull the anger a bit. Bishara was using terms and arguments from the academic study of nationalism, and he adopted the then-prevalent position that nationalism is a purely modern phenomenon with no solid basis in humanity's history beforehand. As far as the modernists – such as Ernest Gellner, Eric Hobsbawm, Benedict Anderson, and others – were concerned, not just the Jews, but all nations were "imagined" or created within the past two centuries.

But Bishara and his supporters' adherence to the modernist view weakens their position. The study of nationalism has headed in another direction, and many authors have convincingly refuted the modernist argument, pointing to the ancient roots of national identity. More than that, all modernists have to jump through hoops to square their thesis with the history of the Jewish people, while non-modernists such as Adrian Hastings and Anthony Smith point to the Jews as the model of pre-modern nationalism, even arguing that the Jewish nation was an inspiration throughout history for other, newer nations to emulate.

Another significant weakness in the position of Bishara and his supporters is that alongside their negation of the existence of a Jewish nation or its subsequent right of self-determination, they support the right of the Palestinians to the same. To deny the existence of the Jewish people as such, even though they have millennia of history as a separate people behind them, and to recognize the right of Palestinians, who are a new nation which would likely not exist were it not for the Jewish return to their land, is a clear and irresolvable contradiction. One cannot hold both positions and be logically coherent.

The question of the right of the Jews to fulfill self-determination in the land of Israel is a discussion we cannot explore here. Suffice to say that this right has been internationally recognized on several occasions.

ARGUMENT 3: THERE IS NO NEED TO ENSHRINE ISRAEL'S NATIONAL STATUS IN A BASIC LAW

Which brings us to an internal Zionist debate. Those who criticize the Basic Law initiative claim that Israel's status as a Jewish nation-state is already anchored in various laws, and thus has no need to be upgraded to a constitutional level. A version of this argument claims that Israel's status as a nation-state is already anchored by the Declaration of Independence.

Evaluating this argument first requires a discussion of the following two questions:

- What is the purpose of a supreme, constitutional level of legislation?
- What contents do democracies choose to include in constitutional legislation?

We cannot discuss these questions here. We will suffice with the fact that most democracies do indeed have a constitution, and most of these include structural principles alongside basic values, some of which are formulated in the language of rights. In nation-states, the sections discussing basic values tend to include articles that anchor the national character of the state.

Thus, for instance, constitutions often enshrine the special status of members of the nation living abroad and the state's obligations to the same, the special status of the national language, and the commitment of the state to protect and cultivate the national culture. The anchoring of these principles in the constitution does not replace their status in regular legislation. Rather, such anchoring is meant to strengthen it. In light of these facts, one can confidently say that Israel's attempt to constitutionally enshrine its status as a nation-state is far from unique.

Furthermore, for a generation, Israel had no Basic Laws enshrining human rights. Despite this, legislation and judicial rulings effectively protected these rights. Israeli academics have taken pride in this effective protection of human rights and argued that Israel can serve as a model even for countries that already enshrine the protection of human rights in their constitution. This fact did not prevent a group of Knesset members from passing, in March 1992, two Basic Laws protecting human rights: Basic Law: Human Dignity and Liberty and Basic Law: Freedom of Occupation. If there is no need to anchor Israel's nation-state status in a Basic Law, why was there a need to do so with human rights?

As for the Declaration of Independence, it is a vague document written under heavy time pressure and meant primarily for the countries of the world that may have supported the establishment of a Jewish state in the land of Israel but did not give their assent to its unilateral establishment at the time of its announcement. One might add that the Declaration of Independence was never meant to serve as a law, and certainly not as a constitution. In light of this, it is no surprise that when the Supreme Court was asked to grant the Declaration constitutional status, it summarily refused to do so, even denying it the status of a regular law. In such circumstances, the idea of adopting the Declaration of Independence in its current vague version as part of the Israeli constitution is nothing short of foolish.

ARGUMENT 4: THE TIMING ISN'T RIGHT

There are those who argue that the relationship between the Jewish majority and the Arab-Palestinian minority is close to boiling point.

Therefore, passing the Basic Law will increase tensions and would have been better set aside for a more appropriate time.

This argument cannot be so easily dismissed. The reality in the State of Israel is different compared to other countries. The Israeli Palestinians' state is at war with their brethren, and as far as many are concerned, the State of Israel or part of it was established on the ruins of their houses and their land. On the other hand, Palestinian terrorists are killing Israeli Jewish citizens, causing the latter to cut off contact with the Israeli-Palestinian public. In such unique circumstances, and with such weighty historic and present background, a great deal of sensitivity, wisdom, and effort is required to build bridges and not burn them.

The proposals for a Basic Law: Israel – The Nation-State of the Jewish People were each formulated in a manner entirely congruent with international human rights documents. These documents emphasize the following principles:

1. National groups have the right to self-determination in their own nation-state in which they may preserve and cultivate their national identity.

2. Members of minority groups in a nation-state are entitled to full individual equality as well as the possibility of preserving and cultivating their own unique culture.

3. The individual rights of members of minority groups and in particular their right to preserve their unique culture are part of the social fabric in which the minority accepts upon itself the obligation to uphold the cohesion and independence of the state in which it lives.

There are those who argue that precisely by unequivocally establishing these guidelines within a Basic Law, the Israeli Palestinians will accept their part of the deal and the flames will die down. They may be right. But although water puts out fire, sometimes it's best to let a scalding pot cool before rinsing it off.

ARGUMENT 5: THE BASIC LAW WILL LEGITIMIZE THE ORIGINAL SIN OF THE "CONSTITUTIONAL REVOLUTION"

The "constitutional revolution" – which according to the Supreme Court took place in the early 1990s with the legislation of the two aforementioned Basic Laws – turned Israel from a parliamentary democracy into a constitutional one. Many in Israel, including public figures and academics, believe that both the manner in which the Basic Laws were passed and the way they were used by the Supreme Court are problematic. Even those who support the revolution agree (at least formally) that it would be preferable if the Knesset would conduct a public and political discussion leading to the adoption of a fully-fledged constitution to replace the present collection of Basic Laws.

Such an appropriate process began, during the term of the 16th Knesset, in the Knesset Constitution, Law, and Justice Committee when chaired by MK Michael Eitan. Unfortunately, the process took a negative turn during the term of the 17th Knesset, when the Committee was chaired by Menahem Ben-Sasson, and it has since completely stalled. One of the arguments made recently against the Basic Law is that it will signal to the court and its supporters that its opponents accept the present status quo, thus putting an end to the possible adoption of a complete constitution by the Knesset in the near future.

Another argument of the same type expresses concern regarding the manner in which the Supreme Court will interpret the Basic Law: Israel – The Nation-State of the Jewish People. Indeed, since the constitutional revolution, not one additional Basic Law has been passed. Some religious members of Knesset have joked that they will refuse to pass even the Ten Commandments, since the court will interpret them in a manner contradictory to their language and the intent of their author.

These arguments also cannot easily be dismissed. The public criticism against the constitutional revolution, still being heard even after it has been in force for a generation, did indeed serve as a kind of incentive for the adoption of an entire constitution. It is also true that the Supreme Court has been very creative in interpreting the existing Basic Laws, and there is no guarantee they will not do the same with the recently passed nation-state Basic Law.

Nevertheless, in my opinion, these two arguments are overstated. The constitutional revolution took place over twenty years ago. The moral force of the opposition to the Supreme Court's conduct fades the more time passes. One can legitimately argue that if the Knesset did not use its power to intervene in the Supreme Court's behavior, then this demonstrates acceptance of the court's actions. I highly doubt that avoiding passing a new Basic Law would have truly maintained the dying embers of the opposition to the revolution.

The fear of distorted interpretation also seems exaggerated to me. As part of the attempt to preempt this and prevent any loophole through which the Supreme Court could twist the words of the Basic Law, I have heard such fantastic methods of interpretation that even the old Jewish scholastics would have rejected as impossible. The Supreme Court is not staffed by power-drunk tyrants but by loyal public servants committed to the values of democracy. I do not believe they will turn legal night into day and vice versa.

ARGUMENT 6 & CONCLUSION: THERE IS NO CONSENSUS

A constitution enjoys supremacy over all other legal norms in force in a political unit, and can therefore be used as a tool for removing certain matters from the political field and drawing the borders in which the political game is played. In light of the limitations a constitution can impose, it is no wonder that many political and constitutional thinkers doubt the legitimacy of having a constitution, arguing that it runs contrary to the democratic principle of majority rule. I cannot do justice here to the debate and the arguments for either side. I will only note that because of this problem, the legitimacy of a constitution is dependent (among other things) on a public consensus in its favor. Of course, complete unanimity is impossible, but massive public support certainly is necessary. In contrast to an ordinary law that enjoys legitimacy even it was passed by a small majority, a constitution enjoys legitimacy only if a large majority of the public supports it.

In my opinion, most of the principles included in the various proposals for the Basic Law: Israel – The Nation-State of the Jewish People are proper and justified. I also believe that in a nation-state like Israel with a constitutional regime, such principles should be included in a constitution alongside structural principles and a commitment to protecting human rights. But when it turned out that many within the Jewish-Zionist majority objected to the Basic Law, for whatever reason, the law should probably have been shelved, rather than passed by a bare majority.

Who Needs the Nation-State Law? The State of the Jews, Fears, and Fearmongering

Israel Bartal

I am a proud Israeli patriot. I was born in a Tel Aviv suburb less than two years before David Ben-Gurion announced, in the city's museum building, the establishment of the State of Israel. My earliest childhood memory is from the day after the Declaration of Independence was proclaimed, the day the Egyptian Air Force bombed the city. I remember looking at the big fire that erupted at the factory just a few hundred meters west of my parents' house. Every time I recall sentences from Israel's Declaration of Independence, the discordant din of airplane engines mixed with the sound of explosions and the screaming of air-raid sirens echoes in my ears.

I was born in Mandatory Palestine to parents who escaped pre-Holocaust eastern Europe in the nick of time, and I grew up in the tumult of wars, in the democratic State of Israel. Perhaps due to this foundational experience, I viewed the Declaration of Independence as an appropriate response – as did many of my peers – to the violent resistance of the neighboring regimes to the establishment of a state in which the children of the ethnic-religious group into which we were born would realize their right to self-determination. And indeed, the Declaration of Independence explicitly refers to the battle for the home that the small Jewish community found itself in at the time of its formulation, while simultaneously and explicitly declaring a universalistic political-social vision in which "Judaism" and "democracy" are one and the same:[1]

---

1 "The Declaration of the Establishment of the State of Israel," The Knesset, http://www.knesset.gov.il/docs/eng/megilat_eng.htm.

We appeal – in the very midst of the onslaught launched against us now for months – to the Arab inhabitants of the State of Israel to preserve peace and participate in the upbuilding of the State on the basis of full and equal citizenship and due representation in all its provisional and permanent institutions.

We extend our hand to all neighboring states and their peoples in an offer of peace and good neighborliness, and appeal to them to establish bonds of cooperation and mutual help with the sovereign Jewish people settled in its own land. The State of Israel is prepared to do its share in a common effort for the advancement of the entire Middle East.

For many of my generation – the first native-born generation – this text was a source of pride due to its wonderful blending of the best universal concepts of equality, liberty, and progress with an explicit, unequivocal stance regarding the right of our ethnic-religious group to live its own life, and sustain its cultures, in a state of its own. As the years went by, I became a historian, researching the annals of Jewish nationalism. I learned to identify the multifaceted nature of this foundational text, and I was exposed to the gap between its promise and the political, social, and cultural reality created in the State of Israel. Yet, I never would have thought that one day someone would come and try to violate – using arguments of bolstering national resilience, no less – the brilliant balance between "nationalism" and "democracy" bequeathed to us for all generations, by the founders of the State of Israel.

THE NATION-STATE LAW AS A POLITICAL MEANS TO UNDERMINE THE SUPREME COURT'S STANDING

In the past decade, radical nationalist trends in Israeli society have grown stronger, trends that testify to the insecurity of their bearers and disclose an increasing disconnection (to the point of outright denial) to the historic Zionist discourse. Worst of all, these trends demonstrate a historical misunderstanding of the heterogeneous character of Israeli society. One of the prominent manifestations of this radicalism is expressed in the struggle of a group of politicians against the authority of the Israeli legal system. In the stormy parliamentary politics of Israel's capital, Jerusalem, the nation-state law, in its various forms, is a tool in the hands of its proponents against the Supreme Court. Yariv Levin, who was at that time a member of Knesset and serving as Chairman of the Coalition, stated this explicitly:

> The State of Israel is a Jewish country in which there is a democratic regime, not a country that belongs to all its citizens and infiltrators [meaning immigrants from Africa] and in which there exists, at its margins, Jewish life. This fundamental principle upon which the State of Israel was established is being eroded at an ever-swifter pace by the rulings of the Supreme Court, and therefore it is necessary to halt this post-Zionist process and anchor the state's basic identity and values in a Basic Law.[2]

Here, a prominent political leader presents the Supreme Court as the enemy of the State of Israel's Jewish character leading a "post-Zionist process" (in the political discourse of the radical Israeli right, "post-Zionist" is the accepted code for "anti-Israel"). According to Levin, a respected member of Knesset, "Judaism" and "democracy" are not two concepts that function as one, as intended in the formulation agreed upon by those who signed Israel's Declaration of Independence, but two separate and distinct systems, whereby the rise of one necessarily comes at the expense of the other. Consequently, whoever wishes to protect Judaism must engage its great enemy: the Supreme Court that supports the democratic system. This approach on the part of Levin also ignores another fundamental issue characterizing the Declaration of Independence: the historicization of the Jewish people. The Declaration says,

> The land of Israel was the birthplace of the Jewish people. Here their spiritual, religious, and political identity was shaped. Here

---

2 Moran Azulay, "Zehu khok ha-le'om: ha-s'ara ha-gedola ba-derekh," *Yedioth Ahronoth*, June 5, 2014, http://www.ynet.co.il/articles/0,7340,L-4527054,00.html.

220 · DEFINING ISRAEL

they first attained to statehood, created cultural values of national and universal significance and gave to the world the eternal Book of Books.[3]

Accordingly, this is an ingathering of people with a historical connection to the land due to its history and not due to any religious beliefs, patterns of behavior, or symbols. The Jewish nation, according to the signers of the Declaration, created cultural assets in a historical process, and was hence shaped by history. The text does not define what "Judaism" is, but rather talks about what Jews share! But Levin, like his partners subverting the Declaration of Independence, in contrast speaks of the state's "Jewish identity" and of "Jewish values"; abstractions that have nothing to do with the secular, manifestly Zionist, discourse, which was accepted by Orthodox and atheists alike.

Note that the Declaration speaks of a "Hebrew Community" in Israel, not a "Jewish community." That same "Hebrew Community" was created, according to the text of the Declaration of Independence, through the connection of a "nation" without a state to the land with which it has a historic affiliation, and in which it created something totally new, revolutionary, and unprecedented:

> In the Second World War, the Hebrew Community [in the Hebrew original: *Ha-Yishuv Ha-'Ivri*] of this country contributed its full share to the struggle of the freedom- and peace-loving nations against the forces of Nazi wickedness by the blood of its soldiers and its war effort.
>
> In recent decades they returned in their masses. Pioneers, defiant returnees, and defenders, they made deserts bloom, revived the Hebrew language, built villages and towns, and created a thriving community controlling its own economy and culture, loving peace but knowing how to defend itself, bringing the blessings of progress to all the country's inhabitants, and aspiring towards independent nationhood.

---

3 "The Declaration of the Establishment of the State of Israel," the Knesset, http://www.knesset.gov.il/docs/eng/megilat_eng.htm.

Studying the various versions of the nation-state law proposed over the past seven years demonstrates the continued centrality of the balanced, harmonious text produced by the signers of the Declaration. In the more moderate versions, such as that put forward by Ruth Calderon and others (see P/19/1539), suggestions were made to anchor in special legislation what has already been written and agreed upon in the Declaration of Independence on May 14, 1948, as if there is an imminent threat to the validity of the Declaration of Independence.

The most radical of the new versions of the Basic Law proposals, including the final version that passed, titled, "Israel – The Nation-State of the Jewish People," include a position that actually expresses reservations regarding several assertions in the foundational text of the State of Israel. Some of these have already been set in the Basic Laws promulgated by the Israeli parliament (such as Basic Law: Human Dignity and Liberty [1992] and Basic Law: Freedom of Occupation [1992, amended 1994]), and interpreted by the Supreme Court as having legal significance.[4]

From a historical perspective, the recent, obsessive engagement of Knesset members with drafting a nation-state law seems like another obvious manifestation of the anti-Zionist character of the Israeli extreme-nationalist camp, which managed to create the government of the 20th Knesset with a slim majority.

FEARS AND FEARMONGERING IN THE SERVICE OF THE NATION-STATE BILL

The elites in the Israel that I grew up in did not project fear, weakness, and discombobulation. On the contrary, the political leaders of the slightly more than half a million Israelis, who confronted a simultaneous attack of multiple invading armies that threatened their very existence, did not wail or cry out of fear, even when the

---

4 "The Existing Basic Laws: Full Texts," The Knesset, https://www.knesset.gov.il /description/eng/eng_mimshal_yesod1.htm.

Egyptian Army bombed Tel Aviv, or when the isolated Jewish villages in Gush-Etzion in the Judean Mountains fell to the enemy.

They also did not search for internal enemies to blame for the external dangers. The first Israelis did not require daily scare-mongering operations on the part of their prime minister to remind them that they face an existential threat. I do not recall David Ben-Gurion ever speaking in the whining tones of Benjamin Netanyahu, even in the most difficult and bitter times. The complaining style reveals, to anyone with eyes in her head, that something important has been lost in the Israeli political camp that calls itself "national": simple confidence in our actual presence as Jewish-Israelis in the land.

Insecurity and the use of grievance and fear for political purposes – when Israel currently has the largest Jewish population in the world, numbering over six million Jews, economically thriving and militarily strong – are what stand behind the legislative attempts made against imagined threats from internal enemies that do not exist.

Let's go back, for instance, to the words of Yariv Levin, who speaks of the threat of African immigrants marginalizing Jewish life in Israel. Instead of solving an administrative problem (affecting Tel Aviv in particular), the lawmaker suggests anchoring in a Basic Law the supe-riority of the state's "Jewish character" over its "democratic character."

Paradoxically, the nationalistic, radical right striving to base the Zionist vision currently being realized on fears and fearmongering (and familiarly, since radical right-wing political movements his-torically have depended mostly on fear to ensure their existence), is undermining everything that Zionism represents for us as a country.

WHY MUST THE DECLARATION OF INDEPENDENCE SUFFICE AS A CONSTITUTIVE BASIC PRINCIPLE?

The foundational document read by David Ben-Gurion in the dec-laration ceremony on May 14, 1948 was a consensual text signed by the representatives of various political factions in the Yishuv (the pre-state Jewish community in Palestine), Zionist and non-Zionist alike. The signers even included the anti-Zionist communist, Meir Vilner, and the representatives of the non-Zionist ultra-Orthodox.

For many years, no one questioned the status of this foundational document, suggested changing it, or demanded revoking in some way the legitimacy of even one of its sentences. Furthermore, the Declaration of Independence was granted legal standing when the Israeli legal system was still in its infancy. In the well-known Supreme Court ruling from 1953, Supreme Court Justice Shimon Agranat wrote the following:

> The system of rules according to which the political institutions in Israel have been established and operate demonstrate that this is indeed a state based on democratic foundations. Additionally, the statements made in the Declaration of Independence – and especially regarding the state being based on "the principles of freedom" and the guarantee of freedom of conscience – mean that Israel is a state that advocates freedom. Indeed, the Declaration is not a constitutional law that effectively rules for the enactment of various orders and laws or their annulment, but, to the extent that it expresses the "vision of the nation and its credo" [...] it is our duty to pay attention to the statements declared within it, when we attempt to interpret and give meaning to the laws of the state [...] after all it is a well-known axiom that a nation's law must be studied from the point of view of its system of national life.[5]

In the following forty years, the Supreme Court repeatedly reaffirmed this ruling, which accepted the Declaration of Independence as a tool for legal interpretation. This foundational text was also granted actual constitutive standing in the 1990s following the promulgation of the two Basic Laws on Human Dignity and Liberty, and Freedom of Occupation. Thus, Supreme Court Justice Dov Levin wrote in a ruling from 1994:

> The Declaration of Independence has become a basic, binding constitutional principle. The purpose of the Basic Laws has also

---

5 H.C. 73/53, Kol ha-'Am v. Minister of the Interior, 7 P.D. 871 (1953), 888.

been clearly defined and is legally-constitutionally in force to "anchor in a Basic Law the values of the State of Israel as a Jewish and democratic state" [...] [T]his court has seen fit from its first days to be guided by the principles and values of the Declaration of Independence as an interpretive source for the law, as a stave to which basic protected rights can be attached. These Basic Laws came and created a dramatic change in the status of the Declaration of Independence, in that it is no longer an interpretative source, but rather itself constitutes an independent source of human rights, since the Israeli legislature in promulgating the Basic Law... aimed to provide the Israeli citizen with a civil rights charter on a supra-legal constitutional level.[6]

The power of the State of Israel's founding text – which demonstrates the wonderful political talent of its formulators – lay in its ability to bring representatives of the entire range of opinions in the Jewish Yishuv to affirm it. This was no small feat, considering that the manuscript bears the names of people from the radical non-Zionist left and socialist-Zionists, alongside activists from the right-wing Revisionists and the representatives of the non-Zionist and anti-Zionist ultra-Orthodox parties.

The opinions of the signers (all male, except for Golda Meirson [later Meir]) were at various extremes from each other, and many of their visions regarding the form and character of the Jewish state were at odds. Indeed, those who had reservations about this or that deficiency in the Declaration took care to submit their opinions in writing.

Reading their documented reservations, we must wonder: if they had insisted that the Declaration's final wording represent their various political views, would we have had the privilege of witnessing the Declaration of the state at all? The great compromise put together by the representatives of the various factions was a unique historical achievement. It is difficult to imagine the nationalist-messianic right who support the nation-state law fully understanding the achievement and its significance.

---

6 H.C. 726/94, Klal Insurance Co. Ltd. v. Minister of Finance, 48 P.D. 441 (1994), 461.

This compromise succeeded in presenting harmony between "Jewish values" and democratic ones. Furthermore, the values of democracy are derived from, according to the wording of the Declaration, Jewish tradition. They rely on the vision of the prophets of Israel. And, as mentioned above, the Declaration presents, in straightforward language and without any reservations whatsoever, a commitment to universal and egalitarian values. This, written and declared while in the midst of a war between the various religious-ethnic groups that would later constitute the civil society in the State of Israel.

The classic Zionist texts should be inserted into the public discussion regarding the nation-state laws. Studying the essential material from the beginning of the Hibbat Zion movement in the Russian Empire, to the Declaration of the State of Israel on May 14, 1948, would demonstrate just how far many of the politicians, who for some reason are called "nationalists," have strayed from the vision of the founders and their precursors. This would not be an easy task, if only because Israeli politicians do not frequently cite the writings of Herzl and Jabotinsky.

Finally, the turbulent struggle between the supporters of the right-wing versions of the nation-state law, including in its final form, and their opponents is by no means a confrontation between Zionists and anti-Zionists (which is how the spokespersons for the Israeli nationalist right seek to portray it). Rather, this is a confrontation between the supporters of classic Zionism at its best – those who view the Declaration of Independence as an exemplary Jewish-Zionist achievement and a milestone in the annals of world democracy (even if the word "democracy" isn't mentioned in the Declaration's text!) – and those who have forgotten, or perhaps never knew, what Zionism is.

POST-SCRIPT: ARE YOU FORGETTING ZIONISM OR IS IT ALREADY FORGOTTEN?

In response to the public uproar over the most anti-Zionist (at least for now?) text ever added to the Israeli law books, the prime minister said "the Israeli left must conduct a *kheshbon ha-nefesh* [an accounting of the soul], it needs to ask itself why such a basic principle of Zionism – a Jewish nation-state for the Jewish people in its land – became a vulgar concept for it, a vulgar word, something for which it should be ashamed." My response to the sharp-tongued politician is as a *Yerushalmi* historian, a student of the Zionist historiographical school, as someone who has for decades been studying the history of the Jewish national movement, and who teaches courses in the history of the Zionist idea. There is no doubt in my mind that Prime Minister Netanyahu has ready access to the writings of the forefathers of Zionism. A selection of research articles from the Zionist thought of the late historian and father of the prime minister, Benzion Netanyahu, was published in 2003 – a valuable book, parts of which are used to teach at universities today. Let us consider from this book the beliefs of the most prominent Zionist thinkers, and let us examine two of the leading "Five Fathers of Zionism" (to borrow from the name of the book) that the late historian chose to include in this group. These two, Herzl and Jabotinsky, our prime minister often mentions. He returns to their words again and again to justify the nation-state law.

So what did Herzl think about the non-Jewish minorities who would live in the state that he envisioned? In his utopian novel *Altneuland* he introduced a vision for an improved and flourishing kind of state, whose excellent governing regime would be a model for all of the peoples of the world. The native-born, including Muslims, enjoy an absolute equality of rights in the Herzlian state that would be established by Jewish immigrants. Moreover, their cultural differences would be recognized. Incidentally, in Herzl's vision the Jewish state would have no official language at all! In *Altneuland*, it is the xenophobic who fail politically. In one scene, at an election meeting in the "New Village" – the name of the Zionist settlement established by the first pioneers – a political leader stands up to give a speech about the guiding principles (a kind of "Basic Laws") for the new country and declares the following:

> It would be unethical for us to deny a share of our commonwealth to any man, wherever he might come from, whatever his race or creed. For we stand on the shoulders of other civilized peoples.

If a man joins us – if he accepts our institutions and assumes the duties of our commonwealth – he should be entitled to enjoy all our rights. We ought therefore to pay our debts. And that can be done in only one way – by the exercise of the utmost tolerance. Our slogan must be, now and always – "Man, thou art my brother."[7]

Herzl expresses in the book disgust and revulsion with a fictional political leader who calls for a denial of political rights for various sectors of the population. He ridicules the fictional politician who delivers inflammatory speeches in the name of nationalism.

Could Herzl have been a leftist? Is it conceivable that one of the "Five Fathers of Zionism" as determined by Benzion Netanyahu could envision a country where all people, regardless of religion or ethnic origin, would be citizens with equal rights and obligations? Or do we rather have a problem with our reading comprehension?

Just like Herzl, Jabotinsky, for whom Benzion Netanyahu served as personal secretary, would be completely disqualified from the community of Zionists based on what Benjamin Netanyahu defines for us as Zionism. Jabotinsky had plenty of liberal ideas – a review of his writings reveals he was an atheist, a defender of women's rights, and in general a democrat too. In 1931 the Leader of the Zionist right wrote the following:

All of us, all Jews and Zionists from all streams, want what's best for the Palestinian Arabs. We do not want to remove a single Arab from either the Left of the Right Bank of the Jordan [River]. We want them to thrive both economically and culturally. We can imagine the police in the land of Israel this way: most of the population will be Hebrew, however it is not only the equal rights of all Hebrew citizens that will be guaranteed and also fulfilled; both languages [Hebrew and Arabic] and all religions will have

---

7 Theodor Herzl's *Altneuland* was first published in 1902. A full English translation by Dr. S. Blondheim, first published by the Federation of American Zionists in 1916, is available at the Jewish Virtual Library, https://www.jewishvirtuallibrary.org/quot -altneuland-quot-theodor-herzl.

equal rights and every nation will receive broad-ranging rights to cultural self-determination.

In short, Jabotinsky envisioned a Jewish state in which minorities would enjoy not only full and equal civil rights as citizens, but also cultural autonomy (just as he demanded at the beginning of his career for the Jews of the Russian Empire!).

What does this have to do with the nation-state law, according to which the Arabic language lost the status demanded for it by the ideological forefather of today's Likud? And what about the claim of the necessity to conduct a *kheshbon ha-nefesh* – an accounting of the soul – regarding the concept of a "nation-state?" No. It cannot be done. So instead the politicians invent a new Jabotinsky and direct their public relations people to market the defective goods to consumers. They rely on the fact that today no one bothers to look at the writings of this forgotten liberal nationalist. With a light touch they add one more lie falsifying and distorting the image of our national liberation movement. It is fortunate at least that some veterans in the Likud – including Moshe Arens, Benny Begin, Dan Meridor, and President Reuven Rivlin – still remind the forgetting, and the forgotten, about what the loud anti-Zionist voices don't want to be remembered. The *khesbon ha-nefesh* – the accounting of the soul – must be conducted by those who intentionally and deliberately forget the true ideas of the fathers of Zionism. The nation-state law in its current form is a stain in the pages of Zionist history.

On the Essence
of the State of Israel

Ze'ev B. Begin

An earlier version of this essay appeared in Hebrew in Israel Hayom, *July 10, 2015, based on a speech delivered at the University of Haifa's Faculty of Law, June 25, 2015.*

In ancient times, when a person hired a laborer, he took a pledge from him to guarantee his good behavior. The pledge was generally a garment – which sometimes would not be returned at day's end. Such occurrences are meant to be forestalled by the commandment in Exodus: "If you take your neighbor's cloak in pledge, you shall return it to him before sunset." One might ask if there is any evidence that people followed that rule in those far-off days, and a hint can be found in a citizen's letter to a governor, written in ink on a clay shard and discovered in a small coastal fortress near Ashdod. It was sent to the city's governor some 2,600 years ago and is on display at the Israel Museum:

> My Lord the governor shall hear the word of his servant: your servant was reaping in the granary yard. And your servant reaped, and completed his work as always, before Shabbat. When your servant finished his reaping as always, Yeshayahu ben Shovai came and took your servant's garment. Although I completed my reaping days ago, he took your servant's garment. And all my brothers will respond to me, those who reaped with me in the heat of the sun, my brothers will say Amen – I am blameless. And now please return my garment, and I will ask the Governor to return the garment of his servant, and you shall have mercy

on me, and your servant's garment shall be returned, and I shall not be dismayed.[1]

Thus, 2,600 years ago, in Eretz Israel, the land of Israel, a Hebrew-speaking reaper demanded the return of his garment in accordance with known practice. We find another reference to the same law, which evidently was not always followed, a hundred years earlier, about 2,750 years ago, in the harsh sermon of the prophet Amos (2:8), denouncing those who "lie down beside every altar on garments taken in pledge." As with many of the Torah's edicts, the explicit social obligation lies with the stronger party, while the right of the weaker party is merely hinted at. Another 2,300 years would elapse before an explicit, crystallized and clear expression of innate human rights came to be formulated in 1776 – that found in the United States Declaration of Independence: "We hold these truths to be self-evident, that all men are created equal, that they are endowed by their Creator with certain unalienable rights, that among these are life, liberty and the pursuit of happiness. That, to secure these rights, governments are instituted among men, deriving their just powers from the consent of the governed." In this statement, the basic assumption is that human rights precede the state; that governments are formed in order to uphold them; and that it is the government's duty to secure these innate rights in practice.

I am a Jew from Eretz Israel, and identify with my people both in space and time: with all my brethren wherever they may be, and with my ancestors and the tradition they bequeathed to us. As such, I also bear responsibility toward the future of my people. And this is my approach: after 1,900 years of exile and subjugation, it is a wonderful gift to be a part of the Jewish majority in the State of Israel – the Jewish people's one and only homeland in Eretz Israel.

Yet the privilege of being a part of the Jewish majority in our ancient homeland also gives rise to a duty – that of the majority to reach out to the minority and, constantly and consistently, what-

---

1 The letter composed on this fragment is the only text of the biblical period, other than the Bible itself, in which the word Shabbat is mentioned. Moreover, it appears here to describe a day people refrained from work.

ever the obstacles, to work for the equal rights of all Israeli citizens. Therefore, the character of our state comprises two complementary elements: it is at once the nation-state of the Jewish people while upholding equal rights to all its citizens.

When I say this, I am not closing my eyes to political platforms, proposed by some Arab leaders in Israel, that seek to fundamentally alter the character of Israel, or to viewpoints holding that Israel was conceived in sin and born in evil. I am not ignoring plans designed to transform Israel from being the nation-state of the Jewish people to "a state of all its nations," that is, to empty it of its deep historical meaning and thereby to deny its raison d'être. But none of these exempt us, members of the Jewish majority, from the perpetual effort to improve the situation, to constantly and vigorously strive to realize the noble principle of equal rights for all Israeli citizens. In doing so, we are not acting generously, but rather perform our duty.

In the spirit of the foregoing, I wrote in the report that I submitted to the Cabinet in early 2013 on the Status of Bedouin Settlement in the Negev: "The implementation of the principles of social justice to Bedouin children in the Negev and to their families is the obligation of the state which must, within a few years, advance a reasonable solution that will help them exploit their talents and realize their natural right to the pursuit of happiness just like any other child in Israel." The Cabinet resolved to adopt that report.

In the ancient times of our example, the reaper demanded justice of the city's governor. But if officials are the ones causing injustice – even unwittingly – who will hear the grievance? This pertains not only to the formal executive branch but also to our parliament: In our parliamentarian democracy the Knesset is actually controlled by the coalition majority and therefore small parties sometimes impose legislation through coalition bargaining. Legislation is thus affected by partisan considerations, which may produce unbalanced laws that harshly impinge upon civil rights. The need for an effective Supreme Court, sitting as a High Court of Justice, is thus underlined. This is in line with our proud biblical tradition, of prophets standing firm against the executive branch of those times, namely kings, a rare exception in the ancient world. If the majority fails to accept that it must voluntarily restrain itself, then the mechanisms that can impose such restraint must be safeguarded and reinforced.

In Psalms it is written: "But the Lord sits enthroned forever; he has established his throne for justice, and he judges the world with righteousness; he judges the peoples with uprightness. The Lord is a stronghold for the oppressed, a stronghold in times of trouble." That is to say, a fortress for the disadvantaged, the downtrodden. The High Court of Justice is a stronghold for the weak, its task being to uphold the rights of the individual and of minority groups, and to protect them where needed from arbitrary decisions by the government and even by the Knesset. Therefore, even if it errs, and I have sometimes thought that its rulings were in error, the existence of the High Court of Justice as a living and active organ and the implementation of its rulings by the authorities is the real test of liberty in our country. We must protect the court and prevent any impairment of its ability to fulfill its important role, so that we may follow the verse in Leviticus, and the similar version in Numbers: *"You shall have the same rule for the sojourner and for the native."*

The essence of the State of Israel needs to be explicitly enshrined in law. Four hundred years ago, in France, Cardinal Richelieu said: "if it is self-evident – write it down." To this I would add: and if it is not self-evident, all the more so – it should be written into law. In 2011, accordingly, I came up with an abridged formulation of Israel's Declaration of Independence, in 2015 I submitted the Basic Law Proposal: The State of Israel (see 2015, P/20/1587), and in 2016 I tabled a very similar proposal in the Knesset entitled "The Essence of the State of Israel." This bill affirms that "Israel is the nation-state of the Jewish people, based on the foundations of liberty, justice and peace as envisioned by the prophets of Israel, and upholding equal rights for all its citizens." Together, the two principles conveyed in this sentence make a whole. They are both essential – not one without the other – and both are absent from our law book. The time has come for their legislation.

On the Dangers of Enshrining National Character in the Law

Nir Kedar

The controversy over the Basic Law: Israel – The Nation-State of the Jewish People (hereinafter: "the nation-state law") revolves mainly around its content. The questions raised in the debate are, for example: does the law discriminate against non-Jewish Israelis (mainly the significant indigenous Arab minority)? Or, will this law reshape the relations between Israeli and non-Israeli Jews?

I wish, however, to elaborate on preliminary questions: Do we need this law? Do Israelis need to enshrine Israel's Jewish character in their laws? Is it wise to do so? Following Lilienblum, Herzl, Jabotinsky, and Ben-Gurion, I answer with an emphatic "no!" The nation-state law is superfluous and dangerous: it will not secure Israel's character as a Jewish state and has the potential to ignite a heated *Kulturkampf* in Israel and the Jewish world. Its approval by the Knesset is a gross mistake.

The wish to enshrine Israel's Jewish character in the law has two motives. First, laws that declare Israel as the Jewish people's nation-state are perceived by many Israelis to be an adequate response to the anti-Zionist attacks on the legitimate right of the Jews to self-determination in such a state. Since it is doubtful whether a declaratory law announcing Israel as the nation-state of the Jewish people is a wise and effective response to the (unjust) attacks on Zionism's legitimacy, I will not discuss that claim here.

The second motivation to codify Israel's Jewish character is to fortify the state's Jewishness in light of the (imaginary) threats that, according to some, jeopardize Jewish culture. Thus understood, this law is the legal equivalent of the seminars and school curricula that strive to inculcate Jewish identity among Israelis and "strengthen" it (whatever that means), or of the *Reshet Gimel* radio station that plays only "Hebrew music" (i.e., Arabic, Greek, American, Russian, or other music with Hebrew lyrics). The exact purpose of *Reshet Gimel* and the "Seminars for Jewish Identity" may be vague, and even ridiculous, but they are harmless; the nation-state law, on the other hand, is also dangerous. I will focus on the difficulty, futility, and perils inherent in the attempts to enshrine Israel's Jewish character in legal norms.

In opposition to the confidence of the drafters of the nation-state law, national identity is very difficult to define. Anthony Smith has reminded us that "even ethnic communities, so easily recognizable from a distance, seem to dissolve before our eyes the closer we come and the more we attempt to pin them down."[1] History demonstrates that one hundred years of efforts to express Jewish identity and culture in formal documents have amounted to nothing.

Modern Jews (in and outside Israel) have always been divided as to the definition of "Judaism," "Jewish culture," "Jewish law," or "Jewish state," and have not known how to translate these into formal laws and documents. Consequently, the Zionist movement and, later, the State of Israel, have avoided the cultural debate over the exact character and definition of Jewish identity and never codified a definition of this identity in its legal documents. Strange as it may sound to the enthusiastic proponents of the nation-state bills, since Israel's Declaration of Independence the Israeli parliament has persistently declined all attempts to declare the state's Jewish character in law. Paradoxically, the legislation of this Basic Law is clearly a post-Zionist step.

I.

Zionism was born out of the modern transformation of Europe and its Jews. The massive processes of modernization and secularization

---

1 Anthony D. Smith, *The Ethnic Origins of Nations* (Oxford; New York: B. Blackwell, 1987), 2.

stimulated among many Jews sentiments of bewilderment as well as tensions between their traditional beliefs and practices and modern principles and lifestyles. Zionism's ultimate aim was to solve this identity conundrum by enabling the Jews to be (as Israel's first prime minister, David Ben-Gurion, put it) "one hundred percent Jewish and one hundred percent free." In other words, the Zionist ultimate end was cultural, but the means to achieve it were *political*: Jewish immigration to Palestine and the establishment of an independent state, or at least sovereignty of a lesser degree, in which Jews would form the majority and in which modern Jewish culture would be able to exist freely over many generations.

Zionism believed that without Jewish sovereignty no Jewish culture could flourish over time. Reality in Europe showed that even in places where Jews had achieved emancipation and equality, it would be impossible to ensure the long-term existence of Jewish culture and its resistance to depletion and assimilation. It was even less possible to ensure the future of Jewish existence, both physical and cultural, in places where Jews had been persecuted. Therefore, from its inception, the Zionist movement focused all its energies and resources on the creation of a Jewish state and refused to take part in the cultural debate regarding modern Jewish identity (such as the one promoted by Ahad Ha'am, or the "Democratic Faction" at the turn of the twentieth century). In particular, it declined the formal attempts to define Judaism, the "Jewish people," or "Jewish culture" (and subsequently Israeli culture).

Already at the end of the nineteenth century the Zionist majority had rejected in its entirety Cultural (or "spiritual") Zionism, which attracted many intellectuals and continues to do so to this day. The Lovers of Zion (*Hovevei Zion*) rejected it, as did later Herzl and his supporters, the leaders of the labor movement, and even the Mizrahi religious party and the Revisionist right-wing Zionists. Cultural Zionism remained marginal throughout the twentieth century – both before and after the establishment of the State of Israel.

The Zionist movement regarded the attempts to fight over the contours of Jewish culture and the definition of Jewish identity as hopeless and even dangerous. Many considered them hopeless because cultural renaissance alone could not rescue Judaism from its predicament, and certainly not the Jews from theirs. What was the point of bickering endlessly over the questions of Jewish culture when there was no institutional, social, and political guarantee that would ensure its existence? Furthermore, Zionist orthodoxy always regarded cultural approaches such as Ahad Ha'am's as dangerous to Zionism. According to most Zionists, the cultural lure of the belief that they could preserve Jewish heritage and at the same time shape a modern and enlightened Judaism to bestow upon the Jewish masses concealed a rocky road with an unclear route and destination that would lead to a *Kulturkampf*, and even jeopardize the unity of the Zionist movement and its ability to cope with the monumental challenges it faced.

Therefore, in the course of Zionist history, the potentially dangerous cultural debate was always rejected in favor of the effort to establish an independent state. The dominant Zionist position was that the character of the Jewish state would be Jewish by definition, as most of its citizens would be Jewish and because the national framework would express and support the culture of the Jewish majority. Thus, for example, when Vladimir (Ze'ev) Jabotinsky was asked by the Royal Committee in 1937 what would be the special Jewish characteristics in the constitution of the future Jewish state, he replied:

> I do not think that it is desirable that a constitution of any state will include special paragraphs explicitly guaranteeing its "national" character. I think that it is a good sign for a constitution if we would find in it fewer paragraphs of this kind. The best and most natural way to guarantee the "national" character of a state is by the fact that it has a certain majority. If the majority is English than the state is English, and there is no need for any special guarantees. Therefore, by pronouncing the words "Hebrew State," I mean a community, or a country that enjoys a sufficient degree of self-government in its internal and foreign affairs, and that has a Jewish majority.[2]

---

2 Ze'ev Jabotinsky, *Ketavim*, vol. 5 (Speeches) (Jerusalem: Eri Jabotinsky, 1948), 224.

Ben-Gurion and most of the Israeli elite shared the same opinion. A major reason Israel refused to adopt a single constitutional document was to refrain from a bitter *Kulturkampf* on the exact legal definition of Israel's identity. For that reason, the nascent state adopted a series of Basic Laws instead of a comprehensive document with a fancy (and precarious) preamble. For one hundred years the Zionists and Israelis as a whole successfully rejected the temptation to define Jewish culture or anchor Jewish identity in their laws and formal documents.

Alas, since the 1980s, the Knesset has chosen to pursue another path: formal (yet vague) legal declarations now assert that Israel is a "Jewish and democratic state," whose judges must rule according to ethical and political principals taken from "Jewish heritage." Apparently, the members of Knesset who coined these nebulous legal formulas hoped that such declarations would both express Israel's Jewish character and enable Israelis to avoid the perilous culture war involved in the attempts to delineate Jewish and Israeli culture.

These relatively new ventures are superfluous and perilous, as is the nation-state law. Clearly, identity and culture are not dependent on formal legal declarations. The Jews in Israel were sure of their Jewish and Zionist identity even before 1992, the year in which Israeli law first declared Israel a "Jewish and democratic state," and it can be assumed that they would continue to adhere to their Jewish identity were their laws silent about the state's Jewishness or were they to obligate judges to refer to principles of "Jewish heritage" in certain cases.

Israel's Jewish character would not be damaged even without a Basic Law declaring and explaining its Jewish identity. Israel would still be the country of more than six-and-a-half million Jews living full, vibrant, and diverse Jewish lives, with or without a nation-state law. It is also evident that enshrining the state's Jewish character in law neither reinforces Jewish identity nor reinvigorates Jewish culture nor protects it from the (imaginary) dangers of diminution and destruction. Jewish culture in Israel is not at all in danger, and history shows that codifying the expressions "Jewish heritage" or "Jewish and democratic state" have not strengthened Israel's Jewish character in the least.

II.

The attempts to enshrine Jewish identity in legal documents have the potential to inflame a dangerous *Kulturkampf* among Israeli Jews, as well as between Israeli Jews and non-Jews, and between Jews in and outside Israel. In order to appreciate the danger of such endeavors let's look at the grim history of the supposedly innocent declaration of Israel as a "Jewish and democratic state" included in the 1992 Basic Laws. Similar to the nation-state law, the drafters of the 1992 legal declaration sought to express the idea of Israel as the nation-state of the Jewish people. But in fact they coined an unfortunate phrase that seems to place Judaism and democracy as two confronting "values."

The phrase "Jewish and democratic state" ignites societal tensions, rivalries, and schisms because it creates the mistaken impression that Jewish society in Israel is composed of two sectors: Jews versus democrats, religious versus secular, proponents of Jewish culture versus modern-day "Hellenists" who prefer "universal" (or "Western") values such as citizenship and democracy over Judaism. This, of course, is a sad mistake. Never were there two such camps in Israel. All Jewish Israelis – religious and secular – enjoy Jewish identity and conceive of Judaism as their national culture. True, they have varying conceptions of Judaism, but the fact is that close to one hundred percent of Israeli Jews define themselves as Jewish.

Similarly, the overwhelming majority of Israelis are devoted to democracy, the rule of law, human rights, and the idea of universal citizenship. This well-established "democratic identity" explains Israeli society's success in establishing a law-abiding democracy despite the harsh circumstances in which the state was established. Jews never saw a contradiction between their Jewish religion or culture and being citizens of a democratic state. This destructive "tension" was contrived only during the 1990s, and the new Basic Law threatens to intensify it.

The futility and dangers of enterprises such as the Basic Law: Israel – The Nation-State of the Jewish People must be stressed. Anthony Smith warned: "the most perplexing feature of investigation into ethnic and national phenomena [is] the curiously simultaneous solidity and insubstantiality of ethnic communities and nations," and that "it is easier to 'grasp' nationalism ... than nations."[3] The purpose of strengthening an identity or a "national character" is in itself an ill-defined and suspicious target, but more importantly the very existence of a cultural debate over the legal definition of a Jewish state endangers Israeli society as it exacerbates divisiveness and creates a distorted picture of cultural opposition between a "Jewish" camp and a supposedly "non-Jewish" (or "less Jewish") "democratic" or "universal" faction.

It should also be admitted that in spite of its innocent appearance the nation-state law was formulated and promoted mainly by specific nationalist and religious groups who believe that Israel has become "too democratic" at the expense of its Jewish identity. According to some politicians and intellectuals who favor the nation-state law, it is not only a reply to the unjust anti-Semitic attacks on Zionism's legitimacy, but also a wake-up call to those Israelis who "abandoned Zionism" and forgot "what it means to live in a Jewish state." Not only do these groups draw a distorted picture of "Judaism" versus "democracy," but they do so from a worldview that in practice gives priority to their unsophisticated nationalistic Zionism and their narrow conception of Judaism over a richer and more pluralistic, open, and democratic Jewish culture. This is a narrow post-Zionist worldview, which clearly deviates from the democratic-civic heritage shared by the Zionist movement and Israeli society, and from their longstanding refusal to join the futile and dangerous Jewish cultural dispute.

The desire to strengthen Israel's Jewish identity stems from an unfounded fear that Jewish culture is in danger. But in fact the opposite is the case: more than six-and-a half million Jewish Israelis maintain a free, diverse, and thriving Jewish culture. They speak, read, and write in Hebrew and conduct lives rich with Jewish-Hebrew art, literature, theater, music, cinema, and popular culture. Roughly one hundred Hebrew books are published weekly in Israel: works of reference, prose and poetry, sacred and profane. Never in the history of

---

3 Smith, *Ethnic Origins of Nations*, 2.

Jews has there been a Jewish cultural blossoming of such impressive scope and diversity as there is today in Israel. This is true of both secular and religious Jewish cultures. Under these circumstances, the fear for the fate of Jewish-Israeli culture is groundless. Israel is better off without a nation-state law.

Medina Yehudit and the Jewish Nation-State Law

Amnon Lord

In years past nobody thought that Israel, which was proclaimed in its Declaration of Independence as *the* Jewish state, should need someday to define itself in a Basic Law as *a* Jewish state – a state of Jewish nationality. It was a given. A notion that was embedded in the consciousness of the Israeli leadership. The basic ideological dispute waged at the state's birth went along two lines: the first was around the question of establishing a constitution. The second was defined as the struggle against so-called religious coercion. This latter debate was in fact the beginning of the struggle against the Jewish identity of Israel.

The debate concerning the constitution faded away a few years after the establishment of statehood. It seemed that the main leaders of this political struggle were expelled from the arena, and there wasn't any real political force represented by a strong party that wanted to carry on with the debate; those who favored establishing a constitution were marginalized or left the country all together. The constitutionalists' main stronghold had previously been the right-wing Herut Party, led by Menachem Begin. Those promoting a constitution included Knesset members like Hillel Kook, Eri Jabotinsky (son of the legendary revisionist leader Ze'ev Jabotinsky), and Shmuel Merlin. As independent personalities with strong Zionist and intellectual records they became a threatening opposition to Begin, and by the early 1950s they were expelled from the party, with Kook and Merlin leaving Israel for America. Although Begin was far more drawn to Jewish religious tradition than was the founding prime minister, David Ben-Gurion, they shared a preference for a public role in the political sphere for the religious parties. Time and again Ben-Gurion had a choice between forming a coalition government with the religious parties or with the strong ultra-secular leftist Mapam, and he favored the religious parties, believing that in the public sphere and the educational system there should be a Jewish religious presence.

The struggle against "religious coercion" continued. It involved many issues, such as the demand for public transportation on Shabbat, the right to sell pork, as well as the right not to be defined as of Jewish nationality or religion (depending on the individual in question) in the population registry or on identification. From the 1950s through the 1970s and until the early 1990s (and in today's fight against Jihadist terrorism), Israel was consumed by fierce national struggles based on its national identity as Jewish or Zionist. And as usual in Israel, internal ideological conflicts were mixed with the country's foreign policy. As Ben-Gurion and Moshe Sharett struggled to preserve Israel as Zionist, they also thought that it was Israel's duty to fight against anti-Jewish powers abroad. The progressive forces in Israel who struggled against "religious" presence thought it was none of Israel's business if the Soviet Union led by Stalin conducted an anti-Semitic drive including the persecution of Jewish artists and the Doctors' plot, designed to spark pogroms. On this there were no differences between the doveish foreign minister Moshe Sharett and his hawkish opponent Ben-Gurion. Both attacked the Soviet Union, drawing parallels between Nazism and then current Communist policy. Sharett in fact stated in the Knesset in 1952 that those who give support from home to anti-Zionist propaganda abroad commit treason.

The same struggle continued on a different level after the Six-Day War in 1967, and culminated with the 1975 UN resolution equating Zionism with racism. The Soviet and anti-Zionist struggle against Israel became entangled more and more with the Arab war against Israel. Currently, the political struggle that progressives lead towards a so-called "state of all its citizens" is part of the Palestinian struggle.

It is because political powers within Israel began to doubt Israel's right to exist as a Jewish state, and to act as one, that the idea of a

Basic Law to define Israel as the Jewish nation-state came about. This is the reason I support the Basic Law: Israel – The Nation-State of the Jewish People. The point when everything that was taken for granted in the Jewish state started to disintegrate is well known. It was in 1992 when the Knesset passed, as though while sleep-walking, two revolutionary Basic Laws, on Human Dignity and Liberty and on Freedom of Occupation. "Since signing them into law," writes Gideon Sapir, "there's no dull moment in the State of Israel. The court uses those Basic Laws as a platform for the creation of a whole constitution."[1]

Menachem Mautner elaborates on the reasons for this wild judicial activism led by Justice Barak and his followers. Mautner has argued influentially that judicial activism in Israel gained legitimacy and unbalanced political power after the historical electoral revolution of 1977, which propelled Likud to power and Menachem Begin to the position of prime minister.[2] After that, everything from national security to questions of values or budget policy came under Supreme Court scrutiny. It went along with the imperialistic encroachment of the judicial branch of the government, with the result that in Israel today it's easier for a man to become a woman on paper, especially on government-issued identification, than it is to register someone as Jewish who is not halakhically so.

The "constitutional revolution" became the alternative route for Israel's Labor party and the left to continue its 50-year-old political hegemony. It also opened the gates for Arab Palestinian irredentism, as Israeli Arabs saw an opening for a new kind of struggle for equality. Instead of civil equality they sought equality in national rights. This struggle gained steam when in 2003 the Supreme Court reversed the decision to block the Balad party from running for the Knesset. The judges, of course, argued for the right of every citizen to vote and to be elected. However, their predecessors in 1965 had denied a similar Arab nationalist party, by the name of Al Ard, the

---

1 Gidon [Gideon] Sapir, *Ha-Mapekha ha-khukatit* (Tel Aviv: Yediot Sefarim, 2010), 15.

2 See Menahem Mautner, *Mishpat ve-tarbut* (Ramat Gan: Bar-Ilan University Press, 2008); *idem, Mishpat ve-tarbut be-Yisrael be-fetakh ha-meʿa ha-ʿesrim ve-ʿakhat* (Tel Aviv: Am Oved, 2008); *idem, Law and the Culture of Israel* (Oxford; New York: Oxford University Press, 2011).

right to run candidates for Knesset. Those judges, like Moshe Landau and Alfred Vitkon, who belonged to the founding generation, invoked the lessons for the defense of democracy from the Weimar Republic, which was undermined by its own democratic tolerance for undemocratic parties.

The most liberal Supreme Court judge, Shimon Agranat, thus wrote in his famous Yeridor (Al Ard) case (23 October, 1965):

> In accordance to the declaration of statehood, The State of Israel is not only a sovereign state, independent, freedom seeking, characterized as a regime with government of the people (i.e., – democracy), but it was also established as a "Jewish state in the land of Israel." The deed of its founding was done primarily on the basis of the natural and historic right of the Jewish people to live in its own right like all nations, in its own sovereign state, and in that act there was an expression of the aspiration through the generations for the salvation of Israel (Geulat Israel).

Indeed, the leader of Balad was none other than Azmi Bishara, who was later accused of being a Hezbollah agent and fled the country. It is clear that Balad is a party designed to gain a parliamentary foothold for the Palestinian and Islamist struggle. A democracy should not allow that, but it's probably too late now.

One might say that the Supreme Court's judicial activism allowed an unintended consequence: who would have thought that within Israel a judicial and legal struggle against the state's Jewishness would take place? In the name of equality, the country slid to the precipice. Historically, the greatest enemies of the Jewish people have used legal venues in their struggle. In the 1990s, in Israel, this struggle became internal lawfare.

The attorney Zvi Hauser, who served under Benjamin Netanyahu as Cabinet Secretary, explained to me one of the reasons for this development in an interview a couple of years ago. The Knesset actually creates, according to Hauser,

> an arrangement of laws of super-principles in the form of Basic laws. But the principles that any constitution is meant to agree upon touch on three elementary arrangements. Out of those

three, only two were written into Basic Laws. One is the institutional structure of the state – regarding the president, the government, the military and so forth. The second anchor regards human rights in the Basic Laws from 1992. The Supreme Court with a list of verdicts built a set of judicial precedents and built a constitutional foundation for the entire subject of human rights in Israel. The third legal anchor was not written into law, and this is the arrangements in regard to the national identity of the country.[3]

The main reason for this fundamental omission is that the Israeli Zionist center did not recognize the judicial and cultural process which had evolved in the preceding decades, and had no answers to it other than cries and whispers. There are problems that Israel is currently facing and will face in the future; strategic problems that are not measured by territory nor by the number of missiles amassed on the other side of the border. According to this perception of the Israeli reality, neither the disintegration of Israel's social frameworks nor the disintegration of the state is physical. We are not talking about ruined buildings as a result of rockets or the death toll of terrorism. The threat is rather the deconstruction of the basic principles that create a broad consensus upon which a society may exist.

The formula that surrounds the disputes in Israel is whether the state is both "Jewish and democratic." This expression, which was written in the law in the aftershocks of the 1984 elections when the Kahane movement won a seat in the Knesset, forbade a movement designated as racist from running in the general elections. "Jewish and democratic" again formulated the verdict which defined the Kahane organization as a terrorist organization in 1988, and later on, in 1992, it entered the text of the Basic Law: Human Dignity and Liberty. One wonders how Israel existed as a democracy all those years without the artificial invention of the "Jewish and democratic" formula. Yet over the years it has become clear that those two words strip the Jewish dimension of all meaning while creating an unnecessary dichotomy.

---

3 Amnon Lord, "Koakh Zvika," *Makor Rishon*, February 21, 2014 (Yoman Supplement).

National identity in Israel is anchored on three levels. The first is declarative – by the Declaration of Independence from 1948. Although it's a foundational text, the Declaration retains no constitutional status, and for many years there was a fierce struggle in the Knesset about the nature of a future constitution. There were those who demanded that the Declaration be integrated as it is into the proposed constitution; but the "progressives" were against this. For a time it seemed that both sides had given up: pushing the constitution through the Knesset was on hold, and, for a while, the Basic Law: Israel – The Nation-State of the Jewish People was frozen as well. But the Basic Law was revived, and proposed in new versions, before being pushed to pass into law by the Knesset. There also remain the other two levels which anchor Israel's Jewish national character: the Law of Return, and the word "Jewish" in "Jewish and democratic" as it appears in the Basic Laws. The problem is that "democratic" always trumps Jewish and the opposition has already declared the nation-state law as racist.

The result is that the Arab struggle within Israel aims at constituting the Arab minority as an equal national community within Israel, which means collective equality – not just civil rights, religious rights, cultural autonomy, and voting rights – all of which are secured in Israel. This struggle threatens to undo the basic arrangement of 1948, that Israel is the Jewish state, or as phrased in the Declaration of Independence, "The land of Israel was the birthplace of the Jewish people." There is a sense that many intellectuals and judges already consider Israel as a Jewish and Arab state, basically a binational entity.

The political momentum unchecked leads in that direction. This binationalism is de facto what Ayman Odeh created with the Joint List in the elections to the 20th Knesset. The Arab parties, and especially Balad, had worked for years to convince all the Arab citizens to vote for nationalistic Arab and Islamist parties, and not to give their vote to any Zionist Israeli party; the creation of a united Arab party only strengthened that trend. Not only does this electoral trend represent a divide along nationalistic lines, it also makes the "democratic" definition an empty verbal game which can be used to cover destructive intentions. It actually represents a clear aim to serve the Palestinian national war against Israel and destabilize the political system in Israel. Although this aim is not declared, it can be ascertained from the published platform of "The Future Vision of the Palestinian Arabs in Israel" which was published in 2006 by the National Committee for the Heads of the Arab Local Authorities.[4] This document formulates assumptions that deny any legitimacy to the State of Israel and the legitimacy of its democracy. Basically, the activity of the Joint List members of Knesset is along the lines of those assumptions, with the political result being a clear separatist movement. It includes supportive utterances for anti-Israeli terrorism, demonstrative actions of disrespect for national symbols, and the beginning of a policy to appeal to international institutions against the State of Israel.

The people of Israel should have the legal tools wherewith to fight in defense of their democracy. When a movement is elected to the Knesset, its members are basically immune from any attempt to curb their activities. It seems that only a Knesset member who is found to be complicit in terrorism, like Basel Ghattas, might be banned from parliamentary life.[5] It should be possible to ban a party which is against the existence of Israel from running for Knesset, as it was decided in the Al Ard case in 1965 and in the Kahane case. Obviously, because of the separation of powers, there is a great chance that the Supreme Court will always rule against such a ban in any particular case.

No law can protect Israeli society from its own unintended consequences. And this is why some Jewish nationalists are against the Jewish nation-state law. Many Israelis don't trust their intellectual elites, including the judges who preside over the judicial system. A reason for this trust gap between the public and the establishment has to do with academic trends. In Israel it seems that a small num-

---

4 "The Future Vision of the Palestinian Arabs in Israel," The National Committee for the Heads of the Arab Local Authorities in Israel (2006), http://www.adalah.org /uploads/oldfiles/newsletter/eng/dec06/tasawor-mostaqbali.pdf.

5 Raoul Wootliff, "Arab MK Signs Plea Bargain, Agrees to Go to Jail," The Times of Israel, March 16, 2017, http://www.timesofisrael.com/arab-mk-signs-plea-bargain -agrees-to-go-to-jail/.

ber of academics can create support for a radical departure from a traditional historical concept such as the meaning of Nazism or the Holocaust, not to mention from interpretations of whatever might be the latest dispute in the country. Such trends lead to propagandistic interpretations of the past which place Israel on a historical continuity with Nazi Germany – in the exact fashion of old Stalinist theories. Irresponsible definitions of apartheid or racism are easily disseminated by a few intellectuals through the media. While all of this intellectual activity is perfectly legitimate in an open society, it also creates a dangerous mistrust of any institution, including the judicial system. This radical intellectual instability seems to ensure, according to those right-wing intellectuals who oppose the nation-state law, future failure in the interpretation of any constitutional law, including the nation-state law.

Nonetheless, it could also be said that clear legal definitions of Jewish values and Jewish attributes achieved by the law's passage might contribute to some sanity in the Israeli political sphere. A final argument in its favor is the need for a stronger legal instrument to fight international anti-Israel lawfare. It is absurd that the Jewish state would allow free activity for organizations that promote anti-Jewish hatred and destabilization of the country. Yet of course, an open society should allow *some* of the activities which seek its own destruction; thus, the Jewish state is obliged to allow anti-Jewish activity and anti-Jewish hatred, because it is democratic. You are free to produce a film which would be a blood libel against the IDF, but state funds don't have to support you. There should be some limitations on financial support for anti-Jewish activity, and in parliamentary representation. It should be remembered that ever since the Durban UN convention in late August 2001, an international strategy for the gradual destruction of Israel had been decided upon, and the fight against it is not military, but legal and political. There is a ground plan for the isolation of Israel on every level, to mobilize all international institutions to deny legitimacy from Israel, and basically to build around Israel a wall of boycotts and sanctions that will bring about its collapse. A vast network of NGOs is mobilized just for that purpose. The Jewish nation-state law will strengthen the ability of Israeli society to resist this anti-Jewish struggle.

Enshrining Exclusion: The Nation-State Law and the Arab-Palestinian Minority in Israel

Yousef T. Jabareen

Since the establishment of the State of Israel, relations between the indigenous Arab-Palestinian minority and the Jewish majority – including state authorities – have been fraught with tensions related to the divergent national identities of the two groups.[1] This divide contributes to the tremendous challenge of creating a definition of the State of Israel and drafting a constitution inclusive of all of Israel's citizens. The definition and constitution significantly impact the Arab-Palestinian minority due to majority-minority relations and the status of Arab citizens generally. The Arab-Palestinian minority would gain from ensuring that legislation, and particularly legislation with constitutional status, will reduce deep and long-standing inequalities between Arabs and Jews rather than exacerbate them. Understandably, the nature of the process – and the extent to which it incorporates the principles of democracy – impacts real human lives and their status in the country.[2]

However, this is not the legislative trend in Israel. This has been particularly clear with the recent passage of the Basic Law: Israel – The Nation-State of the Jewish People. Under discussion and continuous revision since 2011, it passed into legislation in its final form on

---

1 For general reading, see As'ad Ganim, *The Palestinian-Arab Minority in Israel, 1948–2000: A Political Study* (Albany: State University of New York Press, 2001) and Claude Klein, *Israel as a Nation-State and the Problem of the Arab Minority: In Search of a Status* (Tel Aviv: International Center for Peace in the Middle East, 1987).

2 See Aeyal Gross, "The Constitution, Reconciliation, and Transitional Justice: Lessons from South Africa and Israel," *Stanford Journal of International Law* 40, no. 1 (2004): 47–104.

July 19, 2018. This Basic Law creates and deepens existing inequalities between Jews and Arab-Palestinians in Israel.[3] Furthermore, due to its constitutional status, it clearly and definitively establishes the legal and social status of the Arab-Palestinian community in Israel as lower than that of the Jewish majority. The law addresses the formal definition of the state and its symbols along with issues of central importance to Arab-Palestinian citizens such as immigration, citizenship, land rights, culture, religion, and more. Therefore, the law formally establishes Jewish national belonging as the basis for group-based privileges in the areas noted above without creating a provision for similar collective rights for the Arab-Palestinian national minority, compromising one-fifth of the country's population. Thus, this legislation contradicts relevant principles of international law and creates a formalized legal bias in favor of the Jewish majority and to the detriment of the Arab minority. This constitutional basis for state-sanctioned discrimination will further and substantially erode the equal citizenship rights Palestinians are entitled to on an individual basis while also deepening the rift between Arab-Palestinians and Jews in Israel by further entrenching and consolidating deep-rooted discrimination against and exclusion of the Arab minority.

THE BASIC LAW AND INTERNATIONAL LAW

The Basic Law stands in violation of the fundamental rights of citizens according to established norms of international law. In particular, it is injurious to the principle of equality and non-

---

3 On April 30, 2018, when this draft of the nation-state bill was brought for the first reading in the Knesset, I submitted a law that I drafted, and that was signed by fifteen lawmakers, entitled Basic Law: A Democratic State, Multicultural and Egalitarian. See Orly Noy, "Defying Racist Legislation: New Bill Seeks to Turn Israel into a True Democracy," +972, February 6, 2018, https://972mag.com/defying-racist-legislation-new-bill-seeks-to-turn-israel-into-a-true-democracy/132921/, and Gideon Allon, "Arab MK Drafts Bill to Counter What He Calls 'Jewish Supremacy,'" *Israel Hayom*, January 31, 2018, http://www.israelhayom.com/2018/01/31/arab-mk-drafts-new-law-to-counter-jewish-supremacy-bill/.

discrimination on the basis of national origin, race, or religion. Israel has signed a number of relevant treaties including the International Convention on the Elimination of all Forms of Racial Discrimination,[4] the International Covenant on Civil and Political Rights, the International Covenant on Economic, Social and Cultural Rights[5] and the International Convention on the Rights of the Child.[6] Two documents specifically address the issue of minority and indigenous rights: the 1992 United Nations Declaration on the Rights of Persons Belonging to National or Ethnic, Religious and Linguistic Minorities,[7] and the 2007 United Nations Declaration on the Rights of Indigenous Peoples.[8]

In the context of international law, the Basic Law makes a mockery of international legal standards and norms and Israel's stated commitment to uphold them. The Arab-Palestinian community in Israel is a substantial national and indigenous minority and, as such, is entitled to full civil individual equality as well as collective equality. The collective rights granted to minorities are inherent rights derived from the groups' existence as a group, which distinguishes it from the majority. As I have explained elsewhere, these rights are meant to ensure substantive equality and provide the group with

---

4 "International Convention on the Elimination of All Forms of Racial Discrimination," Office of the United Nations High Commissioner for Human Rights, http://www.ohchr.org/EN/ProfessionalInterest/Pages/CERD.aspx.

5 "International Covenant on Economic, Social and Cultural Rights," Office of the United Nations High Commissioner for Human Rights, http://www.ohchr.org/EN/ProfessionalInterest/Pages/CESCR.aspx.

6 "The International Convention on the Rights of the Child," Office of the United Nations High Commissioner for Human Rights, http://www.ohchr.org/EN/ProfessionalInterest/Pages/CESCR.aspx.

7 "United Nations Declaration on the Rights of Persons Belonging to National or Ethnic, Religious and Linguistic Minorities," Office of the United Nations High Commissioner for Human Rights, http://www.ohchr.org/Documents/Issues/Minorities/Booklet_Minorities_English.pdf.

8 "United Nations Declaration on the Rights of Indigenous People," United Nations, http://www.un.org/esa/socdev/unpfii/documents/DRIPS_en.pdf. See James Anaya and Siegfried Wiessner, "The UN Declaration on the Rights of Indigenous Peoples: Towards Re-empowerment," *Jurist*, October 3, 2007, https://www.jurist.org/commentary/2007/10/un-declaration-on-rights-of-indigenous-2/.

individual and collective protection under the law.[9] Accordingly, international law is intended to equalize the inherent power imbalance between minority and majority populations – a prerequisite for self-actualization on the individual and collective bases within any given society.[10]

In line with international law, the granting of collective rights involves granting Arabic a status equal to Hebrew in law and in practice, the equitable distribution of all public resources including effective representation in public institutions and decision-making bodies, and fair and just arrangements for immigration and citizenship.[11] Such collective rights should also involve Arab-Palestinian self-steering in the realms of education, religion, culture, and media, as well as the recognition of Palestinian peoples' historical rights, such as the right of return for people displaced from their homes and villages, recognition of land rights, and the placement of religious matters and properties in the hands of the community.[12]

Furthermore, the Basic Law directly violates the UN's 1947 partition plan as outlined in Resolution 181.[13] This resolution, instrumental in bringing about the establishment of the State of Israel, called on the two states (Israel and Palestine) to adopt a "democratic constitution." The framers meant to ensure equality; resolution 181 notes: "No discrimination of any kind shall be made between the inhabitants on the ground of race, religion, language or sex. All persons within the jurisdiction of the state shall be entitled to equal protection of the laws." Addressing the two states' constitutional

---

9 Yousef T. Jabareen, "Toward Participatory Equality: Protecting Minority Rights under International Law," Israel Law Review 41, no. 3 (2008): 635–76.

10 See Will Kymlicka, "The Internationalization of Minority Rights," *International Journal of Constitutional Law* 6, no. 1 (2007): 1–32.

11 See Yousef T. Jabareen, "The Arab-Palestinian Community in Israel: A Test Case for Collective Rights under International Law," The George Washington International Law Review 47, no. 3 (2015): 449–80.

12 Amal Jamal, "The Political Ethos of Palestinian Citizens of Israel: Critical Reading in the Future Vision Documents," *Israel Studies Forum* 23, no. 2 (2008): 3–28.

13 "UN General Assembly Resolution 181 (11). Future Government of Palestine," United Nations, November 29, 1947, https://unispal.un.org/DPA/DPR/unispal.nsf/0/7F0AF2BD897689B785256C330061D25.

requirements, resolution 181 declares that "The Constituent Assembly of each state shall draft a democratic constitution for its State" and that each constitution shall include instructions "guaranteeing to all persons equal and non-discriminatory rights in civil, political, economic and religious matters and the enjoyment of human rights and fundamental freedoms, including freedom of religion, language, speech and publication, education, assembly and association." The Partition Plan also addressed holy places and religious and minority rights. While non-discrimination is a central feature of resolution 181 – a resolution fully adopted by Israel – the Basic Law codifies discrimination and exclusion.

DISCRIMINATION AND EXCLUSION ENSHRINED IN LAW

I will now examine the various clauses of the proposed legislation and analyze their clear adverse impact on the Arab-Palestinian minority in Israel.

The National Home of the Jewish people

The opening section of the final version of the Basic Law legislated in 2018 entitled "Basic Principles," clarifies the definition of the State of Israel as follows:

- The opening of Article 1 notes that "The land of Israel is the historic homeland of the Jewish people, in which the State of Israel was established."
- Article 1 (b) of the law states that it aims to define the identity of "the State of Israel [as] the nation-state of the Jewish people, in which it exercises its natural, cultural, religious, and historical right to self-determination."
- Afterwards, Article 1 (c) states the "The right to exercise national self-determination in the State of Israel is uniquely that of the Jewish people."

Accordingly, the law rejects the principle of self-determination for non-Jewish groups and the notion that the country and/or region can be a homeland to other national groups.

Importantly, a provision in earlier versions of the law that specified the aim of the bill "to anchor the values of the State of Israel as a Jewish and democratic state, in the spirit of the principles in the Declaration of the Establishment of the State of Israel" (see document E, Netanyahu's proposal, November 23, 2014), was omitted in the most recent version. In addition, a provision in earlier versions of the bill that addressed the democratic aspect of the state, noting that "The State of Israel is a democratic state based on the foundations of freedom, justice, and peace as envisaged by the prophets of Israel, and upholding equal rights for of all its citizens (see 2015, P/20/1587)," was also omitted. Indeed, the words "democracy" and "equality" do not appear at all in the final text.

Also of significance, for the first time, the law gives constitutional status to the "land of Israel" as opposed to the country or State of Israel. This nuance intends to give added weight and legitimacy to the Jewish people's claim to have a relationship with the historical land of Palestine; from the viewpoint of the text, historical Palestine is considered to be the exclusive historical homeland of the Jewish people.[14] By reaffirming the historical land of Palestine as the "land of Israel," and "the homeland of the Jewish people," in which they alone enjoy the right to self-determination, the Basic Law denies the right to self-determination for Palestinians in a sovereign state, alongside Israel. Furthermore, Article 3 states that "Jerusalem, complete and united, is the capital of Israel." These statements contradict international consensus which recognizes the right of Palestinians to an independent Palestinian state alongside Israel with Jerusalem as the shared the capital of the two states.

Interestingly, the opening statements of many regular Israeli laws define Israel as a "Jewish and democratic" state. Former president of the Israeli Supreme Court, Aharon Barak, in addressing the defi-

---

14 Walid Khalidi, ed., *All that Remains: The Palestinian Villages Occupied and Depopulated by Israel in 1948* (Washington, D.C.: Institute for Palestine Studies, 1992).

nition of the state as a state which favors the Jewish national group, wrote as follows:

> What, then are the "core" characteristics shaping the minimum definition of the State of Israel as a Jewish state? These characteristics are derived from Zionism and Jewish heritage. At their core stands the right of every Jew to immigrate to the State of Israel, where the Jews will constitute a majority; Hebrew is the official and principal language of the State and most of its holidays and symbols reflect the national revival of the Jewish people. The heritage of the Jewish people is a central component of its religious and cultural legacy.[15]

The Basic Law, which enshrines the Jewish characteristics of the state and does not include any reference to its democratic aspects, represents a significant departure from the status quo. As it begins with the Jewish element, the law displays a clear preference for this aspect of the definition and, more importantly, includes Jews who are not Israeli citizens. From a democratic perspective, particularistic statements, such as "The State of Israel is the nation-state of the Jewish people, in which it exercises its natural, cultural, religious, and historical right to self-determination," and "The right to exercise national self-determination in the State of Israel is uniquely that of the Jewish people," clearly exclude the 20 percent of Israeli citizens who do not belong to the "Jewish people" while also challenging their civil and democratic rights. Accordingly, this legislation not only negatively impacts feelings of belonging of Arab-Palestinians who are an indigenous community, but also gives this sentiment of exclusion constitutional backing. In fact, the Basic Law is the "law of laws" as it anchors the identity of the state and determines who is sovereign, and it will also affect the interpretation of the other Basic Laws.

The legal definition of the State of Israel causes concern. The clear bias in the law's formulation is not only problematic in prin-

---

15 A.B. 11280/02, The Central Elections Committee v. Ahmed Tibi, P.D. 57(4) 1 (2003), 22.

ciple, but also reflects an obstacle in practice to the achievement of substantive equality for the Arab-Palestinian minority in Israel. This group requires redress from decades of institutionalized injustice and discrimination.[16] Furthermore, constitutional preference for the Jewish majority facilitates the granting of group-based rights and privileges to the Jewish majority while providing legal support for discriminatory policy towards Arab-Palestinians on the individual and collective levels. This law has taken the pre-existing very problematic situation and codified it in constitutional law with all the troublesome social and political implications this entails.[17]

Defining the state as the nation-state of the Jewish people within the constitution creates a constitutional hierarchy of citizenship with Jewish citizens being awarded favored status. Arab-Palestinian citizens have now seen themselves downgraded from being entitled to equal citizenship rights to de jure being second class citizens. Indeed, this law has permanently established Arab-Palestinian citizens' lower-ranking status.

The leadership of the Arab community in Israel has developed alternative – and more inclusive – definitions of the state, including "Democratic State, Multi-Cultural and Egalitarian," "A State for all its Citizens," "A State of all its Nations," "A Jewish and Arab Democracy," and "A Multi-Cultural and Bi-Lingual State."[18] A policy paper drafted in 2007 by the Association for Civil Rights in Israel (ACRI), the country's foremost human rights organization, is instructive here. It noted that:

> "State of the Jewish people" (or other similar expressions) is a loaded term with many possible interpretations, and, by making it binding in the constitution, it creates a dangerous opening

---

16 David Kretzmer, *The Legal Status of the Arabs in Israel* (Boulder, CO: Westview Press, 1990).

17 See Yousef T. Jabareen, "Constitution Building and Equality in Deeply-Divided Societies: The Case of the Arab Minority in Israel," *Wisconsin International Law Journal* 26, no. 2 (2008): 345.

18 "The Future Vision of the Palestinian Arabs in Israel," The National Committee for the Heads of the Arab Local Authorities in Israel (2006), http://www.adalah.org/uploads/oldfiles/newsletter/eng/dec06/tasawor-mostaqbali.pdf.

which could justify discriminatory and racist policy towards non-Jews and it raises a concern that [such a clause] could subordinate the safeguarding of rights while justifying the discriminatory application of such rights.[19]

State Symbols

Article 2 of the final Basic Law gives constitutional status to the current state symbols – all of which have exclusively Jewish connotations. Under the heading "State Symbols," the national anthem is Hatikvah, the flag is white with two sky blue lines close to the margins and a Star of David in sky blue positioned in the flag's center, and the state's symbol is a menorah with seven branches, olive branches on both sides and the word Israel at its base.

Needless to say, all of these are national Jewish symbols and the national anthem, in particular, is a Jewish Zionist anthem which, due to its lyrics and symbolism, Arab-Palestinians can never adopt or identify with. Furthermore, the State's Flag, Anthem and Emblem Law of 1949 and the State Seal Law of 1949 already granted formal legal status to the flag, anthem, emblem, and seal. Granting constitutional status to these symbols deepens Arab-Palestinians citizens' already acute feelings of alienation. Alternative Jewish perspectives on the issue of state symbols (and other aspects discussed here) have been proposed, such as in a leading research project through the Jerusalem Institute for Israel Studies, arguing instead for "Inclusive Citizenship as a Framework for Jewish-Arab Relations in Israel."[20]

---

19 "The Association's Position Regarding Constitutionally Establishing the Nature of the State as 'Jewish and Democratic,'" The Association for Civil Rights in Israel, http://www.acri.org.il/he/1487.

20 See "Towards Inclusive Israeli Citizenship: A New Conceptual Framework for Jewish-Arab Relations in Israel. Points for Public Discussion," Jerusalem Institute for Israel Studies (2011), http://jerusaleminstitute.org.il/.upload/citizenship[1]en.pdf.
See also Yitzhak Reiter, "Inclusive Citizenship as a Framework for Jewish Arab Relations in Israel," The Romanian Journal of Society and Politics 8, no. 1 (2013), 14–35, http://rjsp.politice.ro/sites/default/files/pictures/yitzhak_reiter.pdf.

Downgrading the Status of Arabic

Article 4 states that: "(a) Hebrew is the state language. (b) The Arabic language has a special status in the state; regulating the use of the Arabic language in state institutions or by them will be set by law."

Since the founding of the state, Arabic has been, at least on the legal plane, equal in status to Hebrew. This law downgrades the status of Arabic from being an official language alongside Hebrew to having a "special" status. Arabic is a central component of the culture, tradition, and identity of the Palestinian Arab minority. While, in practice, Arabic is far inferior to Hebrew in Israel's linguistic landscape, the removal of this key collective cultural right represents a dangerous precedent which could have far-reaching consequences. Beyond being a violation of the status quo, this change is a violation of the basic rights of an indigenous minority. Arabic is part of the identity, heritage, and culture of the Arab minority, and denial of its recognition as an official language symbolizes denial of this group's collective rights and status in the state.

Immigration and Citizenship

Article 5 addresses immigration and citizenship. It stipulates that the automatic right to immigrate and achieve citizenship belongs exclusively to Jews as follows: "The state will be open to Jewish immigration and to the ingathering of the exiles."

The Basic Law codifies existing patterns of discrimination in immigration and citizenship that already appear in the Law of Return,[21] the Citizenship Law,[22] and the Law of Entry into Israel.[23] According to the Law of Return, for example, Jews and their family members – including family members who are not necessary recognized as Jews and are not in need of protection – are immediately

---

21 "The Law of Return 5710 (1950)," The Knesset, http://www.knesset.gov.il/laws /special/eng/return.htm.

22 "Nationality Law, 5712 – 1952," Refworld, http://www.refworld.org/docid/3ae6b4ec20 .html; "The Citizenship and Entry into Israel Law (temporary provision) 5763 – 2003," The Knesset, http://www.knesset.gov.il/laws/special/eng/citizenship_law.htm.

23 "Entry into Israel Law, 5712 – 1952 Refworld, http://www.refworld.org/docid /3ae6b4ec0.html.

eligible for citizenship due to their "return." This broadly applicable law also grants such immigrants a number of substantial economic benefits and privileges.

The Law of Return stands in stark contrast to immigration policy granted to non-Jewish spouses of Israeli citizens who, in the best-case scenario, are only granted citizenship rights after a long, arduous, and frustrating process (needless to say, Palestinians – either citizens or otherwise – are not entitled to any form of economic benefit by virtue of immigration). Even worse, non-Jewish spouses who are Palestinians from the occupied Palestinian territories find acquisition of citizenship – or even legal residency inside Israel – virtually impossible, following a 2003 draconian amendment to the Citizenship Law (family reunification).[24]

In line with a preference for Jewish immigration, Article 6 in the law, entitled "The Connection to the Jewish People," strengthens the rights of Jews in Israel and abroad vis-à-vis Israel. Article 6 (c) focuses on the Jewish people in Israel and abroad when it states that "The state shall act to preserve the cultural, historical, and religious heritage of the Jewish people among the Jews of the Diaspora." Article 6 (a, b, and c) is formulated as an obligation and a duty which is constitutionally bound and requires the state to work on behalf of the Jewish people.

Legalizing Housing Discrimination and Segregation

Article 7 of the law promotes Jewish-only settlement. It reads: "The state views the development of Jewish settlement as a national value, and shall act to encourage and promote its establishment and foundation." This phrasing legalizes discrimination and exclusion against Arab Palestinians in housing and development exclusively on the basis of ethnic and national belonging.

The nation-state law codifies and gives constitutional weight to

---

24 "The Citizenship and Entry into Israel Law (temporary provision) 5763 – 2003," The Knesset, http://www.knesset.gov.il/laws/special/eng/citizenship_law.htm. See also "Challenging the Citizenship Law Banning Family Unification," Adalah: The Legal Center for Arab Minority Rights in Israel," https://www.adalah.org/en/content/view /6598.

discrimination based on ethnicity. This legitimizes further discrimination and exclusion of the Arab minority.

National discriminatory projects that seek to Judaize spaces, encourage Jewish-only settlement, and create "demographic balances" become worthy causes that justify discrimination against Arab-Palestinian citizens on the level of individual and collective rights. Article 7 affirms the principle of apartheid in housing, land, and development: a separate legal track is formally created based on the principles of encouraging, promoting, and establishing Jewish settlement in the areas where both Arabs and Jews live.[25] Thus the Basic Law determines the national interest in the state in accordance with the collective Zionist interests.

This legislation blatantly undermines internationally recognized standards of equality and democracy and contradicts basic standards of decency and fairness. As such, it directly weakens the economic and social well-being of a significant minority of Israel's citizens and impairs their feelings of belonging. Indeed, it establishes a legal standard which prioritizes resource allocation to those that are recognized in the law – Jews – at the expense of Arab Palestinians in Israel. This, and the weakening of Arabic, will increase socio-economic gaps and decrease integration in the job market, in higher education, in welfare, and in other important national institutions.

Hebrew Calendar

Article 8 contains further evidence of Jewish content relating to the official state calendar. It determines that "The Hebrew calendar is the official state calendar." This article reflects the status quo as established by the Law of the Use of the Hebrew Calendar – a law relevant for the Jewish majority only.[26] A parallel and more inclusive law recognizing the calendar of the Arab minority does not exist.

---

25 Hussein Abu Hussein and Fiona McKay, *Access Denied: Palestinian Access to Land in Israel* (London; New York: Zed Books, 2003).

26 See "Law of the Use of the Hebrew Calendar, 5758 – 1998," http://www.nevo.co.il /law_html/Law01/p220m2_001.htm.

Days of Rest

Legislation that establishes national holidays in Israel also discriminates against the state's Arab-Palestinian citizens. Similar to the examples above, the Basic Law makes the Jewish calendar and these holidays constitutional. Article 9 (a) states "Independence Day is the national holiday of the state," while 9 (b) notes that "The Day of Remembrance for Fallen Soldiers of Israel and Holocaust and Heroism and Remembrance Day are official state memorial days." Article 10 establishes that "Shabbat and Israeli holidays are the regular days of rest in the state; those who are not Jewish have the right to observe days of rest on their Sabbath and holidays." This also establishes state-sanctioned discrimination in rest days and holidays – giving legal sanction to those which have special meaning for the Jewish people, without recognizing the holidays of the Arab-Palestinian minority. The law fully recognizes Jewish holy days and the Jewish population's right to take days off on their holidays. In contrast, the law does not recognize nor name the holy days of other groups – mainly the 20 percent of the population that is Arab. The allowance to "rest on their Sabbath and holidays" does not correct the imbalance embedded in law, and given these poor protections for Arabs, and Arabs' disadvantaged social and legal position, they are dependent on the goodwill of their (often Jewish) employers for those days off.

The authors strengthened the wording compared to existing versions of laws in relation to Jewish holidays and rest days. Whereas Jewish holidays are the designated days of rest in the state, other groups (which are unnamed) "are entitled to rest" – a right conditional upon government decisions.

Legal Entrenchment

This Basic Law further entrenches legislation of this nature while creating serious obstacles to its repeal. Article 11 states that "This Basic Law shall not be amended, unless by another Basic Law enacted by a majority of Knesset members."

Thus, it will be very difficult to challenge the many problematic issues outlined here. Indeed, this law not only deepens exclusion of Arab-Palestinians but also entrenches and normalizes it.

CONCLUSION

The bill promotes the collective rights of the Jewish majority without granting the same rights to the Arab-Palestinian indigenous national minority. As such, it conflicts with current trends in international law that increasingly recognize the unique rights of both national and indigenous minorities. Indeed, it consolidates a hierarchy that gives preference to the majority over the minority, creating a group-based ethnic classification – and Jewish formal superiority. This reflects a common dualism in Israeli legislation in general, and constitutional law specifically, in all manner of rights pertaining to Arab-Palestinians: a full individual and collective approach for Jews and a narrow individualistic approach for non-Jews. This dangerous Basic Law more firmly entrenches these norms within Israeli society while creating serious barriers to overcoming them. Thus, its passage has exacerbated ongoing exclusion, increased feelings of alienation, and has led to a further weakening of civil and democratic values.

The provisions established by the law and their emphasis on the Jewishness of the state contradict internationally accepted fundamental rights – primarily equality and non-discrimination – as central to all citizens within democracies. On the domestic level, the Basic Law further threatens the legal and social standing of Israel's indigenous Palestinian minority as it makes basic democratic principles subservient to the Jewish element. This divides Israeli citizens into two groups: first class citizens (the Jewish majority), who are fully recognized in the definition of the state and its laws and enjoy recognition of their individual and collective legal rights, and second or third-class citizens, who are excluded nationally and denied any group recognition. The Arab-Palestinian minority is now in a constitutionally established and supported position of disadvantage, and the government can no longer hide behind the pretense of equality.[27] Preexisting Israeli legislation has already codified the unequal status of Arab-Palestinian citizens; this Basic Law makes Arab-Palestinians' status even more precarious. Indeed, this represents a deathblow to Arab-Palestinians' civil and constitutional rights.

The Basic Law should serve as a serious wake-up call regarding the state of democracy in Israel. As phrased by the human rights group Adalah, it has the characteristics of apartheid "in that it seeks to maintain a regime in which one ethnic-national group controls an indigenous-national group living in the same territory while advancing ethnic superiority by promoting racist policies in the most basic aspects of life."[28] Adalah further notes that "A colonial regime is expressed in this Basic Law by the imposition of a constitutional identity of Jewish ethnic supremacy and control, without consent and cooperation, which denies the connection between the Palestinian natives (citizens and residents) with their homeland."

Therefore, passage of this law signals a dangerous deterioration in the basic rights of the Arab-Palestinian minority in Israel and moves Israel one step closer to an apartheid system. Indeed, it affirms the principle of apartheid by introducing formal separate legal tracks based on ethnic belonging in main areas of life, including in housing, citizenship, immigration, state symbols, the calendar, and days of rest. It thus constitutionally sanctions institutionalized discrimination.

---

27 Yousef Jabareen, "Israel Just Dropped the Pretense of Equality for Palestinian Citizens," *Los Angeles Times*, July 20, 2018, http://www.latimes.com/opinion/op-ed/la-oe-jabareen-israel-nation-state-bill-20180720-story.html.
28 See Adalah's position paper, "Proposed Basic Law: Israel – The Nation-State of the Jewish People, UPDATE 16 July, 2018," https://www.adalah.org/en/content/view/9569.

Religion, Religious Ideologies, and the Nation-State Law

Kalman Neuman

Why did the various versions of the new proposals prefer the terminology of "nation-state" to the old, time-tested "Jewish State" which has a track record from Herzl, through the 1947 UN resolution and the Israeli Declaration of Independence, up to the Israeli Basic Laws, which speak of a "Jewish and Democratic" state? One reason seems to be the intent to somehow decouple the "Jewish-democratic" combination and focus on the Jewish element as an independent factor. However, another motivation is to avoid a confrontation with one of the major obstacles to Israel's constitutional legislation – the intra-Jewish debate on religion and state. The term "Jewish state" may be interpreted by some as mandating a relationship between the state and the Jewish religion.[1] Israeli proponents of separation of religion and state might be in favor of describing Israel as a secular nation-state but are wary about possible (even if incorrect) interpretations of "Jewish state" that would legitimate religious coercion.

On the other hand, the equality clause which appears in the Begin version of the law (2015, P/20/1587)[2] is problematic for those (first and foremost, the religious parties) who wish to preserve the present

---

1 Even former Supreme Court President Aharon Barak has said that the "Jewish state" formula precludes a full separation of religion and state. See "Individual Freedom in a Jewish and Democratic State," *Haaretz*, March 25, 2018, https://www.haaretz.com/opinion/.premium-individual-freedom-in-a-jewish-and-democratic-state-1.5935245.

2 "Israel is the nation-state of the Jewish people, based on the foundations of freedom, justice and peace as envisioned by the prophets of Israel, and upholds equal rights for all its citizens." See 2015, P/20/1587.

arrangements regarding religion and state (and perhaps even extend religious legislation). In particular, it is highly probable (at the least) that the Supreme Court would interpret "equality" as prohibiting discrimination against secular, Reform, and Conservative Jews, as well as against Jews and non-Jews seeking to marry and couples seeking single-sex marriages. Any such ruling would jeopardize the present situation in which the state's marriage and divorce law is under the jurisdiction of one's respective religious community – whether Jewish, Muslim, Druze or Christian – and existing legislation that all Jews are subject to the Orthodox rabbinical courts. Therefore, given the composition of the governing coalition in the 20th Knesset or any other imaginable one which includes the religious parties (whether Haredi or Religious Zionist), the Begin version is probably a non-starter.

Even the other versions under consideration have ideological implications for various Orthodox groups within Israeli society.[3] I will attempt to reflect the possible approaches towards the nation-state law on the part of two distinct and important parts of Israeli society, whose religious ideologies clearly impact their attitude to the proposed law. With some hesitation, I will try to describe their perspectives with the necessary caveat that I am an outsider looking in.

THE HAREDI COMMUNITY

When talking about the Haredim we are talking about approximately 13 percent of the Jewish population in Israel. They are characterized, like ultra-Orthodox Jews over the world, by an insular lifestyle which renounces various aspects of modern society and by a rejection of the Zionist attitude toward the State of Israel. The various Haredi groups reflect religious and ethnic differences, different degrees of withdrawal from broader society, and distinctions in their stance

---

3 Using common nomenclature, the term "religious" refers to Orthodox. As is well known, the number of Reform and Conservative Jews in Israel is rather small, and they are not politically distinct.

regarding the State of Israel, ranging from an extreme fringe which refuses to take any part in the political process and eschews government funding, to groups who entertain a pragmatic attitude and judge the state by the extent to which it addresses the needs of the community. The Haredi community is represented in the Knesset by three different political parties. All share in a rejection of the ceremonies of Israeli civic religion, such as the celebration of Independence Day. This continues to be true, despite a recent process that has been described as "Israelization" of the Haredi population, which I will mention later.

I suggest that the deliberations regarding the nation-state law would highlight the tension between the Haredi commitment to ideology and the implications of reality, a tension typical of many aspects of Haredi life. From the purely ideological perspective, a law declaring Israel as a nation-state and, thus, the Jewish people as a nation, is inimical to the Haredi worldview. In fact, the rejection of Jewish nationalism was the basis for the Haredi objection to Zionism, which defined the Jewish people as "a nation among all nations" and denied that accepting the Torah as its basis is a *sine qua non* of Jewish peoplehood. Haredim often quote the words of the ninth-century Jewish thinker Sa'adia Gaon, "Our nation is a nation only in its Torah" (the original reads: Toras – referring to the Oral as well as Written Law). Isaac Breuer, one of the most profound anti-Zionist thinkers, saw the goal of the Jewish people as the establishment of "the Torah State" in which "the people of the Torah" would accept the absolute sovereignty of the Torah and reject the belief in the popular sovereignty of the nation.

How then are Haredim to address the existence of a secular (or at least a "non-Torah") Israel, even if they reject the extreme position of total non-cooperation espoused by fringe elements? In fact, many Haredim refrain from addressing this question, because of the possible implications of different answers to the Haredi ideology. One possible solution would be to ignore the claim of the State of Israel to be the embodiment of the Jewish people and the realization of Jewish history, and to treat it as a federation of communities – "a diasporic existence in the land of Israel." This has in the past suggested to various non-Haredi Israelis that the Haredim might develop a "civic" attitude towards the state. Such pundits often hoped that as a group that dwells apart from the Zionist hegemonic culture, Haredim could even find common ground with the Arab population in Israel.

This probably was wishful thinking on the part of Israeli liberals. Much has been said and written in recent years about the "Israelization" of the Haredi population: its greater identification with Israeli culture, its representation in popular television series, its greater participation in the work force and (to a limited extent) in the Israel Defense Forces. However, the bridge to "Israelization" does not occur through some nebulous "Israeli" civic identity, but through a connection to the more "Jewish" sectors and aspects of Israeli society. This process started in 1977 with the participation of the Haredi parties in a government led by Menachem Begin, who was perceived as rejecting the Labor Zionist ethos of creating a "new Jew," and which saw Zionism as a transformation of Judaism. Begin, although not observant in the Orthodox sense, did not try to meddle with Jewish traditions, was comfortable using phrases like "with God's help," and was seen as a more "Jewish" politician. Forty years later, the Haredi rank-and-file (with the exception of an extreme fringe and some ideological purists) see themselves as part of the hegemonic Jewish sector of Israeli society and demand their rights as part of that sector. It is perhaps best to describe the Haredi conceptualization of the state as an extended *kehilla,* a Jewish autonomous community in which non-Jews are tolerated, but not seen as equal partners. It is precisely their perception of Israel as a "Jewish state" and of their type of Judaism as the only authentic one that undergirds their sectorial demands, such as exemption from army service for Haredi men and women, and supports their claim that the public sphere should reflect "Jewishness" in a traditional sense, based on Jewish law (halakha). Thus, they wish to sustain and even extend the so-called "status quo," which, for example, allows only Orthodox marriage and divorce, limits activity (such as public transportation) on the Sabbath, exempts Haredim from military service, and recognizes Orthodox Judaism as the de facto state religion.

The Haredim have perceived – accurately, in this observer's opinion – that there is a correlation between positions on issues of religion and state and the discourse regarding the state reflected in the nation-state law. "Jewishness" in the religious sense and "Jewishness" in the national sense are not always distinct. Israelis, especially those who define themselves as secular, who prefer a robust and inclusive "Israeli" identity based on individualistic and liberal values to a "Jewish" one, are very often those who support separation of religion and state and a minimal presence of Judaism in the public sphere. On the other hand, those – often those who are more observant of Jewish tradition – who give priority to "Jewishness" over "Israeliness" call for more manifestations of Jewish religious tradition in the public sphere, even at the expense of individual rights. This is the basis for the identification of the majority of Haredim with the right wing and nationalist wing of Israeli politics, which in general (although not unanimously and unconditionally) is more accommodating to Haredi expectations regarding the public sphere. It would therefore stand to reason that the Haredi rank-and-file will support legislation that enhances the ethnic-national definition of the state. Despite this, in the run-up to the final vote on the bill, some Haredi leaders (such as MK Yisrael Eichler, member of the Agudat Yisrael party) voiced their concern that the concept of a "nation state" is a secular one. Therefore, the courts could define "who is a Jew" and "what is Jewishness" based on secular categories and ignore the dictates of Halakha (Jewish religious law).

Ultimately, though, the attitude of Haredi politicians to the law was based on pragmatic considerations. In fact, after gaining concessions in the final version of the law (including the outrageous amendment of paragraph 6 [b], which limited the state's work for the unity of the Jewish people to the Diaspora, ignoring the need for such work within Israel) the Haredi parties supported the law as part of coalition horse-trading, probably because of their urgent need for government support for a law exempting Haredim from army service.

Ironically, the Haredim were not affected by the ruling which triggered much of the motivation for the nation-state law. The Ka'adan case in 2000, which prohibited the state to allocate land for a community that excludes Arabs, refers only to a community which is defined only as "Jewish," and includes exemptions for communities of minorities such as Haredim or Druze, which are not considered discriminatory. On the other hand, Haredim have often been among the most vocal proponents of strict immigration laws in order to minimize non-Jewish immigration, particularly regarding labor migrants and "family unification" of Palestinian spouses from the two sides of the Green Line. Legally buttressing the identity of Israel as a Jewish nation-state could plausibly justify immigration policies that would be explicitly intended to limit the number of non-Jews in the state.

In general, the Haredim are also suspicious of the Supreme Court. One of their leaders famously quipped that they would be opposed to accepting the Ten Commandments as a constitution, if its interpretation would be entrusted to the Court. It therefore stands to reason that their support of the law will be combined with great circumspection about its possible implications and legal interpretations.

THE KOOKIANS

The other ideological group that I will describe are the adherents of messianic Zionism, identified first and foremost with Rabbi A.I. Kook (d.1935) and with his son Rabbi Z.Y. Kook (d. 1982), who applied the thought of his father to the political reality of the State of Israel. The Kookian attitude, which sees the state as part of an irreversible process leading to the final redemption, has de facto (and especially since 1967) become the dominant philosophy among Israeli Religious Zionists, who, despite their commitment to Orthodox Judaism, are sociologically, ideologically, and politically distinct from the Haredim. The majority of Religious Zionist rabbis, educators, and communal leaders subscribe to this worldview.

For them, the establishment of the State of Israel is not only a renewal of Jewish nationhood but is part of the messianic process, which in the deepest sense is the unfolding of the true nature and destiny of the Jewish people. The Jewish nation-state is not only a preparation for the ideal state but is already such a state-in-waiting. The Kookians therefore see the state as a sacral entity. It has the status of a Jewish monarchy in which the authority of a king has been transferred to the will of the people. Indeed, the state's democratic nature reflects the general will. This gives religious sanction to the notion of popular sovereignty, as long as its *demos* is the Jewish people. The Kookians have conceptualized the status of non-Jews in Israel in varying ways, but in no way do they really entertain a notion of equal citizenship. Non-Jews are at most "tenants" who are to be treated fairly.[4] In fact, while the Kookians have not proposed disfranchising non-Jews, during a few months in 1974 Rabbi Z.Y. Kook went as far as to deny the legitimacy of the Rabin government, as its support in the Knesset depended on Arab MKs (it is notable that Menachem Begin, then the head of the opposition, explicitly rejected such an argument).[5]

The Jewishness of the state defines its meta-historical role, and anything that bolsters that Jewishness fortifies its messianic destiny. The Kookians are therefore comfortable with a state based on ethno-republican values (even if it doesn't conform totally to Jewish law) and are apprehensive of liberal-individualist values. Their ideology is in accord with the collectivist ethos which dominated Israel in its early years. The transformation of the worldview of Israeli elites from ethno-republicanism to liberal individualism, as has been described by Oz Almog, is, for the Kookians, a demoralization of Israeli society and a rejection of the values that the true essence of the Jewish people and the State of Israel represent.[6] Therefore, they deride

---

4 See "Ba'al ha-bayit ha-hagun," Yesodot, http://www.yesodot.org.il/article/891/2205/. Yesodot is an organization dealing with the relationship between Judaism and democracy.

5 "Ha-keytsad memshalat mi'ut," *Maariv*, June 7, 1974, http://bit.ly/2JEYW3m.

6 This is the central thesis of Almog's massive book *Pereda mi-Srulik: shinui 'arakhim ba-elita ha-Yisraelit* [*Farewell to 'Srulik': Changing Values among the Israeli Elite*] (Haifa: Zmora Bitan and Haifa University Press, 2004). Israel, which was founded as a revolutionary society, has undergone routinization in which secular Israeli society has created a new culture which he refers to as "the democratic faith": "The new civic faith includes a number of secular rituals which have in common 'worship

this process, spearheaded by the Supreme Court and personified by former Chief Justice Aharon Barak, as "post-Zionism."

For example, one of the ways that the state realizes its true essence, according to the Kookians, is by practicing and abetting the cardinal obligation of the Jewish people to settle the land, which is itself part of the realization of the messianic vision. The Ka'adan ruling, which prohibits the state from establishing settlements which are exclusively Jewish, is therefore a rejection of Zionism, and of the raison d'être of the state itself. The nation-state law is intended to undo that process and direct the Supreme Court away from "post-Zionism" back to the days when it was clear that the needs of (what they see as) the Zionist project take precedence over anything. To achieve their goal it is also necessary to limit the power of judicial review and to change the method of appointment to the court, but the law is a first step in that direction.

The nation-state law is therefore for the Kookians a reiteration of the true sacral essence of the state, and hopefully a bulwark against the erosion of that essence. Its declarative aspect is in itself vital, while its practical elements are also important. They are less concerned with the imposition of halakha in the public sphere than with the strengthening of Jewish national identity in the framework of the State. The clause in some of the drafts, absent in the final version, which describes the role of Jewish law as an inspiration for Knesset legislation and mandates the teaching of Jewish tradition in all Jewish schools (without, for example, requiring education for democratic values) probably reflects the demands of this group. Indeed, for Rabbi Kook the son, the judiciary and educational systems were always described as a blot on the sanctity of the state. Even if the practical import of those nebulous clauses seems dubious, they have an important symbolic impact.

---

of self' [freedom, individualism, striving for personal achievement] and 'worship of the world' [preservation of the environment, participation in global markets, engagement with other nations and varied cultures, and toleration of the stranger and the other].... 'The democratic faith' develops through three depth-processes which changed Zionist culture from the foundations and created a triad of new values – capitalism, democracy and globalism" (p. 26, my translation).

One additional consideration must be mentioned, even if it is not always articulated publicly. It must be remembered that the primary political project of the Kookians (to which they have harnessed the political and social capital of the entire Religious Zionist sector) is the expansion of Jewish settlement and political rule over "The land of Israel," and more specifically over the West Bank/Judea and Samaria. In order to respond to the claim that annexation of the territories would require giving the vote to their Palestinian inhabitants, many proponents of annexation have suggested that Israel demand a process of "naturalization," which would include an oath of allegiance to the state before granting them Israeli citizenship. A prominent religious Zionist politician, Tzipi Hotovely, presently Deputy Foreign Minister, has described the nation-state law as part of a plan to eventually annex those territories.[7] Evidently this means that the law – or a similar one – could be used to prevent enfranchising West Bank Palestinians, if they refuse to sign on to the definition of the state as a Jewish nation-state.

The nation-state law, which has attracted attention mostly regarding its repercussions on the status of non-Jewish citizens of Israel, is thus meaningful also as part of the culture wars within Israeli-Jewish society. The questions of the role of Jewish religion as part of the "Jewish identity" of the state, the different religious attitudes towards the establishment of Israel, and the robust correlation between membership in the "religious" (Orthodox) sector and right-wing politics, make the law a necessary bulwark for the very existence of the state for some, and a unnecessary and possibly dangerous statement of intent for others.

---

7 Tzipi Hotovely, "Tokhnit khamishat ha-shalavim le-erets Yisrael ha-shlema," *Makor Rishon*, July 7, 2013, https://www.makorrishon.co.il/nrg/online/1/ART2/487/799.html.

Double Decolonization and the Loss of Hegemony

Nahum Karlinsky

SPRING

Spring in Palestine/Israel is beautiful but brief. Red anemones carpet the Negev/Naqab fields; the hills around Jerusalem are painted with pink-white blossoms of almond, pear, and apple trees, like an impressionist painting; the clear chilly air exudes the fragrance of wildflowers and is full of the hymns of birds and newly energized bees. You only have two or three weeks to give in to this intoxicating magic before the hot east wind, the *Sharkiya*, arrives, bringing with it the harsh reality of summer, somehow unexpected and always unwelcome.

I was driving from Kiryat Gat, the development town in the northern Negev where I grew up, to Jerusalem where I attended university. Beside me sat the bright-eyed young woman who would later become my wife. I wanted to share with her the landscape of my childhood and youth, the thrill of spring in the Negev. Retracing the defining experiences of my early years, I took her to the "secret" spot where my brothers and I loved to play and picnic: a hidden well with several palm trees that thrived on its waters; hedges of cacti – the famous prickly pears known as sabras – lining the slopes of the *wadi*; dilapidated and overgrown stone ruins.

The magic dissipated abruptly. She spoke quietly: "You know, this was someone's home. You know, this was a Palestinian village before 1948...." No, I did not know. Or, rather, I did not want to know. But from that moment on, I could not "un-know." The *Sharkiya* had arrived.[1]

---

1 She experienced a similar "eye opening" moment a few years before, while working

Since that day, and on subsequent journeys of discovery, I have not been able to overlook the evidence that had been there all along, hidden in plain sight, lurking in Israel's blind spot. I cannot ignore the Palestinian histories, embedded in neighborhoods like Talbiyeh, Katamon, or the Greek Colony of Jerusalem, in Beer-Sheva, Jaffa, or in Kiryat Gat itself, which was built on the lands and properties of the displaced inhabitants of al-Faluja and 'Iraq al-Manshiyya. Yet, at the same time, this difficult legacy does not contradict my deep attachment to my homeland or the weight of thousands of years of Jewish history that I carry with me.

SUMMER

Unlike the brevity of spring, summer in this part of the world feels endless. At times, the only escape from the scorching heat that sits on your shoulders like a heavy weight is to immerse yourself in the cool waters of the Mediterranean Sea.

In the summer of 2014 I was sitting with my brother in his modest home, overlooking the Mediterranean, contemplating that option. He lives in one of the kibbutzim that border Hamas-controlled Gaza. But swimming was not an option. It was early July 2014 and a war between Israel and Hamas had just begun.

The combative rhetoric that fell upon us from both the government and the army promised a swift and decisive victory, like the one of 1967 – a victory that would crush Hamas once and for all. But we had our doubts. After all, we had heard those words and been exposed to this rhetoric many times in the past. Indeed, Hamas rockets fell upon the kibbutz until the very last day of the war. Hamas had not been vanquished, and the immense gap between the high rhetoric and our sobering reality was clear to all.

As mentioned, that sobering reality did not come as a complete surprise. The consistent erosion of the image of the invincible Israeli

---

as a translator and as a "local" liaison to a prominent American newspaper. See Gannit Ankori, *Palestinian Art* (London: Reaktion Books, 2006), 9–10.

warrior and the declining ability of the Israeli army to win decisive military victories have been part of Israeli discourse and consciousness since the 1973 Yom Kippur War. However, a totally new feature surfaced during the 2014 war between Hamas and Israel: a radical Jewish religious-extremist turn, which transformed this military confrontation into what can be characterized as the first religious-oriented war of the modern State of Israel. This shift was accompanied by an unprecedented hyper-nationalist campaign against Arabs in general, and against the Arabs citizens of the State of Israel in particular. Thus, the 2014 Israel-Hamas war brought to the surface the existence of deeper and broader currents in Israeli-Jewish society, currents that also underlie the recently passed Basic Law that goes by the name Israel – The Nation-State of the Jewish People.

WINTER AND AMALEK

One of these currents is the denial of the Arabs' right "to be" on their homeland. In the weeks before the 2014 war broke out, as well as during the fighting and even in its aftermath, Arabs in Israel were targeted in the streets of Israel's multi-ethnic/multi-national towns, especially in Jerusalem. Their social media accounts were monitored by vigilante Jewish citizens; Facebook, Twitter, and readers' comments on online news outlets became sites of hate speech and verbal violence. Calls demanding the boycott of Arab-owned businesses grew in number and volume – most conspicuously voiced by Israel's (at that time) Foreign Minister Avigdor Liberman.[2]

This campaign took place in spite of the fact that a dominant trajectory of Arab-Jewish relations in the State of Israel over the last forty years – as Sammy Smooha convincingly argues – had been characterized by a continuous commitment to "mutual rapprochement" and coexistence. Smooha's pioneering scholarship demonstrates that the Arabs in Israel see themselves as Israeli citizens, affirm Israel's

---

2 "Lieberman's Racist Incitement Must Be Condemned," *Haaretz*, October 28, 2015, http://www.haaretz.com/opinion/1.606483.

right to exist, do not wish to leave the state, support friendly relations between Jews and Arabs, and that the Israeli component in their self-identification trumps its Palestinian counterpart.[3]

Yitzhak Rabin's second term as Israel's prime minister (1992–1995) has been the highest point, so far, of positive Arab-Jewish relations inside Israel. Yet, Rabin's assassination by a religious-extremist Jew in November 1995 marked a change of direction in these relations. Since then, and especially since the outbreak of the second Palestinian uprising against Israeli occupation in late 2000, the relations between Arab and Jewish citizens of Israel entered a worsening trajectory.

Scholars put most of the blame for this deterioration at the doorstep of Israel's government and parliament. According to Elie Rekhess, "anti-Arab legislation introduced in the Knesset was a major factor in the Arabs' increased sense of estrangement and fear and also reflected Jews' distrust of them." Rekhess cites the findings of the Mossawa Center (a prominent Arab advocacy group in Israel), that "in 2009 there had been twenty-one 'discriminatory and racist' bills proposed in the Knesset – 75 percent more than the previous year." Among the proposed bills Rekhess mentions are the Citizenship and Entry into Israel Law, the Loyalty Oath, the Nakba Bill, the Acceptance of Communities Bill, and the initiative to legislate a Basic Law: Israel – The Nation-State of the Jewish People.[4] I believe there is no need to elaborate here on the content of these proposed bills. Their titles speak for themselves.

Other scholars emphasized that on top of the anti-Arab legislation initiatives, additional dimensions, like government policies, public opinion, and public discourse also contributed to the worsening process. In addition, all scholars agree that the Israeli government's refusal to prosecute police officers who were involved in the killing of thirteen Arab citizens of Israel during civic demonstrations in October 2000 has also been a major reason for the deterioration

---

3 Sammy Smooha, "Arab-Jewish Relations in Israel," United States Institute of Peace, Dec 13, 2010, http://www.usip.org/publications/arab-jewish-relations-in-israel.
4 Elie Rekhess, "The Arab Minority in Israel: Reconsidering the '1948 Paradigm,'" *Israel Studies* 19, no. 2 (2014): 187–217. The quotes are from p. 192.

in Arab-Jewish relations inside Israel.[5] Hence, the hyper-nationalist rhetoric and the violent physical campaigns against Arabs during the summer of 2014 enflamed old hostilities and incited new ones. In many ways, for the first time since 1948, attacks against Arab citizens of Israel succeeded in presenting the Israeli-Palestinian conflict as encompassing the entire area between the Jordan River and the Mediterranean Sea.

The second deep current in Israeli-Jewish culture is the return of religion in general, and the growing usage of Jewish religious reasoning in explaining and justifying the Palestinian-Israeli conflict in particular. The extreme manifestation of this new state of mind is the National Religious messianic theology. Indeed, in the wake of Israel's continuous withdrawal from the "Greater Israel" territories, which began immediately after the 1973 war and continues to today, the National Religious camp has been undergoing a process of religious radicalization. An important result of this process has been the development of a "counter" militaristic-extremist halakha by this camp. Another outcome of the above processes has been the theocratization of the Israeli military.[6] Signs of these processes and of this worldview's penetration into mainstream Israeli society and politics appeared even before the 2014 Gaza War. However, its most glaring expression – so far – was during that war. A day before the opening of

---

5 See Smooha and Rekhess; also Nadim N. Rouhana and Nimer Sultany, "Redrawing the Boundaries of Citizenship: Israel's New Hegemony," *Journal of Palestine Studies* 33, no. 1 (2003): 5–22; Nadim N. Rouhana and Areej Sabbagh-Khoury, "Settler-Colonial Citizenship: Conceptualizing the Relationship between Israel and its Palestinian Citizens," *Settler Colonial Studies* 5, no. 3 (2015): 205–25. On the Palestinian-Arabs in Israel see also Ilan Peleg and Dov Waxman, *Israel's Palestinians: The Conflict Within* (Cambridge; New York: Cambridge University Press, 2011); Amal Jamal, *Arab Minority Nationalism in Israel: The Politics of Indigeneity* (London; New York: Routledge, 2011).

6 See the pioneering studies by Stuart Cohen, Motti Inbari, and Yagil Levi: Stuart A. Cohen, "Safra ve-sayfa uma she-beneyhem: 'Itsuv hilkhot tsava u-milkhama ve-Yisrael, 1948–2004," *'Iyunim Bitkumat Yisrael* 15 (2005): 239–74; Motti Inbari, *Messianic Religious Zionism Confronts Israeli Territorial Compromises* (New York: Cambridge University Press, 2012); Yagil Levi, *Ha-Mefaked ha-Elyon: Ha-teokratizitsya shel ha-tsava be-Yisrael* (Tel Aviv: Am Oved and Sapir College, 2015); idem, "Religious Authorities in the Military and Civilian Control: The Case of the Israeli Defense Forces," *Politics & Society* 44, no. 2 (2016): 305–32.

the Israeli offensive, Colonel Ofer Winter, commander of the Givati Brigade, sent his soldiers a declaration explaining the purpose of the war and its justification in purely religious terms. While the Israeli government presented the war as an act of self-defense, Winter, who was educated in one of the government-funded National Religious army preparatory academies (situated in an Israeli settlement in the West Bank), presented it as a religious war against the entire "Gazite" people. The "Gazites," the ancient Philistines (Joshua 13:3) who were identified by Winter as modern-day Palestinians, were portrayed by him as a nation that "curses, reviles, and defames the God of the battalions of Israel."[7] In other words, to Winter the war was not a war in defense of the modern Jewish and democratic State of Israel, but rather a religious war against those who blaspheme Israel's God.

In other parts of his declaration, Winter evoked the words that, according to Jewish law, a special priest (*kohen mashuakh milkhama*) is supposed to say before Israel launches a war. Perhaps most worrying, Winter used language one might interpret as identifying the Palestinians as Amalek – one of the ancient nations that, also according to Jewish law (halakha), should be completely wiped off the face of the earth. This possible interpretation can be inferred from the very identification of the "Gazites" as a nation that defames the God of Israel – a trait characteristic of Amalek – and from Winter's usage of the loaded term *le-hakkhrit* – to make extinct – that is mentioned in Jewish law many times in reference to what one should do to the seed of Amalek. (It should be stressed, however, that since Maimonides' rule on this issue, rabbis have forbidden the fulfillment of this commandment in our times.)

Be that as it may, in sermons delivered during the war and now available online, and in a clear deviation from the accepted halakha, a few leading rabbis of the radical (and leading) wing of the National Religious camp supported Winter and interpreted the war as a special "commanded war" (*milkhemet mitsva*) for the conquest of

---

7 Gili Cohen, "Makh"t giv'ati la-mefakdim: 'H" Elokey Yisrael, anu nilkhamim keneged oyev ha-mena'ets shemekha,'" *Haaretz*, November 7, 2014, http://www.haaretz.co.il/news/politics/1.2373864.

the "land of Israel" and against Amalek, who was identified as the Palestinians. In these rabbis' interpretation, Amalek is defined as any nation that "wants to kill Israel" or that prevents the people of Israel from settling the "land of Israel." Indeed, on the website of a leading National Religious Youth Yeshiva, Yeshivat Netiv Meir, and in direct relation to the 2014 war in Gaza, the identification of both the ancient Philistines and the modern Palestinians as Amalek is made very clear: "we are at war now against the modern Philistines, Amalek of Eretz Yisrael."[8]

Other rabbis categorized all the Palestinians in Gaza as *rodefim* (pursuers), meaning that they are all equally suspected of supporting or encouraging violent acts against Israeli Jews.[9] Similar identification of civilian Gazans as *rodefim* appears to have been expressed by colonel Winter himself in an interview he gave during the war to Israel's most popular newspaper, *Yedioth Ahronoth*.[10] According to Jewish law, in extreme situations one is even required to kill a *rodef*. Here, however, and in a sharp contrast to the accepted halakha, the law of *rodef* was now applied to the entire Palestinian population. In fact, a continuity exists here, as already during the First Intifada (1987–1993) leading rabbis of the National Religious camp began to categorize all Palestinians as *rodefim*.[11] In other words, the same worldview that produced the Jewish Underground of the 1980s – a messianic organization that conspired to blow up the Dome of the Rock and the Al-Aqsa Mosque in the hope that such an act would hasten the coming of the Messiah (which is the same worldview that allowed its followers to openly contemplate declaring Prime Minister

---

8 From "Palestinians – then and now," which appeared on www.netivmeir.co.il but has since been taken down. I have a printed copy of this text.

9 See the "virtual Torah lessons" on the website of Bnei David Eli, such as the following on "internal trends" in Israel's war: http://www.bneidavid.org/Web/He/VirtualTorah/Lessons/Default.aspx?subject=&rabi=24&name=.

10 See Oren Persico, "Sa'ir la-'Azazel," *Ha-'ayin ha-shvi'it*, August 15, 2014, https://www.the7eye.org.il/121859.

11 Gerald J. Blidstein, "The Treatment of Hostile Civilian Populations: The Contemporary Halakhic Discussion in Israel," *Israel Studies* 1, no. 2 (1996): 27–45.

Rabin as a *moser* [informer]) – has now reached the highest ranks of the Israeli army.[12]

Winter's declaratory order clearly undermined the chain of command and the authority of the democratically elected government of Israel. One would have supposed, then, that Winter's superiors would have removed him from his command immediately. But they did not. Not only was he allowed to remain in command, but he also became the Israeli "face" of the war. The army deliberately embedded journalists with him, advertised photographs of him taken during combat, and his interviews, comments, and photographs became a central part of Israel's public relations campaign. The religious fervor did not subside when the 2014 Gaza War ended. During the following months – leading up to the crisis of the nation-state laws – more Israeli settlements were established in the midst of one of Jerusalem's Arab neighborhoods, Silwan, and an intensifying campaign launched by right-wing members of the Knesset and Jewish religious activists for the establishment of the Third Jewish Temple on Haram al Sharif/ the Temple Mount brought Jerusalem to the brink of a dangerous religious conflict.

To an outside observer, the debate over the bills and the general radicalization and theocratization of Jewish-Israeli politics and discourse, manifested so clearly during the 2014 Gaza War and its aftermath, may seem irrational, self-destructive, and a danger to Israel's vital interests. However, this supposedly irrational conduct is completely rational if we shift our angle of vision: this mode of behavior is characteristic of societies in the final stages of their colonial decline.

DOUBLE DECOLONIZATION

Israel in 2018 is in the throes of the last phases of decolonization from territories it captured during the 1967 war: the Sinai, the Gaza

---

12 See Michael Karpin and Ina Friedman, *Murder in the Name of God: The Plot to Kill Yitzhak Rabin* (New York: Metropolitan Books, 1998).

Strip, the West Bank and the Syrian/Golan Heights. This continuous process of military decline and withdrawal, which began as early as 1967 and continued during the War of Attrition (1967–1970) became most apparent at the time of the 1973 Yom Kippur War. Indisputably, the 1973 war marks a watershed in the balance of power between Israel and its neighboring Arab countries. In the wake of that war Israel was forced, for the first time, to withdraw from territories it captured in 1967.

The war shattered the myth of the invincible Israeli army, and, in fact, the 1967 war was the last military campaign that Israel actually won. Starting with the War of Attrition (1967–1970) between Egypt and Israel, Israel was never able decisively to win any war with its Arab neighbors or to curb the Palestinian uprisings against its rule over them in the occupied territories. These included two wars in Lebanon (in 1982 and 2006), two Palestinian uprisings (Intifadas) against Israeli military occupation (1987–1992; 2000–2005), and three wars (or military "operations") against Hamas in the Gaza Strip (2008–2009, 2012, 2014). Some of these wars Israel did not win; others, it lost.

Significantly, after each of these military confrontations Israel was forced to withdraw from territories it occupied, or to give up on demands it insisted were crucial before the confrontation broke out. Thus, immediately following the 1973 war Israel was forced to withdraw from the Suez Canal and parts of the Sinai, steps the state's leadership consistently and vehemently refused to take before 1973. As is well known, the Israeli-Egyptian peace treaty in 1979 stipulated full Israeli withdrawal from the Sinai and the complete evacuation of Israeli settlements there. The evacuation of the city of Yamit and of fifteen Israeli agricultural settlements in that region in 1982, as well as the evacuation of other Israeli settlements in the Sinai in the wake of the Israeli-Egyptian peace treaty, was an important milestone in Israel's decolonization process.

This process did not stop there. The First Lebanon War was accompanied by rhetoric that would repeat itself in the following confrontations, including in the 2014 Gaza War. This Lebanon War ended, however, after many years of conflict, with a unilateral and panicked retreat, images of which brought to mind pictures of the fall of Saigon. As it is well known, the goal of the First Lebanon War was to crush the Palestinians' military forces stationed in that country, and consequently to "solve the Palestinian Problem." However, only five years passed since the Israeli invasion of Lebanon in 1982 and the Palestinians in the occupied territories opened up a popular revolt against Israeli occupation, known as the First Intifada (1987–1992). At first, Israel tried to subdue that popular revolt. Eventually, however, Israel was forced, once again, to take steps that consistently and vehemently it had refused to take before: to withdraw from major Palestinian cities, to acknowledge the Palestinian Liberation Organization (PLO) as the official representative of the Palestinian people, and to establish a framework for a future Palestinian state. The overall trajectory is therefore clear. Indeed, following its failed attempts to crush the Second Intifada (2000–2005), Israel was once again forced to withdraw from territories it occupied and to completely evacuate its settlements in the Gaza Strip (the so-called "Disengagement"). Finally, the unsuccessful 2014 war against Hamas pushed Israel to ease restrictions it imposed on Gaza's civilian population – restrictions it opposed easing before the war.

The watershed events around 1973 also instigated a parallel, inner process of cultural and social change, which I will term as an inner social and cultural decolonization. The foundational hegemonic regime and culture of the state, Ben-Gurion's *mamlakhtiyut* (statism), has been continuously challenged or fractured since 1973. True, there were attempts before 1973, mainly bottom-up economic and social ones, to challenge that core "civil religion" of *mamlakhtiyut*. However, they were all defeated. Only when that keystone of Ben-Gurion's system, the invincible soldier and the "code of security," was shattered in 1973, did the system begin truly to be challenged. This inner social and cultural process, seen by its advocates and participants as a "freedom movement" away from the cultural and social yoke of Labor's Gramscian *mamlakhtiyut*, prompted the rise of diverse heretofore-marginalized groups that did not conform to the hegemonic socialist and secular brand of Jewish nationalism. Hence, Jews who came from Muslim and Arab countries (Mizrahim), women, Holocaust survivors, and religious Jews of both "traditional" and ultra-Orthodox (Haredi) communities began to express their distinct identities.

The social and economic system of the state also changed from its socialist orientation to a capitalist-driven system. Moreover, growing numbers of Israelis emigrated from Israel, creating an Israeli diaspora that undermined the very premise of Zionism's ideals of "negating the Diaspora" and the "ingathering of the exiles." In addition to its impact on the Jewish population of Israel, this process of inner decolonization facilitated the integration of Israel's Arab citizens into the social and economic fabric of its society, while encouraging them to demand collective recognition and rights much like other groups.[13]

It should be emphasized that these two decolonization processes influenced each other. Hence the emergence of the political and ideological right in Israel, previously suppressed during much of Ben-Gurion's tenure as prime minister. Significantly, the emergence of the messianic Religious Nationalist movement took place not after 1967, but rather in 1974, as a reaction to the fear that Israel was losing ground in the territories it occupied during the Six-Day War.

Today, Israel's *mamlakhtiyut* has lost its hegemonic hold on the majority of Israel's population. The decline of the symbolic and authoritative "center" of *mamlakhtiyut* lowered the cultural and social walls between Israeli subcultures, and a more multicultural and even hybrid type of culture began to emerge. Thus, Mizrahi music and cuisine became dominant societal features while the economic

---

13 This brief outline is based on a model explaining the rise and the continuous decline of Israel's collective identity that I have developed. See Nahum Karlinsky, "Hirhurim 'al limudey Medinat Yisrael," in *Sefer Yovel le-Yisrael Bartal*, ed. Gershon Hundert, Jonathan Meir, and Dimitry Shumsky (Jerusalem: Zalman Shazar Center, in print). See also Charles Liebman and Eliezer Don-Yehiya, *Civil Religion in Israel: Traditional Judaism and Political Culture in the Jewish State* (Berkeley: University of California Press, 1983); Ian Lustick, *Unsettled States, Disputed Lands: Britain and Ireland, France and Algeria, Israel and the West Bank-Gaza* (Ithaca, NY: Cornell University Press, 1993); Baruch Kimmerling, *The Invention and Decline of Israeliness: State, Society and the Military* (Berkeley: University of California Press, 2001); Gershon Shafir and Yoav Peled, *Being Israeli: The Dynamics of Multiple Citizenship* (Cambridge; New York: Cambridge University Press, 2002); Guy Ben-Porat and Bryan S. Turner, eds., *The Contradictions of Israeli Citizenship: Land, Religion and State* (London; New York: Routledge, 2011); Anita Shapira, *Israel: A History* (Waltham, MA: Brandeis University Press, 2012).

and social gaps between Mizrahim and Ashkenazim narrowed. Secular Jews became more traditional, and espoused diverse religious approaches, from "new age" Judaism to the Haredi type. Haredi communities, on their part, have experienced an ongoing process of Israelization, similar to the one Israel's Arab citizens went through.

At the same time, central institutions that were established during Israel's formative years, like its three branches of government, its internationally recognized pre-1967 borders, or the state's educational systems, have proven to be stable and resilient to change. As these institutions are fundamentally Western in their orientation and structure, important aspects of *mamlakhtiyut* continue to guide Israeli culture and society. Hence, one can characterize the many divisions and ongoing conflicts inside Israeli society as a continuous struggle to control the state's fields of cultural and political production.[14]

Israeli society has still failed to construct an alternative identity that might replace Ben-Gurion's statism. A major reason for this failure relates to the accelerated pace of the external process of decolonization, which is much faster than its inner counterpart, and hence does not leave sufficient time for the inner process to forge a new collective identity.

Postcolonial studies have stressed the psychological difficulties that colonizers encounter when they face the reality of decolonization. Colonizers, who are used to imposing their will on the colonized by force, refuse to accept the fact that at a certain turning point the colonized peoples are no longer afraid of them and are undeterred by their might. Consequently, the colonizers resort to using even more force, hoping that this will allow the situation to revert back to its previous "normal" state.[15]

Brute force, nonetheless, only feeds the process of decolonization. Violence hardens core traits of national and personal identity, such as language, religion, and family relations. In contrast, as scholars

---

14 See Pierre Bourdieu, *The Field of Cultural Production: Essays on Art and Literature* (Cambridge, UK: Polity Press, 1993).

15 Albert Memmi, *The Colonizer and the Colonized* (Boston: Beacon Press, 1965); Frantz Fanon, *The Wretched of the Earth* (New York: Grove Press, 1968); Alistair Horne, *A Savage War of Peace: Algeria, 1954–1962* (London: Macmillan, 1977).

of conflict resolution and reconciliation have shown, addressing the emotions of the other side – especially their self-esteem and their personal and collective honor – can help bridge gaps and even halt the process of colonial withdrawal and retreat.[16]

Since 1973 Israel's usual reaction to its apparent loss of influence has been to use more force. But there were two exceptions to this mode of behavior: Menachem Begin's 1979 peace treaty with Egypt and Yitzhak Rabin's 1993 Oslo Accords with the PLO. Undoubtedly, in both agreements, vital security, as well as economic, social, and political interests played a major role. It is also clear that in both cases the main goal was to nip the decolonization process in the bud.

Prime Minister Begin understood that Israel could not afford to sustain an open military confrontation with Egypt. Indeed, the peace agreement with the largest and most influential Arab country has proven itself to be a cornerstone of Israel's security. Rabin, who was defense minister when the First Intifada broke out and was instrumental in the failed attempts to crush it, also realized that this perpetual cycle of violence only weakened Israel. Significantly, both leaders used symbolic language and gestures that addressed the other side's emotional needs for recognition and respect. Rabin's assassination by Yigal Amir, a religious Jew who was immersed in the more extreme version of National Religious theology, succeeded in halting the Oslo process and most probably prevented the establishment of a Palestinian State in the West Bank and the Gaza Strip. It did not, however, stop the process of decolonization. Rather, it exacerbated and accelerated it.

The Second Intifada (2000–2005) was more violent and bloodier than the first. Led by the hawkish veteran army general Ariel Sharon as prime minister, Israel launched a wide-range military campaign against the Palestinians in an effort to crush the uprising. After five

---

16 Roger Petersen, *Understanding Ethnic Violence: Fear, Hatred, and Resentment in Twentieth-Century Eastern Europe* (Cambridge, UK: Cambridge University Press, 2002); Daniel Bar-Tal, "Why Does Fear Override Hope in Societies Engulfed by Intractable Conflict, as It Does in Israeli Society?" *Political Psychology* 22 (2001): 601–62; Yaacov Bar-Siman-Tov, ed., *From Conflict Resolution to Reconciliation* (New York: Oxford University Press, 2004).

288 · DEFINING ISRAEL

long years during which thousands of people on both sides were killed and wounded, Israel evacuated its settlements from the Gaza Strip and from an area in the northern West Bank. In contrast to the first Palestinian uprising, this time Israel's withdrawal was unilateral and no agreement with the Palestinian leadership was reached. In addition, Israel built walls between it and Palestinian communities in the West Bank and the Gaza Strip. The decolonization path was clearly marked on the ground.

DENIAL AND COERCIVE HEGEMONY

Since the 2005 unilateral withdrawal from Gaza, the debate's focus in Israel has shifted away from security concerns to notions of perception and consciousness. The reality of Israel's continued weakness, and the inability of the majority of Israeli Jews and their leaders to accept that reality and take the emotional and conscious leap that Begin and Rabin took, has led Israelis to adopt a variety of psychological defense mechanisms. The two most conspicuous ones can be termed as "soft" and "coercive" denials. The "soft" denial is expressed in many ways: through the imagining of Tel Aviv as a Western, liberal, and conflict-free "bubble" in which one conducts one's life as one would in New York City; through the popularity of TV "reality shows" that help viewers block actuality from their gaze; through the establishment of various political parties that attend to the middle class and consciously avoid any references to the reality of the withdrawal and retreat process.

The "coercive" type of denial, on the other hand, is engaged in an aggressive cultural battle. Thus, the successful effort to pass the Basic Law: Israel – The Nation-State of the Jewish People was just another aspect of this broader campaign. Following the Italian political theoretician Antonio Gramsci's concepts of hegemony, this campaign should be seen as an aggressive attempt to impose on Israeli society a right-wing religiously informed coercive hegemony. Hence, the very existence of Israel's occupation is denied, as well as the reality of bi-nationalism in Palestine/Israel, or the fact that there is a Palestinian people. Thus, any form of Israeliness or any Zionist outlook that accepts the reality of the existence of a Palestinian collective is defined as illegitimate, non-Jewish, and anti-Israeli. In the variations of the proposed bills and in its final form, as well as in other restrictive legislation, policies, and public discourse, the Jewishness of the state trumps its democratic foundation. "Democracy" is therefore a code word for the mirror on the wall that should be smashed. It is a code word for the danger inherent in free speech and freedom of expression, or in institutions that enable these notions to be actualized, like universities or the judiciary.

A variety of non-governmental organizations, like the Institute for Zionist Strategies and Im Tirtzu, that were established either during the withdrawal from Gaza or after Israel's unsuccessful Second Lebanon War in 2006, target civil-rights NGOs and Israeli academia. For example, supporters of these organizations and their ideology have secretly filmed the classes of "suspected" faculty, and the heavily edited films were then broadcast on prime-time Israeli television, purportedly showing Israeli academics' "betrayal" of Zionist ideology. Moreover, these organizations have close personal and ideological ties to Cabinet members and members of the Knesset. The battle over the monitoring of thought crimes and the organizations that support these "crimes" was also waged in the Knesset itself, in a long list of anti-democratic laws and proposals.[17]

In a final example – one with which I have intimate familiarity – from 2011–2013 the Council for Higher Education, which is controlled by the Ministry of Education, tried to shut down the Department of Politics and Government at Ben-Gurion University of the Negev, claiming that its faculty was post-Zionist or even anti-Zionist. Consequently, the university was forced to make changes to the department's syllabi and to hire new faculty. It seems that the government backed down from this attempt only after it realized that closing down the department would only add more fuel to the already blazing BDS movement.

The double paths to decolonization, the external and the inter-

---

17 See "Anti-Democratic Legislation Initiatives," The Association for Civil Rights in Israel, August 2, 2012, http://www.acri.org.il/en/2012/08/02/update-anti-democratic-legislation-initiatives/.

nal, which have characterized Israeli politics and culture, have not changed in the years since the 2014 Gaza War and Netanyahu's attempts in that year to pass a nation-state law. True, combatant rhetoric continues: there are growing calls for the annexation of the Golan/Syrian Heights, as well as areas in the West Bank, or certain cities there. At the same time, the external decolonization process continues. In 2017, Israel completed the evacuation of the Amona settlement in the West Bank and the destruction of several buildings in Ofra, the jewel in the crown of Israeli settlements. It did not do this willingly, of course, but rather due to the danger that the International Criminal Court (ICC) would interfere if Israel did not follow Israel's own Supreme Court's ruling to evacuate these areas.

Cultural and social decolonization, especially the never-ending symbolic and cultural clashes between Mizrahi and Ashkenazi Jews continues as well. Interestingly, the two processes have been personified in the colorful and outspoken character of Israel's minister of culture and sport, Miri Regev. For her, as for many Israelis, the struggle against Ashkenazi cultural hegemony is also a struggle against an Ashkenazi Western worldview that supports the right of national self-determination for all peoples, including the Palestinians.[18]

The nation-state law should be seen, therefore, as yet another desperate effort to deny the reality of Israel's decolonization and of the existence of a Palestinian people that regards the same land as the Jews' as its homeland. It is not a coincidence, therefore, that most of those restrictive bills and measures, including the various versions of Basic Law: Israel – The Nation-State of the Jewish People," were introduced after Rabin's assassination and after the outbreak of the Second Intifada. It is also not a coincidence that the first bill was brought before the Knesset just a few months before the Palestinian Authority began its drive to gain acceptance for Palestine as a full member of the United Nations. The declaration in several versions of the proposed law, as well as the one that passed, that "the

---

18 Ruth Margalit, "Miri Regev's Culture War," *The New York Times Magazine*, October 20, 2016, https://www.nytimes.com/2016/10/23/magazine/miri-regevs-culture-war .html?_r=0.

right to exercise national self-determination in the State of Israel is uniquely that of the Jewish people," was written to challenge that reality. Some versions went even further. In Netanyahu's proposal, his statement that the "land of Israel is the historic homeland of the Jewish people and the place where the State of Israel has been established," insinuates that the territorial boundaries of the State of Israel are equal to the entire land of Israel, and that only the "Jewish people" can claim national rights over it.

ETHNIC CLEANSING OR HOPEFUL SPRING?

The law is mostly declaratory in nature. Yet the international community has already indicated its opposition. An increasing number of European parliaments have been passing resolutions that recognize Palestine as a state. The Palestinians themselves, including Arab citizens of Israel, obviously do not accept it. Finally, many Israeli Jews reject this law as well.

Nonetheless, rhetoric plays an important role in ethnic and national conflicts. "Hypernationalist mobilization rhetoric," writes Chaim Kaufmann, "hardens ethnic identities to the point that cross-ethnic political appeals are unlikely to be made and even less likely to be heard."[19] Thus, the law purposely antagonizes "outsiders" and raises boundaries between Israeli Jews and Palestinians. In addition, the law also aims to coerce moderate Israelis to choose between two polarized sides rather than opt for a conciliatory "third way."

Such an emotionally charged atmosphere is fertile ground for the commitment of atrocities and eventually ethnic cleansing. The cases of Rwanda, the former Yugoslavia, and other sites in our contemporary world, as well as the scholarship on ethnic and national conflicts, attest to this observation. Does Israel stand at such crossroads? The answer is not decisively negative. The political right, which has been controlling Israeli politics over the last forty years, projects a strong

---

19 Chaim Kaufmann, "Possible and Impossible Solutions to Ethnic Civil Wars," *International Security* 20, no. 4 (1996): 136–75.

sense of despair and frustration at the reality of Israel's continuous process of decolonization. As a result, there are some who openly discuss options of "population exchange" or "transfer" of all Arabs, including Arab citizens of Israel, to areas beyond the borders of the State of Israel.[20] Some influential rabbis of the National Religious camp even use terms like "cleaning" the land of Israel of Arabs.[21] In such an atmosphere, one should hardly be surprised to learn that in a survey conducted by the well-respected Pew Research Center between October 2014 and May 2015, almost half (48 percent) of Israeli Jews agreed that "Arabs should be expelled or transferred from Israel." While 36 percent of Israeli secular Jews supported the expulsion of Arabs from Israel, 71 percent of National Religious Jews (so-called *dati*) supported the ethnic cleansing plan.[22] It is not unthinkable to assume that under certain circumstances such phrases and openly discussed options will be translated into actions.

Luckily, the processes of inclusion – of creating new and more inclusive, tolerant, multicultural, and hybrid forms of Israeli identity – are gaining more ground, as more people realize that, indeed, force did not solve Israel's main existential issue. The struggle over the creation of a new Israeli symbolic "center" has not yet been decided.

---

20 "An Arab-Israeli Dilemma: Might They Want to Join Palestine," *The Economist*, January 18, 2014, http://www.economist.com/news/middle-east-and-africa/21594353 -avigdor-liebermans-radical-ideas-population-transfers-are-gaining-ground -might. See also the official plan from September 2017 of the National Union faction (which is part of the right-wing religious Jewish Home party) to essentially annex the occupied territories, deny Palestinians there voting rights, and to facilitate their transfer elsewhere: Martin Sherman, "Into the Fray: The Smotrich Plan – A Step in the Right Direction, but…" *Arutz Sheva*, September 15, 2017, http://www .israelnationalnews.com/Articles/Article.aspx/21018; Yotam Berger, "Israeli Party Approves Plan to Coerce Palestinian Departure," *Haaretz*, September 13, 2017, https:// www.haaretz.com/israel-news/.premium-israeli-party-approves-annexation-plan-to -coerce-palestinian-departure-1.5450326.

21 "Hardline Rabbi Calls to 'cleanse' Israel of Arabs," *The Times of Israel*, October 1, 2014, http://www.timesofisrael.com/hardline-rabbi-calls-to-cleanse-israel-of-arabs/.

22 "Israel's Religiously Divided Society," Pew Research Center, March 8, 2016, http:// www.pewforum.org/2016/03/08/israels-religiously-divided-society/.

Too Jewish?

Moshe Koppel

In 2004, the Knesset's Constitution, Law, and Justice Committee, under the chairmanship of Michael Eitan, held hearings regarding the drafting of a constitution for Israel. Eitan asked me to prepare drafts for a proposed chapter on Israel as a Jewish nation-state. The committee members who took the keenest interest in this chapter were the late Rabbi Avraham Ravitz, of the Haredi (ultra-Orthodox) United Torah Judaism (Yahadut ha-Tora) Party, and Reshef Chen, of the anti-Haredi Shinui Party.

Despite the somewhat challenging cast of characters, it proved possible to reach a more or less agreed text for the proposed chapter without as much difficulty as might be expected. The key was to identify those issues where some consensus could be formed, while avoiding controversial ideological pronouncements. When efforts to draft a complete constitution stalled, the Institute for Zionist Strategies, of which I was a member, used the chapter that had been presented to the committee as the basis for a proposed Basic Law, the first of the bills under discussion here. Member of Knesset Avraham Dichter, along with thirty-six other signatories, including most of the MKs of the centrist Kadima Party and some MKs from parties to the left of Kadima, placed this bill on the Knesset's table in 2011 (2011, P/18/3541).

Many people more expert in matters of constitutional law than I am contributed substantively to the draft of the law and the literature surrounding it. Nevertheless, the litany of malign intentions attributed in the pages of this volume (and before that in the *Marginalia* forum) to the drafters of the bill afford me a rare glimpse into a seamier side of my soul, wherein I suffer from, in Nahum Karlinsky's felicitous phrase, the "psychological difficulties that

colonizers encounter when they face the reality of decolonization."[1]
One lives and learns.

But never mind the pop psychology. Let's focus on the arguments
against the legislation, which (for tendentious rhetorical purposes)
I organize into three pairs of claims.

1. The bill is unnecessary since its substance is uncontroversial and
   irrevocably woven into the very fabric of Israeli law and culture.
   Moreover, it is unjust, redolent of fascism, and must be derailed
   at all costs.

2. The bill is unnecessarily concrete, lacking in grand vision and
   soaring poetry. And, by the way, since judges are masters of
   creative interpretation, the drafters' intentions are unlikely to
   be realized.

3. The whole idea of nation-states is utterly passé. Also, we should
   be focusing on more urgent matters, such as creating a Palestinian nation-state.

That each of these three arguments rests on an internal contradiction doesn't matter, because beneath the high rhetoric there is a
single point: the law is, as Jackie Mason would put it, "too Jewish."
Jews have been demoted in the grievance hierarchy; if they insist on
claiming for themselves in their state what dozens of other nations
have claimed in their states, they should at least do so discreetly and
apologetically. With that off my chest, I move on to the substance.
Why do we need this law? Broadly speaking, the law serves two
purposes. The first is to provide a sort of mission statement for the
state and the second is to fill a specific lacuna in Israel's legal system.

If we wish to teach our children that Israel is a Jewish nation-state,
we need to define concretely what that entails. If we wish to demand
from others that they live peacefully alongside us however we choose
to define ourselves, we ought to flesh out that definition. This definition cannot be achieved in a non-binding declaration; an operational
definition must be made explicit in a law with some teeth.

---

1 See in this volume Nahum Karlinsky, "Double Decolonization and the Loss of
Hegemony."

As a mission statement, the law is as careful about what it does not include as what it does include. It is based on the discussions described above and seeks consensus across a broad range of Zionist Jews. There is no mention of the Rabbinate and scant mention of religious legislation (essentially a bromide giving tradition its due respect). Nor is this bill, in its different versions, as some have insinuated, a foolhardy attempt to "inculcate Jewish identity."[2] The thought that the state ought to pro-actively inculcate any sort of identity is, in the Israeli case, mainly rooted in the secular socialist utopia for which Israel Bartal apparently hankers.[3]

The drafters of these bills have a more modest goal: the state should serve as a framework in which the majority of citizens already committed to some form of Jewish identity are able to manifest that identity in the public sphere. Specifically, what these bills demand is that this Jewish identity be given expression in Israel's choice of language, symbols, calendar, immigration policy, and so on. (The fact that Hebrew, as Israel's national language, was omitted in some versions of the bill is, as Alexander Yakobson notes, absurd.)[4] All these are sufficiently fundamental that they should be anchored in a Basic Law. In fact, I suspect that most innocent observers of Israel would be surprised to hear that they haven't long been anchored in a Basic Law.

The second purpose of the law is a more formal matter. Just as judges must adjudicate between conflicting civil and human rights – say, my right to free speech versus your right to privacy, or your freedom of movement versus my property rights – so too they must adjudicate between the collective right of the majority to self-definition and other rights that might conflict with this collective right. This does not mean that being a Jewish nation-state is incompatible with being a democracy any more than that free speech is

2 See in this volume Nir Kedar, "On the Dangers of Enshrining National Character in the Law."
3 See in this volume Israel Bartal, "Who Needs the Nation-State Law? The State of the Jews, Fears, and Fearmongering."
4 Alexander Yakobson, "A Manual on How Not to Write a Constitution," *The Marginalia Review of Books*, February 16, 2015, https://marginalia.lareviewofbooks.org /manual-write-constitution/.

incompatible with the right to privacy; rights and values bump up against each other and from time to time they need to be adjudicated.

Let's be clear about the terms of the debate. This bill seeks to anchor the Jewish collective right to self-definition alongside other rights already anchored in other Basic Laws. It does not call for the superiority of this particular right. Israel's legal system occasionally faces cases in which its special national character, specifically its interest in maintaining a strong Jewish majority, is in tension with other rights. This Basic Law would require that judges *balance* Jewish collective rights against the rights of individuals. (This is not the current practice. For example, in cases involving the constitutionality of laws regarding, respectively, family unification and infiltrators, Israel's interest in maintaining a Jewish majority was neither raised by the state's attorneys nor considered by the court.) Those who argue in favor of the status quo, in which Israel's Jewish character is referred to only fleetingly in Basic Laws and has been rarely invoked in recent jurisprudence, are effectively arguing *against* the attempt to achieve such balance.

One note on the phrasing of the law: ambiguity in a law is usually not a virtue, but an invitation. It invites judges to interpret and, often, to exceed their legitimate authority by legislating from the bench. Let us not play pretend. This law, in its different drafts, was not written in a cultural vacuum: Israel's judges since Aharon Barak have never resisted an invitation to legislate. The kind of grandiose language that invokes vaguely defined liberal principles would do more than just invite judicial activism. It would lay out a broad red carpet. "Equality" is an especially irresistible term. Do we care to define it? Are we talking equality of opportunity or equality of outcomes, equality among individuals or equality among collectives? If the national culture suits the majority better than it suits some minority, has equality been achieved? If not, do we wish to give unelected and – due to the nature of the judicial nomination process – essentially self-perpetuating judges carte blanche to remedy that problem against the will of the legislature? For those who wrote this law, the answer is "no" and the language of the law reflects that.

In short, this law is necessary for restoring a lost balance between national rights and individual rights in Israeli law. It is necessary also for the purpose of clarifying to ourselves and to others what we mean – and, no less significantly, what we do not mean – when we assert our right to a Jewish nation-state. In any event, I'm grateful that some of the discussions this bill has engendered have contributed to the goal of clarifying what a Jewish nation-state is or might be.

What is a Nation-State For?

Yehudah Mirsky

An odd and simple-minded question, perhaps, given the ubiquity and centrality of nation-states in our world, but still worth asking, especially when first principles are on the table.

"The state," Max Weber lucidly said, "is an association that claims the monopoly of the legitimate use of violence, and cannot be defined in any other manner."[1] It is the prerequisite for survival beyond the clan, both within society and beyond its territory. More than just the guarantor of survival, the state is, in its illiberal forms, the ensemble of legal instruments for political and socio-cultural practices through which the majority, or at least the ruling elites, impose their will on everyone else. It is, in its liberal forms, the ensemble of legal instruments and genuinely democratic frameworks for political and socio-cultural practices through which citizens, qua individuals, work out their respective claims for power and freedom. This freedom in turn can take many forms, from, for instance, freedom *for* one's own ethnic group, to freedom *from* one's own ethnic group.

Broadly autocratic, oligarchic, and repressive governance has been with us for a very long time, as has the state's monopoly on legitimate coercion within a given territory. Liberalism, on the other hand, and the nation-state, both arose in the West at the same point in history, and in some respects, arose together. Both arose in response to deep changes in the nature of identity – of meaningful belonging.

The late Shmuel Noah Eisenstadt wrote that identity takes three forms – primordial (we could say ethnic, or kinship), civic (or social),

---

1 See Hans H. Gerth and C. Wright Mills, eds., *From Max Weber: Essays in Sociology* (Oxford: Oxford University Press, 1946), 334.

and transcendent (the realm of ultimate values). Eisenstadt, in a sense, restates Aristotle's reconstruction of the concentric emergence of the polis from the family to village to city-state, but he replaces Aristotle's serene teleology with the structural and existential anxieties of modern sociology. In a stable group or individual, the three dimensions of belonging more or less work together, or at least not too much at cross-purposes with one another. When the structures holding those identities together come apart, our responses to this fissure alternate between liberation and terror.[2]

So it was in Western Europe after the Catholic Church gave way in the Protestant Reformation: after much bloodshed, the Westphalian order of semi-nation-states came to provide, after 1648, the framework for meaningful and hopefully secure collective belonging. In this prying loose from the c/Catholic framework, salvation was now something to be attained by the believer's own relationship with God rather than via participation in the Church qua body of Christ. This individuation was accompanied by the corresponding end of the identification of the body of the monarch with the body politic. These developments had deep implications for the individual, as person, and as a unit of meaning in his (for centuries, his) own right. Meaningful collective belonging now sought an anchor sunk deep in the territory of the state and the linguistic and cultural inheritances of its inhabitants.

There are, needless to say, many stories to be told here; many more than can be encompassed in a broad-brush essay such as this. But the one that concerns us is the story of the collapse of transcendence and immanence into one another – with the ultimate meanings of the religious order now being instantiated in the state, and the subjectivity of the individual coming to be seen as one with the subjectivity of the nation. These processes moved in tandem with the other crucial dimensions of the ending of pre-modern corporate

---

2 Eisenstadt used this formulation on many different occasions. The most succinct statement is in the first part of the article he co-authored with Bernhard Giesen, "The Construction of Collective Identity," *Archive of European Sociology*, 36 (1995): 72–102.

life, namely the rethinking of social and political life in terms of equality and freedom.

What has any of this to do with the Jews? Quite a bit.

Relieving or at least coming to terms with the civil inequality of the Jews was central to the new meaning of statehood in modernity – quite literally a stumbling block to the Jews, and, often enough, a foolishness to the Gentiles. In the new, modernizing nation-states, the limited but genuine forms of Jewish collective life, as lived in the pre-modern self-governing Jewish community known as the *kehilla*, no longer made sense. Beyond the technical sticking points of Jews' collective perdurance as pockets within the nation-state, and the persistence of the Jews' distinctive integration of primordial identity and transcendence, now as participants in the culture at large, the Jewish condition presented an unresolved structural conundrum in the emergence of that new statehood itself.

The perceived failure of Western European nation-states to accommodate the Jews gave rise to the political Zionism of Theodor Herzl and others. To the East, even (to put it mildly) compromised efforts at emancipation and liberalization were too much for the Russian Empire to attempt, and thus the ongoing insecurity and misery among so many in the Pale of Settlement, and the emerging nationalism of those around them, gave Zionism its most pressing moral (and much demographic) heft. It was, moreover, the Jewish eastern European struggle to rethink and reconstitute the tradition that gave rise to a different Zionism, as a project of cultural renaissance and, for others, a project of cultural and political revolution – not only against exile but also against Jewish history.

To be sure, Zionism was not the only program on offer to ameliorate Jewish disability. It was one set of answers to the multiple crises of politics, culture, and religion that wracked European Jewry through the nineteenth century. Others included liberalism, socialist revolution, Jewish Diaspora nationalism, assimilationism, and, in its own way, Orthodoxy. Surprising as it may sound to describe that traditionalist party as a modern dispensation it is true – and indeed is indicated in the very term "traditionalist party," namely its being a party, and an "ism." In the coming to be of Orthodoxy, adherents of a more or less organic tradition (necessary caveats notwithstanding) came to see themselves as a minority ideological group within the Jewish world, competing with other Jews for standing and authority – all within the distinctively modern dispensation by which society and history are not givens, but artifacts, to be unmade and made anew. These ideological possibilities mixed and matched within Zionism itself, yielding varieties of Zionism – secular and religious, left and right, universalist and nationalist – in staggering array (too often lost in the fog and in the willed forgetfulness on all sides of today's contemporary polemics). The Holocaust raised the stakes of all these arguments to an unnerving pitch.

At the State of Israel's creation in 1948, it was, above all, the Labor Zionism of Ben-Gurion's Mapai Party that emerged ascendant. Labor Zionism's greatest skill was in institution-building – in its ability to square the circles of nationalism and class, as well as of nationalism and universalism, within a program of Jewish socialist revolution. The creation by its leaders and thinkers – steeped in the classical Jewish tradition but against which they rose in full-fledged, yet deeply dialectical, rebellion – of a new interpretation of Jewish history and of Judaism itself, as radical as it was compelling, became enshrined in the Declaration of Independence. These are but a few of the reasons why Labor Zionism triumphed.

I.

Other contributors to this forum and volume have expertly explicated the ways in which the Declaration of Independence deftly synthesized questions of national identity and civic equality in the new state. I would just add one crucial element. God – to whom all pre-modern and even many modern Jews credited not only the universe but their own souls and survival – appears nowhere in the official language of the Declaration save for an oblique reference to the "Rock of Israel" (a venerable liturgical phrase taken from 2 Samuel 23:3). This near-total omission of the Creator was not lost on the religious signatories, one of whom, Rabbi Judah Leib Maimon, a significant scholar as well as long-time head of the Religious Zionist Mizrahi Party (flown in by Ben-Gurion for the signing from Jerusalem, then under siege), appended to his signature a squiggly three Hebrew characters, *b'h*, a traditional acronym for *be-'ezrat ha-Shem*, "with God's help."

Much of Israel's recent history is the gradual movement of Rabbi Maimon's squiggle – and of other historical squiggles – from the margins of the founding document, and the ethos it meant to enshrine, to its center.

In other words, the nation-state law, the controversies it engenders, and the processes it visibly enacts, simply cannot be understood outside the context of the steady decline of Mapai and its ethos from the mid-1970s to today. Ever since the still-traumatic Yom Kippur War of 1973, the hegemony of Mapai and its overwhelmingly secular Ashkenazi leadership has been in steady decline – and with it the Zionist civil religion it created. Secular Ashkenazi Israel has, to be sure, not gone away, but it has steadily been shunted aside and made to yield in one sector after another to Jewish groups who either were not present at the creation of the state or came to prominence only years after.

Among these were: the Revisionist Zionists, whose forcible exclusion not just from political power and patronage but from national memory and ethos engendered a bitter politics of resentment; Sephardi Jews, who in their countries of origin experienced modernity differently and less conflictually, and for whom it was precisely their very immigration to the new and secular Jewish State of Israel that became their traumatic encounter with modernity (this time wearing a secular Jewish face); Jews of the former Soviet Union, who, on their mass arrival, turned out not to be multitudes of Sharanskys and Nudels, dissident refusenik heroes yearning to breathe free, but normal human beings seeking to improve their lives after having lived in forced estrangement from Jewish life for the better part of a century. In addition, new generations of religious Zionists, whose youth rebellion was directed as much against moderates like Rabbi Maimon as against the elites of Mapai, came forward to press their new vision of Zionism as the paradoxical engine of the messianic redemption that would, by extending Israeli sovereignty to the biblical heartlands of Judea and Samaria, redeem the Jewish people and save the human race. For their part, Israel's ultra-Orthodox Jews, rather than accepting Labor Zionism's preferred role for them as inhabitants of a Judaic Colonial Williamsburg, have grown in numbers and in social and political clout, proving once again that people relegated by secular elites to the dustbin of history nonetheless have their own ideas. All these trends, taken together with the decline and widespread discrediting of socialism, have driven Israel's Labor Zionism to the ropes for decades.

II.

The Basic Laws of 1992 and the "constitutional revolution" of Justice Aharon Barak, which form the backdrop to the present discussion, must be seen in light of the steady decline in the political power and cultural predominance of the secular elites of the Mapai party, which was overwhelmingly dominant from the State's founding until the mid-1970s – and which has been brilliantly explicated in Menachem Mautner's *Law and the Culture of Israel*.[3] The 1992 Basic Laws introduced "Jewishness" as a substantive factor in law-making. The constitutional revolution of Justice Barak not only established American-style constitutionalism and judicial review in the absence of a written constitution, but also went even farther than the most activist of American judges in its wholesale erasure of political question doctrine, the idea, fundamental to American jurisprudence, that courts cannot rule on issues constitutionally delegated to the executive or on those involving policy judgments.

In many ways, Barak came to see the judiciary as the last ditch of Israeli democracy; and yet, this very stronghold, through the backlash that its forward defense engendered, may have actually helped weaken that democratic edifice. (In a sense, Barak and his

---

3 Menachem Mautner, *Law and the Culture of Israel* (Oxford: Oxford University Press, 2011).

chief sparring partner in public debate, Ruth Gavison, both of whom spent significant time at Yale Law School, each internalized one of the poles of the debates over judicial activism and restraint that have wracked, and in some ways disfigured, American jurisprudence for decades.) One case that emerged as a flash-point was the so-called Katzir decision of 2000, ruling that state resources could not be used to establish Jewish-only communities.[4] This, taken with the tenor of the court generally, unwittingly fed into a perception in more right-wing circles that the judiciary did not recognize the legitimacy of the Zionist enterprise as a whole.

Overwrought though much of the criticism of the court has been, it is crucial to note that in some respects the new right and religious critics of Mapai's inheritors were not wrong. Israel's secular elites had quite deliberately estranged themselves from, and weaned their children off, their own Jewish cultural resources, succumbing to the fate of revolutionaries who give their children an education as different as they can get from their own. Ben-Gurion and his peers had no trouble making the argument to religious Zionists that the Labor Zionist ethos was not only the better defense of Jewish interests but the better interpretation of its values. The successors of Ben-Gurion's generation, however, could not make that argument, if for no other reason than that they no longer share with their religious interlocutors the same language or the same basic understanding of who they are and what they are doing in their own state.

Not that the new would-be elites have all that many answers. As some of the contributors to this volume have pointed out, these laws are as much a sign of desperation as they are of anything. (They have been the occasion for extraordinary political opportunism on the part of Prime Minister Netanyahu and others, though that opportunism was made possible by genuine and unanswered questions.) The law represents a flailing away both at the increasingly complex picture of Israeli democracy, and at a growing recognition that Israel's conflict with the Palestinians is at bottom not about how to

---

4 H.C. 6698/95, Aadel Ka'adan v. Israel Lands Administration, 5(1) P.D. 258 (2000), https://www.escr-net.org/node/365464.

divide the land between two national groups but whether the Jews rightly deserve to have a state at all. That latter impasse has been made exponentially more complex by Israel's settlements in Judea and Samaria, but would have been there even without them.

But desperate measures can lead to disastrous results. To be sure, as Gideon Sapir wrote, building on the terrific work of Alex Yakobson and Amnon Rubinstein, liberal democracies certainly can have strong national identities.[5] And it must be said that a number of the nation-state law's sponsors and supporters, far from being illiberal revanchists, have been classic liberals, genuinely fearful of relentless attempts from multiple quarters to deny Israel's very legitimacy as a Jewish state. And it must also be said that Israel is a polity created not only to provide the physical security of sovereignty but to reconstitute affective ties of community. Staking the legitimate bounds of the latter will be a perennial conversation. Nonetheless, there is no denying that these current proposed laws, in both design and intent, aim to put in place Israel's Jewishness as such (as though such a thing were easily defined in this day and age), as *the* defining interpretive lens through which all other laws, including those governing Israel's Arab minority, are to be scrutinized. Serving as interpretive lenses for legal systems and cultures as a whole is, after all, what constitutional provisions do.

There is, in addition, a curious slippage at work in the very wording of these laws. The phrase at the center of these laws, *medinat Yisrael ki-medinat ha-leʿom shel ha-ʿam ha-yehudi*, translates as "Israel as the nation-state of the Jewish people." In one and the same breath, the warm, historical resonances of the "people" are yoked to the hard edges of the modern "nation," in which peoplehood is tied to the coercive power of the state. This illustrates, if nothing else, the uneasy and still unresolved relationship between the new Israeli

---

5 See in this volume, Gideon Sapir, "Was it Right to Pass a Nation-State Law?"; also Alexander Yakobson and Amnon Rubinstein, *Israel and the Family of Nations: The Jewish Nation-State and Human Rights*, trans. Ruth Morris and Ruchie Avital (London; New York: Routledge, 2009). For some helpful criticisms of their approach, see Chaim Gans, *A Political Theory for the Jewish People* (New York: Oxford University Press, 2016), 74–81.

nationalist dispensation and the very historical identity it is seeking to preserve and protect.

Which brings us full circle, to Weber. States are meant to provide security – and so the terms of meaningful belonging in and through which those states understand themselves are inextricably tied to security. It is all one package, and there are no easy ways out.

What's more, this Israeli story belongs to some larger trends, both regional and global.

Regionally, we are, finally, witnessing the collapse of the nation-state order put together after World War I as the Allies tried to sort out the contradictory promises scattered in all directions under the press of wartime. Middle Eastern states have imploded and exploded all around, and what is coming to replace them is, interestingly, not nationalism. Rather, we are seeing people in Iraq, Syria, Libya and elsewhere turning increasingly to clan-based organization for security, or to a new dispensation of illiberal universalism, namely radical Islam, or, in Egypt, to authoritarians who promise to rein the Islamists in.

Liberalism faces competition from many quarters besides ethnic nationalism. And universalism comes in many forms, not all of them benign. This is so not only in the Middle East. To take a malign example, much of Western anti-Semitism rests on a kind of exclusionary universalism – as does radical Islam – in which rights are denied to those who do not accept our version of what is good for them and humanity. These exclusions, whether they derive from Plato, St. Paul, or Sayyid Qutb have no room for Jews.

Globally, we are witnessing a liberal recession. If once there was a liberal order underwritten by American power, that order is increasingly called into question. As America is unable to impose its will or make full use of its soft power, as demonstrated inter alia by its inability to do much regarding Syria's civil war (out of a mix of healthy caution, diplomatic incompetence, and a sense of impotence), the suasion – soft and hard – of a liberal order diminishes accordingly.

The liberal order faces a triple threat in today's world – Putin's imperial, authoritarian nationalism, China's authoritarian capitalism, and radical Islamic politics. And the ongoing lesson of the unraveling of the European Union is that nationalism cannot be erased or wished away. Not just imagined communities, but every community is held together, as Maimonides understood, by the power of the imagination. Islamist politics is unlikely to win adherents in the West but, nonetheless, like the other two threats, deepens the Western crisis of faith in its own values.

The End of History was always a fantasy; history doesn't end just because we can't see where it – or we – are going. And in good Hegelian fashion, things generate their opposites. Or more precisely, the next stage comes to compensate for the liberal state's deficiencies: its difficulty with giving expression to strong affective ties of kinship and its dependence on religious mind-frames and notions of transcendence that sooner or later will challenge it.

The hardening of Israel's nationalism is, among other things, a harbinger of how the West will respond to the further dangers of Islamist politics, by digging in – a reaction that is paradoxically furthered by Western liberalism's own feebleness in articulating and defending its own values. Western European governments who have continued to support the Palestinians and especially Hamas, no matter their depredations, have done liberalism no favors. In Europe, multiculturalism looks increasingly to have been a dodge to get off the hook and avoid building a genuinely shared civic culture. But nobody is off the hook here. As always when it comes to Israel there is plenty of blame to go around, including in my own mini-camp of Religious Zionist liberals who have been unable to make political traction over the years.

At the same time, we have to accept the fact of American exceptionalism, the ways in which the American model of religious neutrality is in many ways non-transferrable abroad, and then decide what to do after that recognition has sunk in.[6]

---

6 See Yehudah Mirsky, "Separation Anxiety: Can the American Approach to Religion Work outside the West?" a review of Martha Nussbaum, *Liberty of Conscience: In Defense of America's Tradition of Religious Equality*, in *Democracy: A Journal of Ideas* 8 (2008), available online at: https://democracyjournal.org/magazine/8/separation -anxiety.

Is there a way forward?

In her recommendations to the minister of justice, Ruth Gavison powerfully argued that liberal democracy is at times best preserved precisely by letting some large questions go unanswered but endlessly argued.

Perhaps the instruments and practices of liberal democracy – and the package of rights that complements it – are best seen as principles of procedure rather than substance. They aim to facilitate life in common with a minimum of coercion and violence. Yet that latter proviso is itself a matter of both procedure and substance. Violent polities are not internally stable in the long haul (admittedly, at times a very long haul). And if being human means anything, it means there are things that other humans should do to one another only with the greatest reluctance and as a last resort.

There are, of course, as many devils here as there are details.

The advantage of thinking about these constitutional arrangements in procedural terms is that they place to the side the thick questions of substantive belief and identity, or at least bracket them as much as possible, and create some sort of standard of review. If there is a whiff of theology here, it is along the lines of John Courtney Murray's characterization of the religion clauses of the First Amendment as the "Articles of Peace."[7]

Those wishing for a more Hegelian state, or any state that perfectly embodies and realizes our ultimate communal ideals and our most far-reaching aspirations, are, sooner or later, calling for a bloodbath. Yet states cannot simply function as, in Emerson's phrase, joint-insurance companies, because they will not thereby generate the common concern, solidarity, and mutual sacrifice required to sustain them. For that, something more is needed, some sort of thick civic culture (and, if we seek to inspire self-sacrifice, civil religion). And the Israeli problem is that the old civil religion formulated by Mapai is gone and nothing new has yet arisen to take its place.

---

7 John Courtney Murray, "Civil Unity and Religious Integrity: The Articles of Peace," Woodstock Theological Library, http://www.library.georgetown.edu/woodstock/murray/whtt_c2_1954d.

Writing recently about the postwar nation-states of Africa, Samuel Moyn has said the following:

> The nation-state has always been exclusionary and often been violent, offending the cosmopolitanism of the liberals and the desire of Marxists for solidarity beyond borders. The nation-state has also been a severe disappointment for post-colonialists, who believe that new nations succeeded mainly in creating new elites and perpetuating the suffering of their populations at large... But that is no cause to underestimate – just as many anti-colonialists overstated – the possibilities of nationalism, with all its flaws, for progressive politics. While it may seem foolhardy to propose to rescue the nation-state from the enormous condescension of posterity, it is critical all the same to understand why so many of our ancestors chose it.[8]

Why did they choose it? Because in order for statehood to survive, to be able to bring forth the bonds of solidarity and collective responsibility without which even the most solitary life is at the end unlivable, and to endure via anything more than mere brutality and fear, it must speak to some meaningful forms of belonging: managing the necessary ties and nearly inevitable contradictions of primordial bonds, civic associations, and shared pursuits, and ultimate values, which together shape the lived experience of our worlds. Political, social, and even legal institutions are answers not only to instrumental needs but to existential questions. The deep and tangled intermingling of instrumentality and existence, of our own human finitude, will always be with us. What defines us as humans is our need to make some sense of that finitude for the sake of our very survival, and to take heed of the needs, claims, danger, and suffering of other human beings.

The human person, the figure at the center of the very idea of human rights, is not a person in general but a concrete figure, embedded in time and place; and yet, being human also includes being

---

8 Samuel Moyn, "Fantasies of Federalism," *Dissent* (Winter 2015), https://www.dissentmagazine.org/article/fantasies-of-federalism.

dis-embedded and capable of seeing beyond one's own horizon; able to see in the people of other times and places a reflection of oneself. The dynamic tension of the particular and the universal is woven into the very fabric of being human. Living and working that tension to the fullest is a particular burden, and blessing, of the Jews.

Postscript: *The New Liberalism*

In the summer of 2018 the Knesset finally passed a nation-state law, which contained no reference to democracy or equality as core values of the Jewish nation-state. The years since this essay was first written have seen dramatic and perhaps existential challenges to liberal politics in the Western world in general, including the United States. The triple threat to liberalism noted above is now fourfold, with the addition of an American President, and many of his supporters, who affirmatively seek to roll back liberal democracy in the US and around the world.

Much of the discussion of this liberal crisis has turned on discussions of populism and the like, seeing these dramatic shifts in terms of people turning to strong leaders in times of socio-economic uncertainty. True as that is, this new politics must also be seen, as all politics are, as people's trying to answer existential questions and discern the meaning and purpose of their lives, to put the meaning into the meaningful belonging of human identity. The nationalist view of personhood speaks to elements of human being, no less real and compelling than the drives to freedom and autonomy at liberalism's heart. Liberalism is no longer a code word for American power, to the extent it ever was. The new liberalism that our time demands must be forged not by denying the human roots of nationalism, but by working in concert with them. Here, as in so many cases, Israel is a crucial testing ground, and this newly passed law presents an invitation to grapple with the most fundamental issues of our time.

On the Meaning of Israel as a Jewish and Democratic State

A Conversation with Tzipi Livni

INTRODUCTION

Tzipi Livni played a central role in the debates over the nation-state law. After a career practicing law, Livni became a member of Knesset in 1999 and has headed seven ministries and served as both vice prime minister and leader of the opposition. In her second stint as minister of justice (she held this position from 2006–2007 then 2013–2014) Livni commissioned Ruth Gavison to draft a constitutional provision dealing with Israel's identity that would balance the Jewish and democratic aspects of the state's character. Though Livni favored a nation-state law, and even more so a constitution, she adamantly opposed Prime Minister Netanyahu's text as proposed on November 23, 2014 as insufficiently democratic, and the members of her party put forward Livni's proposed Basic Law the next day, November 24 (P/19/2883, sponsored by Elazar Stern, Meir Sheetrit, Amram Mitzna, David Tzur, and Amir Peretz). On December 2, 2014, Netanyahu dismissed Livni and Minister of Finance Yair Lapid, ending the 19th Knesset's governing coalition. In the elections that followed, held in March 2015, Livni's party (known as Hatnua) entered into a political alliance with the Israeli Labor Party to form a center-left bloc that took the name Zionist Union. The new electoral list came second in the number of seats won in the Knesset but did not join the new coalition government headed again by Benjamin Netanyahu and the Likud party. From the opposition in the 20th Knesset, Livni was among the most vocal opponents of the government's proposed nation-state laws and the one that finally passed. I sat down with Livni in the Zionist Union's Tel Aviv office in the summer of 2015 – following the electoral loss and Livni's move into the opposition – for a conversation about the nation-state law and the challenge of clarifying Israel's constitutional identity. Below are excerpts from that conversation.

– Simon Rabinovitch

SIMON RABINOVITCH (SR): In terms of the public's appetite for the law itself, I was wondering what you think about the extent to which the public wants a law clarifying the meaning of the state and the definition of the state.

TZIPI LIVNI (TL): It depends when you say public to which group – or to which "tribe" – you refer.[1] Because I think when I was elected to the parliament I thought this [legal clarification] is something that is needed, because when we say "Jewish democratic state" nobody really knows what it is all about, and we have different translations for the same word. Well, not about democracy, because democracy is something that we have in different states around the world, but what is this Jewish state? What does it mean? For the ultra-Orthodox it is Jewish from a religious perspective, for me from a national perspective – and how can we have these two different values [Jewish and democratic] living in harmony – when I see democracy also as a set of values, when for others it's just a system of elections?

Basically, for me, it was the first chapter of the future constitution. But then during these years – I'm talking about 1999 until now – it has become so dangerous, because everyone inserts his own translation and values, and in a way, as was shown, the

---

1 Israel's President Reuven Rivlin had recently argued that instead of Israelis thinking about the state in terms of majority (Jewish) and minority (Arab), or even Zionist and non-Zionist, today's Israel is composed of four "tribes" of approximately equal size: secular, national-religious, Arab, and Haredi (see my introduction, "Jewish and Democratic According to the Law"). Rivlin proposed that Israeli society focus on a partnership between these sectors based on the starting point that membership in Israeli society recognizes these separate identities. "President Reuven Rivlin Address to the 15th Annual Herzliya Conference," June 7, 2015, http://www.president.gov.il /English/ThePresident/Speeches/Pages/news_070615_01.asp.

law itself also creates lots of dispute and misunderstanding and tension. Unfortunately so, because I think that a few years ago it could have been something that the vast majority would have embraced. Now, because what was put on the table [by the prime minister] would change the balance between the Jewish and the democratic values, the debate was about the need for this law and about the substance.

SR: So do you think that when the term "democracy" is used it's clearer in its meaning than the term "Jewish?"

TL: No. For some, democracy can be used as "system of election" and not for a set of values, and this is part of the reason why I rejected the bill that Netanyahu put on the table, because it referred to democracy just as a system, as a democratic system...

SR: The mechanics.

TL: Yes, and since we had this dispute about what Jewish values mean, on the nature of democracy we can also have a debate. Until now what we have had is a kind of combination in which they [democratic and Jewish values] can live in harmony without real contradiction between these two areas. For those who want to have democracy as something technical, they are also the people who basically want to have the Jewishness of the state as something more religious, which would have a greater impact on the nature of the state.

SR: So why do you think some of the bills have tried to make this correction in balance between the two sets of values? In November 2014 I heard the prime minister saying repeatedly that there is an imbalance between the Jewish and democratic consideration in how laws in general are considered.

TL: Basically it should have come from the Declaration of Independence. It's there. In the Declaration of Independence it's quite clear what it is, what it means; it's more than just two words. But during the past years, because of the bill of *kvod ha-adam ve-khiruto* [the Basic Law: Human Dignity and Liberty, passed in 1992], there was one law that the Supreme Court of Justice in a way used in order to put all of the sets of values of democracy into this law. Now, what the Supreme Court said is that it is a set of values, but the Jewish values – Judaism – represents a kind of democratic value, so they could live happily ever after by having the Jewish and democratic values as basically the same set of values. And for some, especially from the right wing, those who want also to reduce the power of the Supreme Court, what they thought is that if they have another bill that relates just to the Judaism – to the Jewishness of the state – this bill would be the balance. Not balance in the same bill, but balance in two different laws. So one would be *kvod ha-adam ve-khiroto* – for freedom and all this stuff, which is democracy, human rights – and the other would relate to Jewishness. This would force the Supreme Court to judge in accordance with these two bills. Basically it's the same group that acts against the power of the Supreme Court.

SR: Though, of course, the Supreme Court can judge according to any principles it likes.

TL: Because we don't have a constitution, this is the situation. I wish we had a constitution.

SR: What's interesting to me is the sense of threat to Jewish national identity in the state that's articulated by those who want the bill. The way it's articulated is that it's not only democracy versus Judaism, but also individual rights versus national rights.

TL: Yes, it is true. It is true, and it is also true that the ultra-Orthodox don't need this law because, anyway, they said once, since they don't want the constitution, even if we were to write the Ten Commandments they would never accept it. So for them it's less important, because the source of authority for them is the halakha anyway. It's not a constitution.

SR: But when I walk down the street in Tel Aviv, admittedly as an outsider, not just in Tel Aviv, in any city in Israel, I find it difficult to understand the sense of threat to national identity, to the Jewish identity of the state. I read Netanyahu saying that those who oppose his version of the bill are essentially proposing bi-nationalism instead…

TL: This is completely different. As long as we are not dividing the land on the basis of two states for two peoples, the meaning is that this would lead to a bi-national state. It's not about the bills that we write; it's about what we do, because if we don't have a Jewish majority we are going to have a contradiction between these two values. Because without a Jewish majority you cannot just force it – I don't think you can force the minority. I think we can live by an understanding that Israel is the nation-state of the Jewish people, but a state in which all its citizens are equal-rights citizens. This is the entire sentence. In a way, if we want to translate the "Jewish democratic state," the meaning is "nation-state for the Jewish people with equal rights for all its citizens." *This* [the nation-state] is the "Jewish" and *this* [equal rights for all citizens] is the "democratic."

I think that altogether there is another trend, which worries me. When Israelis are looking at their region in the world, they are looking at it from the point of view of a satellite. So we have this tiny place surrounded by all the crazy Islamists – ISIS and Hamas and Hezbollah and terrorists and everybody – and the less Israeli government policy is understood, the more we have clashes with the free world, and especially with Europe. And so Netanyahu, unfortunately, is the one who is kind of brainwashing Israel, that we – well he's not using this word – that Israel can turn into a kind of Jewish ghetto in the Middle East: surrounded, isolated, we are *just there*, we need to keep ourselves focused on *who* we are. He once said in the parliament: it's not about what we do, it's about who we are. So, this is part of it.

Well, you know I'm to blame partially on this. I entered politics because I wanted to reach a final status agreement with the Palestinians, because I believe, as I said, that this is the only way to keep these values living in harmony. And because we've been working since Oslo on the same final status issues, including refugees, what I tried to do with the world was to say listen, the idea of two states for two peoples, the meaning is the end of conflict. So Israel is a Jewish state. When Israel was established it was the solution to an ongoing conflict here: it took the Jewish problem off the international table, we absorbed Jews who came from all over the world, and every Jew is entitled to become an Israeli citizen when landing at Ben-Gurion airport. So the creation of the Palestinian state is the answer for all of the Palestinian people, including the refugees. And also internally Israel is nationally – from a national perspective – Israel is the nation-state for the Jewish people, but yet, all of the Arabs who are living in Israel individually have equal rights. So this was the entire concept.

I got from the [United] States the "Bush Letter" saying that the creation of the Palestinian state is the answer for the refugees, and I convinced lots of leaders in the world to recognize this. And Netanyahu – since he didn't want to say the words "Palestinian state" – just took this Jewish state, just one part of the equation, and altogether this became his flag. This is also the reason why he won the last election [in 2013]. Because as Netanyahu portrayed the danger, the combination between the Arabs living outside, the Arabs who are Israeli citizens, *us*, foreign governments, and all this mess is threatening; it's not threatening like an enemy about to conquer Israel, it is more about the identity of the state.

SR: There is a strange alignment between those who are most pessimistic about a future Palestinian state and those who want most clearly a definition that the state *only* reflects the national rights of the Jewish people.

TL: No, it's not only pessimistic. You have a group there that, even if we had the greatest partner in the world on the other side, they would not sign an agreement because they would not give up even a square centimeter of the land. So for them, this is the only way to give me an answer when I ask them, "What are we going to do?" We cannot continue like this between the Jordan River and the Mediterranean Sea without…

SR: So their answer is a nation-state bill?

TL: No, it's not directly – basically their answer is God. But this can help. It's fate. We had miracles during all these years so maybe we will still have them.

SR: But the problem is that there's a blind spot for those who aren't citizens. You mentioned at the beginning of the interview the "tribes." I read Rivlin's speech where he outlines the four tribes. When he talks about how these four groups need to live together – and we're not talking about majority/minority anymore, we're talking about several minorities – for each of them he always has representative towns: the town of this, the town of that, Tel Aviv or Bnei Barak. He does this twice in his speech. When he talks about the national-religious, the two places he associates with that group are Beit El and Efrat [both in the West Bank]. So, the question is, to me, if you're going to talk about partnerships and all of the rights and privileges of these various citizens of the state, there's one group that he's representing by cities that are surrounded by people who are not citizens of the state.

TL: Yes, but this is not what Ruvi Rivlin thinks about Beit El and Efrat. For him it's going to be part of Israel anyway. He did not want to exclude them from being part of Israel; this was not his intention, not at all.

SR: No, I don't think he was trying to exclude them from being part of Israel. My question is, if one doesn't believe in the impending future of a Palestinian state (as it is clear Rivlin does not), what does one do with all of those who are not citizens?

TL: But they are citizens … ah, you are talking about the Palestinians?

SR: I am.

TL: Well it depends. If you are talking about Jabotinsky's believers, and Ruvi Rivlin is one of them, so for him the meaning of one state is also to give equal rights to the Palestinians.[2] This is the only way he can live with the values of Jabotinsky. If you're not Ruvi Rivlin, you put your faith in God.

SR: But Jabotinsky believed in national rights.

TL: For minorities, yes, for minorities.

SR: The funny thing is, when I read the versions of the bill that say specifically that the right to self-determination in the state is *uniquely* for the Jewish people and talk then about the rights of others as *zkhuyot ishiyut* [individual or personal rights]…

TL: Yes, this is what I said, it's the nation-state of the Jewish people and all of its citizens have equal rights.

SR: My question is why go out of one's way to specify that other

---

2 Vladimir (Ze'ev) Jabotinsky (1880–1940) was a Russian Zionist and founder of the Revisionist Zionist movement, the ideological forebear of today's Likud Party.

groups within the state would *not* have national rights? What is the danger?

TL: Listen, we have a national conflict between us and the Palestinians. And the national conflict is also about land and about each people's right to self-determination in a state of its own. So, there are two options to end this conflict. One is to live in Greater Israel, between the Jordan River and Mediterranean Sea, in one state. But since we need to give everybody equal rights – voting rights – it's going to change from a Jewish state into a bi-national state, maybe an Arab state in the future. In the concept of two states for two peoples we accept and legitimize their aspiration for a state, but the meaning is that the creation of the Palestinian state is the *national* answer for those Arabs who are living in Israel. Because otherwise we are going to have just a state. We are giving part of the land of our forefathers, and our history, and we take some calculated security risks, and to do what? To create a state just for what? The whole idea is to end the conflict based on two states for two peoples; each state gives to the other the [recognition of] the national aspirations of their people.

SR: Theoretically, conceptually, what is the fear of the Arab-Palestinian minority in Israel having some kind of legal recognition as a national minority?

TL: Because since we have this conflict, and this is over land, and this is a tiny place, nobody wants – something Jabotinsky also wrote about – irredentism within the state. Between our two peoples we have an understanding: you're getting your state, you can stay here as respected equal-rights Israeli citizens, but the answer for your national aspiration is elsewhere. Like, in a way, an American Jew.

SR: But Jabotinsky also wrote about…

TL: I know. I'm not trying to say that if Jabotinsky would have lived today this is what he would have wanted. I don't know. This is a way to give my answer according to my beliefs.

SR: I agree that it becomes a bit silly when we start to talk about what people who had no ability to predict the future would have said about a situation that doesn't reflect what they might have imagined.

TL: I don't know, I totally don't know. By the way, he was completely secular, he saw things differently – maybe Jabotinksy would have preferred the idea of one state? I don't know. One state over all of the land with some combination of minority and majority rights. The question is, what are the rights of the group? (By the way, I'm not trying to impose my narrative on them [the Palestinians]. I respect theirs, I would not adapt it, it's theirs.) So basically the idea of solving the conflict is not who has more rights over the entire land, and who is more just; it's not this kind of decision. It's trying to solve the problem we are facing.

SR: But collective rights are not based on land.

TL: I know, listen, we are now in an ongoing conflict. I'm not [like an academic] writing something theoretically. Now this is the situation. They have anyway a kind of rights based on Arabic; they have *some*. It's not like they have to be Jews and Zionists in order to be Israeli citizens. This is my concept; I know Gavison is thinking differently on this.

SR: I won't speak for her.

TL: About collective rights, it's an open issue now. I don't want to speak now about collective rights when we have this [conflict] also because it can turn into something that changes the endgame with their [the Palestinians'] people.

SR: So you think that acknowledging minority rights would have ramifications on negotiations with the Palestinians?

TL: No. What I need from the Palestinians is end of conflict and end of claims.

SR: Can I ask you what you think lies in the future?

TL: I don't think that they will find the common ground to form one bill, and while working on this Ruth Gavison tried and successfully convinced me that to open all of this stuff up right now can just create new problems. We should live with the Declaration of Independence, and that's it.

On the Declaration of Independence as a Basic Law and the Meaning of a Jewish Nation-State

A Conversation with Ruth Calderon

INTRODUCTION

Ruth Calderon was elected to the Knesset in 2013 for the Yesh Atid party, and in her maiden Knesset speech, to press home the point of the value of religious culture in the secular state, she read from the Talmud, called for the creation of a new Hebrew culture, and ended with a prayer. Though secular and vehemently opposed to the political power of the religious in Israel, Calderon nonetheless believes strongly in the cultural and national necessity of religion in the public sphere. Calderon has a doctorate in Talmud from the Hebrew University in Jerusalem and is the founder of two influential institutions: Elul, Israel's first egalitarian and pluralistic beit midrash (house of study), and Alma, an educational center in Tel Aviv devoted to bridging secular and religious Hebrew culture. In July 2013, Calderon tabled a proposal in the Knesset to enshrine Israel's Declaration of Independence as a Basic Law (see 2013, P/19/1539). Before making that proposal, Calderon had worked for about nine months on a committee with several of the key proponents of a nation-state bill in the hopes of reaching a compromise between her bill and others being considered, but was unable to get the members to agree to a version that would guarantee complete equality for all citizens. Calderon was in Boston in June 2017 and we had the opportunity to discuss her efforts to pass a nation-state law with the Declaration of Independence at its center, her work in the Knesset to reach a compromise on the nation-state law, and what it means for Israel to be Jewish and democratic. Below are excerpts from that conversation.

– Simon Rabinovitch

SIMON RABINOVITCH (SR): What was your experience like trying to come up with a "compromise version" of the nation-state law?

RUTH CALDERON (RC): First of all, I think it's the one most important challenge in Israeli legislation today; the question of what is the identity of the state, and what are the values; [the problem of] a constitution, or the lack of a constitution. So I started working on it when the Likud wrote up that bill for the Knesset and I came to my colleagues at Yesh Atid and to Yair [Lapid] and I said, this is terrible.

SR: The Netanyahu version?

RC: Netanyahu didn't really have a version. He kind of adopted pieces and when he adopted pieces of it [in November 2014] then Yair adopted mine [from 2013] and then the coalition fell apart.

An earlier bill suggested Arabic would not be an official language and that really worried me. So Yair said [to me], come up with something better, and I worked with [Israeli philosopher and legal scholar] Moshe Halbertal and we came up with the Declaration of Independence as a Basic Law [in 2013], but it wasn't adopted even by Yesh Atid.

SR: So the party faction did not adopt it?

RC: At that point the party did not adopt it. Some people in the party thought it is better not to even raise the issue. Things that are not written cannot… well, better not to have a conversation about nationality.

SR: This is the Haredi position basically.

RC: The Haredi position, I think, is not wanting to have a sentence "complete equality to all citizens" because they benefit from the fact that there's no equality. But the Yesh Atid people on the left have the opposite concept, and they thought they don't even want to write a national law because they want Israel to belong to all citizens or something like that. And I thought if you leave the platform only to [the right wing], it will always be worse than wording it yourself. And I thought, because there's no agreement, if we go back to a place where we all agreed, in the Declaration of Independence, we might have a majority. And so then there was [Avraham] Dichter and me, and then I came up to Yariv Levin and Ayelet Shaked and I said to them let's try and draft some compromise together. And we met many times, with Moshe Halbertal, and they brought a few lawyers and people that were involved. And Ayelet and I kind of reached an agreement, but Yariv said he's not willing to have the word "equality" in there.

SR: In the first phrase?

RC: Anywhere.

SR: Anywhere.

RC: [No] complete equality, and then Ayelet also withdrew.

SR: [In an earlier conversation Calderon had said to me, "Yariv is a democrat; Yariv believes in democracy."] This is Yariv Levin, the "real democrat" you're talking about?

RC: He is a serious man.

SR: Serious and democratic are two different things.

RC: He's democratic. It's not so shallow, it's not so simplistic. You know we're so used to having the good guys on one hand, and the "creatures" on the other hand. It's not like that. He's a serious man, he's an academic, he's the son of a professor of history, he's a colleague.

SR: I'm not debating his seriousness.

RC: He says that complete equality to them [Arabs], in the demography of Israel, if they have complete national standing like we do, if they have the national rights like we do, they will have the state. It's a fair seeing of facts.

SR: Why?

RC: Because if in this country you would give Native Americans complete rights, they should have the state and not you. They will want a different national anthem, they will want to have a different...

SR: But as an example, they do have national rights; they do independently have a form of sovereignty.

RC: Well, after you killed most of them.

SR: I'm not sure I understand the argument.

RC: 20 percent of Israelis are Palestinians. They want a different national anthem, they want a different flag, they want a different army, and they want a different politics. If they will have it in the same state, they could not recognize Israel as their state. They want to have a different state.

Yariv [Levin] was afraid of the Declaration of Independence and he said that in '48 when you said complete equality and all of that, you didn't yet have such a strong movement of Palestinians who don't want to be citizens of our country and want to build a different country here. At that time it was complete equality to all of the people that stayed here, and we are reaching out for peace to all of the countries around, and there were Arab villages but we told them you will get complete equality as our citizens – I'm trying to be Levin's advocate. But now that they don't want to be our citizens, they don't want to serve in our army, they don't want to be loyal to this country, if you give them the same complete national rights you have to pay for a different national anthem, for a different country, that you as a country, as a state, will pay for. Because when you have equal rights to express your national identity, what I think initially they [the state's founders] meant was that you can celebrate your holidays, you can have your culture and all of that. But what the Palestinian Knesset members say is that we want our national identity to be "here will not be a Jewish state." And Yariv Levin is more worried about that. I think, ok, that's the case, but there's no other way but complete equality for our citizens because this is a democracy. So, it's not that I couldn't see what worries him, but we couldn't reach an agreement. Without equality, not only the Arabs will not have equality, secular citizens will not have equality. And Ayelet, she said ok, equality. But he [Levin] was raised in a very right-wing [environment]. It was fascinating to hear their fears, something we don't usually respect. We don't give time to hearing the fear, and then there's no way to communicate. People come from their worries more than they come from their ideologies.

SR: I would say that not all fears are rational.

RC: Of course, but before you say they're not rational you have to make space to hear them. And in Israel, it's not like something that is coming out of the sky. Yariv was, at that point, the head of the coalition, and the way Haneen Zoabi and the other Arab members of Knesset spoke then was very close to what he's talking about.[1] I'm just believing that they're not all the Arab population. They say this is not going to stay your state, it's a state of all citizens, and we don't want all of your Jewish stuff; it shouldn't be. That's why Dichter wanted a nation-state law – because the question of "what is the identity of the state" is still a question on the table.

SR: Begin has also made an argument for getting the state's identity in writing.

RC: Me too, I wanted to be clear that it is a Jewish homeland, but as a Jewish homeland it must be democratic.

SR: So Ayelet Shaked simply withdrew support or did the effort to compromise end – what were the mechanics?

RC: It was one night: she said, "ok we can make a deal," then the next day Yariv spoke to her and she said "I can't." Some people even in my party said it [the Declaration of Independence] can't be a Basic Law… And I said ok, it might be the preface of a constitution – the Declaration will be the beginning for a constitution. And even for that they wouldn't agree.

Amnon Rubinstein [who is an Israeli legal scholar] and Benny Begin are two logical voices that I identify with, but unfortunately we don't have a majority. And that was a shocking understanding for me. That in the Zionist parties there's no majority for the Declaration of Independence, or for the word *equality*, which is such a simple word. Again, if there would be equality, there would be freedom of religion, which we don't have. Because there's no equality between my ability to celebrate my Jewish life and that of an Orthodox person. The Haredim are worried about that.

---

1 Haneen Zoabi (also Hanin Zoubi) is a member of Knesset elected in 2009 and 2013 as a representative of the Balad party, and in 2015 on the Joint List.

SR: There are implications for everybody. The Haredim, I think, are also worried about the idea of fixing the identity of Judaism along national lines. To do so is essentially an acceptance of the Zionist principle that being Jewish is a nationality.

RC: But they have no problem being paid to live on the national state. We are, as a state, supporting a whole community that works against the state. But you're right.

SR: That's the nature of democracy – democracies are states for all their citizens whether or not certain citizens agree with the principles of the state.

RC: But here it's a national state that supports and gives priorities to people who think it's not a nation-state. But ok. People on the left didn't want the bill – I don't know why – because they didn't want me to say that it's Jewish maybe. So then things became hectic [within the coalition], and it was around the question of the *khok ha-le'om* [the nation-state bill], that the coalition began to dissolve, but you never know if it's really about it or not. And then Netanyahu said the Dichter law is really too severe, and he came up with another law that didn't have equality in it.

SR: And Netanyahu proposed this at a cabinet meeting [November 23, 2014].

RC: Yes, and then Yair Lapid took my law [2013, P/19/1539] and proposed it as an alternative. So then there was Bibi's which was better than Dichter's but with no equality, and there was Yair's, and then they broke. [Netanyahu dismissed Lapid and Livni, and the coalition collapsed.]

Maybe the reason was more cynical than my understanding, but I thought that was the reason the coalition was dissolved. Because the question of the identity of the state is a huge one. You know there's no equality also in land. Arab people and Druze can't build [equitably] on land, and that's not fair and not equal. Education, in culture, and all of that; it's a big issue. And a lot of fear is working in the process. It's very difficult to give complete equality to people who tell you they hate you and they don't accept you. It's much easier to give equality when you know they're loyal citizens.

SR: This is exactly the argument that was made against Jewish emancipation and civil equality for the Jews in Europe.

RC: I don't think it's exact, because Jews in Europe never had [conducted] terrorist attacks in this amount. Bombs every week. Stabbings every week. They never had politicians speak in parliament against the state. Jews were very marginal and very polite.

SR: There was a different basis for opposition to Jewish emancipation – it was theological, it was about the perceived hostility to Christianity – but from the perspective of those who opposed Jewish civil equality in the European states in the eighteenth and nineteenth centuries, it was exactly this argument: how do we give equality to those who hate us?

RC: You are a professor of history and I think we have to be very careful here. Jews in Europe never had national intentions to take over Germany, so that Germany will not be a German state and it will be a Jewish state. When my mom was living in Germany, they [the Jews] wanted to be Germans. They were wishing to be Germans!

SR: When your mother was living in Germany this was after one hundred years in which they'd had civil equality, but much earlier there was a debate.

RC: When my father lived in Bulgaria or my grandparents lived in Galicia they didn't have civil equality, they never wished to be…

SR: Well in Galicia, certainly in Austrian Galicia, they had civil equality, but…

RC: But they didn't want to build a Jewish state in Galicia.[2] And the Arab politicians who are, again, drawing their strength and their budget from the state, they say we don't want this state, we want to change the state to be a state of our nationality.

SR: Of "our" nationality or of all nationalities?

RC: No of their nationality. They want it to be an Arab state. Jamal Zahalka,[3] who was teaching in Alma [Home for Hebrew Culture,

---

2 On Jewish nationalism in Galicia specifically, see Joshua Shanes, *Diaspora Nationalism and Jewish Identity in Habsburg Galicia* (Cambridge, UK: Cambridge University Press, 2012).

3 Jamal Zahalka is a member of Knesset elected in 2003, 2006, 2009, and 2013 as a representative of the Balad party, and in 2015 on the Joint List.

in Tel Aviv] and is a friend of mine, and of course Haneen Zoabi. I had a lot of meetings with her, we became friendly, we had coffee in her office and my office and we became friends – she said "this is my land, you are visitors here, and it's a matter of time and this is not going to be a Jewish state."

I think that you have to be very delicate when you sit here in Boston and you look at it; it's so easy to be judgmental, black and white. It's not so simplistic. It's been sixty-eight years of war and there's daily terrorism. My son wants to take a vacation in Sinai and Da'esh [ISIS] is there. It's your daily worries. It's not something philosophical about religion. Like Egyptians, "they will rise against us" [a reference to Exodus 1:10]. There is a difference between the [biblical] Egyptians saying "the Jews might take over Egypt" and going to the next step of persecution of the Jews. I don't think that exists in Israel – I don't think people want to throw the babies of the Arabs into the Nile [a reference to Exodus 1:22]. But they worry when people tell them we want to take away your homeland and make it our homeland. It's like when you date someone and he says "I'm a terrible man" – you better believe him.

Again, I will fight for democracy and equality. But I want your project to give a fair and serious thought to the ones who are afraid. Who listen to the Arabs with a more worried ear.

I want to say that I think the Arab politicians are more extreme than the Arab population, and I think that when one has equality they don't want to take over the state. Part of it is the problem of the egg and the hen: because they don't have complete equality they feel it's not their home. But the reason that you as a Jew do feel that you are a patriot of America is because you have complete equality.

SR: I'm Canadian, but yes.

RC: But again, it will never be like Canada or America because we built a nation-state and we want the public space to be Jewish. That is the big deal. I know the concept of a nation-state today seems kind of outdated.

SR: I'm not so sure. It's very present in the current political moment. Look at the problems in the European Union today.

RC: I can understand them. Especially when you're not a religious person, living in a public space that offers you meaning by celebrating your nationality is quality of life. It's belonging. It's identity. I think it makes our children a little more grounded. I don't believe in "the citizen of the world." I don't think there is such a thing. I think all of us are very specific people. We come from a certain place and that is precious to me. And because of that I suggested the Declaration of Independence – that tries to balance [different elements]. Some of the Palestinians say you will be out of here, like Haneen, and it will be an Arab state. Some others say it will be a state for all its citizens. Sounds lovely, but it means there's no Shabbat, there's no Hebrew, there's no holidays in the public schools.

SR: That's a very narrow definition of a state of all its citizens. Right now there are already multiple education systems in Israel.

RC: But it's all Jewish. The Arab system is a minority, very small, and they also know and study Hebrew, and they are part of it. It's not a melting pot, of what you have here [in the United States], of a kind of indifferent public space, in the names of the streets, the holidays that are celebrated, the television, the radio, etc.

SR: You're right now drawing a dichotomy between two possible systems. But this isn't a straight dichotomy. There are plenty of national states that are also states for all their citizens. Where the public space is a religious space, the public space is a cultural space of the majority, and yet they still have no problem with the idea of equality.

RC: Like what?

SR: Pretty much all of Europe.

RC: But you see what happens now with Islam in France.

SR: What happens?

RC: There's a lot of threat and people feel that the public space is not French anymore, and that is something they cherish. It's not that they [in France] want to hate the Muslims and throw them away;

332 · DEFINING ISRAEL

they feel that the Muslims don't pledge allegiance to France. It is the beauty of America that people very quickly feel they belong and it's theirs.

SR: There are Muslims in France who would argue with you that you are repeating a particular right-wing, Christian, French perspective.

RC: I'm telling you about my students at Mandel [Leadership Institute in Jerusalem] who would not stand up on Memorial Day, or they would not stand up on Holocaust Day.

SR: These were French Muslim students?

RC: No in Israel, Muslim Israelis – they would not stand up on Holocaust Day. That's ok, it's a democracy. But it's like someone in class intentionally reciting something else during the Pledge of Allegiance. You feel that there's no bond. America found the right balance by saying the street will not be specifically this or that. It's not a nation, it's a place for all of the people who ran away from their nations.

SR: I think there's something you may be missing about American democracy. When people say the Pledge of Allegiance, why they believe in the ideals behind the Pledge of Allegiance is because one of those ideals is that you get to scream and shout during the Pledge of Allegiance should you want to do that.

RC: I never saw anyone dare.

SR: Because they believe in its possibility.

RC: And there is pressure, and fear.

SR: For sure there is pressure, but you also have to believe in those ideals. Perhaps one of the problems that you're articulating is the expectation that Arab citizens should believe in the ideals of the state before they actually have membership in the group.

RC: I think from '48 they had membership in the group.[4] Things became more and more tense as the Palestinian voice became more and more, not just voice – aggression – became more and more present. And so the right wing became much stronger. Why

---

4 Arabs who remained in Israel after the War of Independence became Israeli citizens, but were subject to martial law until 1966.

do people vote for Trump and why do people vote for Netanyahu? It's not because they didn't grow up learning that sharing is nicer than not sharing. It's because of when things don't work out for them, when they get hurt, when they go to the army and come back wounded. We can't think about these things only conceptually. Life also takes a toll. And I'm still a believer [in equality], not only because they deserve it but because I don't want to live in a place where complete equality is not given.

My argument, not from the Palestinian/Jewish side but from the religious/secular side, is that because there's no freedom of religion secular Jews are running away from their own identity and hate Judaism, which is hurting Judaism. It's not easy. Again, the nations in America that are now pledging allegiance were not the natives of this country – the natives are gone.[5] And so nobody feels like Palestinians feel: "we were here before you and you have to go away." Some people came [to the United States] from Germany, some people came from Ireland, some people came from Italy: they were all new to the land. And we [Jewish Israelis] believe that we came back home, and they [Palestinians] believe that they were always home.

SR: I think as you acknowledged, certainly when it comes to the Palestinian citizens of Israel, it is not necessarily the majority viewpoint that all the Jews need to leave.

RC: I hope so. They don't think that all of us need to leave but that the state should not be Jewish. They want a state of all citizens. Again, I can very deeply appreciate living here [in the United States] and seeing how nice it is when everyone is equal. But I would not give up a nation-state. Although today it's very unpopular to talk about nationality, I'm a national Jew, that's what I am.

---

5 As a point of clarification, in the most recent (2010) US census, 5.2 million people, or 1.7 percent of the population, identified as "American Indian and Alaska native alone or in combination." See "The American Indian and Alaska Native Population: 2010," https://www.census.gov/history/pdf/c2010br-10.pdf.

EPILOGUE

Reflections on the Nation-State Law Debate

Ruth Gavison

There is something perplexing, intriguing, and deeply troubling in the debate over Israel's character and whether it should be enshrined in a constitutional enactment. It was reflected in the political debate which took place in Israel in 2013–2014 that generated my being commissioned by the then Minister of Justice Livni to address the question. It was also reflected in the very thought-provoking discussion which was developed first in the *Marginalia* Defining Israel forum and then in this volume. Given the law's passage in July 2018, this may in fact be a good time to look at the question and its presuppositions from two different perspectives. One is a more detached, long-term perspective. As debates about identities and visions and constitutional entrenchments should always be. The other is a short examination of the questions raised by the passage of the law and the immediate response to its enactment.

Most of the participants in the debate here, as well as most of the participants and pushers in the political debate in Israel until enactment, were Jewish. There is a broad consensus among Jews that descriptively Israel – in its history, self-understanding, and social and political realities – has at present, and has always had, elements that are both distinctively Jewish and strongly democratic. More importantly, there is a broad agreement that this is as it should be. There are many debates about the meanings and implications of the key concepts, and about the existing, possible, and desirable balance between such elements – both now and over time – but Jewish advocates for Israel as a fully neutral civic state, indifferent to numbers and cultures, or for a bi-national state in Israel, are rare and marginal.

Not a single Jewish participant in the forum or contributor to the volume fully espouses such a view. Moreover, the Declaration of Independence clearly entrenches this basic duality, reflecting both the Jewish consensus and the position of the international community at the time, in a powerful and evocative way. None of the Jewish participants rejects this canonical and moving Declaration, which has definitely become a part of the constitution of Israel in the substantive sense, even if it does not have formal legal force. It is extensively used in Israel's public school system as the constitutive document of the state.[1]

Moreover, while many Arab leaders object in principle to *any* Jewish distinction of the state or its nature – a position articulated by Yousef Jabareen here – they too accept that in terms of the social and legal reality, Israel is both a Jewish state and a democracy, struggling to balance and negotiate these parts of its vision. Moreover, many of them are even willing to concede that once we accept the idea of self-determination and the legitimacy of a Palestinian state, there is no good reason for rejecting the idea of a Jewish state. The debate should be one about the details of the arrangements in the state concerning the rights of minorities, and the relations of religion(s) and state, rather than about the very fact that Israel is where Jews exercise national self-determination.

Nonetheless, the development of the debate, and the unsuccessful fate of the Begin proposal (2015, P/20/1587), show that the disagreement was not about the details of the various proposed nation-state laws, some of which were indeed objectionable and very unwise, and most of which were amended through the public discussion of the bill in the last two years. This is revealing. It reflects the fact that Israel today, although in many senses it is much more democratic and liberal and affirming of civic equality and the rights of minori-

---

1 I fully expect it to be the case in the future as well. I intend to make a point here of assuring that this is in fact the case. The enactment of the law will of course be mentioned in civics courses – as it should. But it should be added to the chapters about constitutional law and the present Basic Laws, including Basic Law: Human Dignity and Freedom. The nation-state law is one of a series of Basic Laws which together are forming the Israeli constitution in the making, emphasizing aspects and interpretations of the Jewish element in Israel's vision.

ties than it had been at its inception, cannot reaffirm – legally and possibly ideologically – even the principles of the Declaration of Independence (see also 2013, P/19/139). This in itself is not so surprising when we recall that the Declaration was a document signed only by the leaders of the Jews in Israel, prior to the establishment of the state, in order to meet the requirements of the partition resolution and the need to declare the establishment of the Jewish state at the end of the British mandate. Moreover, the Declaration reflected creative constructive compromises among the signers on many of the deep controversies among Jews that were suspended, not abolished, by the need to present a fully unified front against external challengers of the young state. In present-day Israel, Arabs are full-fledged citizens who vote on any such legislation, and Jews do not feel compelled by such historical reasons to suspend their disagreements; especially not in a binding constitutional Declaration, with all its symbolic visibility.

Similarly, and despite claims by Israel Bartal and others that Israel has betrayed its commitments in the Declaration and has become less democratic and less welcoming to non-Jews and to non-religious Jews, the present debate is *not* only or mainly about the internal Jewish debate concerning the relationships within Judaism between religion and national-cultural identity. That this is the case is clarified by the fact that all proposals of the nation-state laws were more than willing to suspend references to this internal Jewish debate in the nation-state law.

As far as I can see, the main difference between the present debate – in the 2010s – and the moment of the Declaration is the unbelievable success of Zionism and Israel as the nation-state of Jews. This success, hoped for but not assumed by the signers of the Declaration, explains the fact that while many Arab leaders, in Israel and outside it, are persistent in claiming that the issue is not 1967, or Arab minority rights, or state and religion within Israel, but rather the Nakba and the very foundation of Israel as a Jewish nation-state, many Jews, within Israel and abroad, feel that the two challenges to Israel's character – the internal Jewish debate and the Jewish-Arab one – need not be separated as they clearly had been in 1948.

This is a reason for celebration: for appreciation of both the achievements of Israel and the road that still needs to be taken to continue the struggle within it concerning the negotiation of democracy, human rights, and Jewish self-determination. This is not a reason, and should not be seen as a reason, for forgetting the difference and the distinction between the two challenges facing Israel: the external challenge of those who think and argue that a nation-state for Jews is in principle unjustified (with implications ranging from the legitimacy of seeking to fight it militarily and extinguish it as a political entity, to de-legitimating it economically and politically in the eyes of the international community and Jews themselves) versus the internal debate, among Jews and Israelis, about the exact social, cultural, and legal arrangements that should obtain in Israel.

It is natural (although not necessary and not inevitable, as shown by many polls taken in Israel) for Arabs to resist the new legislation, but also to resist any ideological and educational affirmation of the Jewish self-determination component of Israel's vision. This fact explains why political leaders of Arabs, and especially non-Jewish members of Knesset in both coalition and opposition parties, did not really and forcefully participate in negotiating the details of the nation-state law. Unlike Jewish members of the opposition, they did not even fight for a short Basic Law: The Vision of Israel Law, a law that would re-state all three components of the vision, including that of Jewish self-determination. They did not want to confer legitimacy on the very process of discussing the law, assuming as they justly did that the final product would include legal statements that they would not be able and willing to live with. This would include a re-affirmation of the fact that Israel is the home of the Jewish people as well of that of all its citizens and protecting personal and cultural rights of all its citizens.[2]

---

2 The language section of the law is a victim of this predicament. There was willingness among the coalition and the opposition to declare explicitly that the law will not harm the status quo on languages as it exists. True, there is a debate on what the status quo is, but there was no intention to change it "against" Arabic. Most analyses of the status quo are that in fact and in law, Hebrew is the primary language of the state while Arabic is secondary. A proposal to reflect this status quo by saying that Hebrew is the language of the state while Arabic is a second official

It is, however, intriguing that some Jews are willing to conduct their struggle concerning the arrangements in Israel on these issues while denying the possibility, reality, or desirability of Israel being committed to Jewish self-determination as well as to democracy and human rights. Thus some Jews on the left claim that Israel cannot be both Jewish and democratic and must be democratic and secular only.[3] Some Jews (mostly religious) on the right think that Israel must be Jewish-religious first and democratic, if at all, second; others believe that the struggle between Jews and Arabs has not been decided in the long term, and that Israel must insist on its Jewish national character vis-à-vis the international community and its own population, so as to make sure that the support among them for the legitimacy of Jewish self-determination as a central component of Israel's vision is not eroded further.

The ideological difference between these three groups – advocates of Israel as a neutral liberal democracy; Israel as a Jewish theocracy or ethnocracy first; and Israel as committed to Jewish self-determination, democracy, and human rights at the same time – is huge. It is the difference between struggling to maintain Israel as Jewish, democratic, and committed to human rights on the one hand, and Israel as either only or mainly democratic and secular, or as only or mainly Jewish and halakhic. Usually, the political and ideological leadership of the Arabs advances a fourth and a different vision for Israel: their vision is a state which does not recognize non-civic affiliations of its citizens, and is therefore in principle a state of all its (religious and national) communities.

---

language may have passed had Arab members of Knesset asked for it. However, they preferred not to negotiate so that they could claim the law, even in its amended formulation, harms the status of Arabic by dispelling the ambiguity of the present situation which is – some of them claim – that Israel is, and should be, a bilingual state, where Hebrew and Arabic are both official languages of equal status; a claim which they are indeed making very forcefully. Indeed, the "demotion" of Arabic in the law is a powerful complaint raised by many in Israel and abroad.

3 A most powerful illustration is Gideon Levy's op-ed, "Enough with 'Jewish,'" in *Haaretz*, September 13, 2015, but there are hints in this direction among the essays here as well. Gideon Levy, "Day le-'Yehudit,'" *Haaretz*, September 13, 2015, http://www.haaretz.co.il/opinions/.premium-1.2730352.

Once this fault-line is clearly drawn again, as it had been in 1948 and the first decades of Israel's life, we can easily distinguish the question of the vision itself from the question of additional legislation with constitutional import on the one hand, and of specific arrangements on the other. The push for legislation was motivated mainly by fears that the line has become fuzzy, and the legitimacy of the Jewish state is eroded. Moreover, it is built on the fact that the rhetoric among many Jewish elites in Israel, including some legal elites, especially after the Basic Laws of 1992 and the "constitutional revolution," became more human-rights and democracy centered. Driving hard against legislation, claiming that a balanced nation-state law like the Begin proposal is the end of democracy,[4] or that nothing distinctively Jewish is consistent with democracy and human rights (as some Arab leaders claim), in turn strengthens these fears considerably and lends them support.

In terms of the constitutional vision of Israel, I still believe that it would have been best to refrain from legislating and from constitutional anchoring, while the discussions of the debate and the legitimacy of the complex vision of Israel should have been maintained and even strengthened. Naturally, talk about visions is declaratory and abstract. It should not be relegated to binding laws and justiciable questions. The legal debate should be concentrated on the arrangements seeking to negotiate Jewish self-determination, human rights, and democracy.

But what should one do now that it did pass? The story of how this law passed is a fascinating illustration of the relationship between constitutional identity and simple short-term electoral politics. I hope to expand on this subject in the future. At this point, I will only say that it illustrates powerfully why constitutions should in fact be entrenched in some way to make it harder to change them by processes controlled by regular politics and without a broader perspective. This applies to the substantive provisions such

---

4 See Uri Weiss, "Benny Begin mityakhes le-'elyonut ha-Yehudim, kfi she-liberal mityakhes le-shivayon," *Haaretz*, July 8, 2015, http://www.haaretz.co.il/blogs/uriweiss /1.2679390, and *idem*, "'Al ha-brakha she-ba-hatsa'at khok yesod ha-le'om," *Kikar ha-Shabat*, November 29, 2014, https://bit.ly/2JyCoSK.

as regime structure and bills of rights as well as to preambles and general declarations. If Israel had a complete constitution, amending its vision in this way would not have been possible. However, part of the problem is that Israel does NOT have a full constitution. As happened in the past, entrenched Basic Laws are passed without the broad support that is required to allow them to perform their main function: to create a shared constitutional framework within which different parties and communities can advance and negotiate their own visions and interpretations.

The nation-state law is not of this shared kind. It was vehemently opposed by both advocates of the neutral liberal state, by supporters of a state committed to Jewish self-determination, democracy, and human rights (a majority of the opposition), and by those rejecting any reference and legitimacy to Jewish self-determination. A consensus of the supporters and the second part of the opposition was in principle possible, but advocates of the law preferred a law dealing exclusively with the Jewish element of the vision. They explained this was required because of their fear of judicial activism and a judicial tendency to deny Jewish self-determination sufficient weight in their adjudications and rhetoric. They feared that adding terms like "equality" to the basic law might lead to judicial interpretations invalidating the Law of Return or establishing a legal basis for claims of a Palestinian alleged "right" of return. Others mentioned the fear that inclusion of "equality" may be the basis for judicial invalidation of the religious monopoly over marriage and divorce.

The response to the law was quick and has been major. In both Israel and outside it the law is described as a game changer, as a proof that Israel has given up on its commitment to democracy (if it ever had any). However, democracy teaches – in many countries – that the way to struggle against even very unacceptable decisions made with substantial democratic credentials is within democratic rules of the game. Unless one succeeds in saying that the allegedly unacceptable decision is one that permits and in fact leads to a revolution. This does not seem to be in the cards in Israel at the moment.[5]

---

5 Debates such as these happen in other countries. After Donald Trump was elected

My own perspective is clear: my long-term interest is the welfare and success of Israel as a country in which the Jewish people exercises its rights to self-determination and is committed to both democracy to all its citizens and to the human rights of all under its jurisdiction. I understand the intensity of the criticisms of the law. I share the feeling of non-Jews that the legislation does not exhibit sufficient awareness of the huge importance of the symbolic and declarative effects of a constitutional Basic Law that does not reflect in any way the commitment of the state to shared and equal citizenship and to equal dignity and respect. Yet I see this as a serious challenge to Israel, one that should be addressed and remedied, not as an event that justifies breaking the democratic rules of the game.

Thus, for example, I hope the law does not lead to a constitutional crisis. The proposed law already generated claims, e.g., by ex-president of the Supreme Court Aharon Barak, that the court could, possibly should, declare the law unconstitutional as it negates the constitutional DNA of the state reflected in the Declaration of Independence. The court will have to face this challenge, as at least the Arab Joint List as well as some NGOs have petitioned and asked the court to abolish the law as unconstitutional. This may create an extremely difficult constitutional moment for all involved: the government, the court, and the opposition. The potential crisis is illustrated very clearly by some reactions made by the minister of justice and her critics, as well as by the arguments made in the Arab sector petition.[6] It is one thing

---

president, there arose a substantial voice that "Trump is not my president." Most Americans, including many who had voted for Clinton, thought that democracy made such a move unacceptable. A similar debate occurred with the Brexit vote in Great Britain.

6 The minister of justice, Ayelet Shaked, said that if the court intervenes here it will create an all-out war with democracy, and expressed disappointment that the court did not reject the petitions out of hand, stating that it had no jurisdiction over the constitutionality of Basic Laws. Many criticized her as leading an anti-democratic counter-revolution seeking to allow the Israeli government to operate with no judicial review. The petition by the Arab Joint List claims that the idea of a Jewish state and Zionism itself are unjustified and racist and that the foundation of the state was grounded on cooperation with colonialist regimes who had no right to authorize the Jewish national home or partition. This line of argument highlights the difference between the position of the political leadership of the Arabs and

to fight against the law and make such claims within the struggle against its legislation. It is quite another to in fact ask the court to declare that entrenching the manifestations of the state's Jewishness in somewhat vague and declaratory ways, negotiated publicly within the coalition, and accepted as legitimate by legal advisors, is legally beyond the power of the legislature.[7] In a way, it is a great boon for supporters of the law that there are these petitions against it, because it is now much easier to attack the petitioners as objecting to the very legitimacy of the entrenchment of Jewish self-determination in the law. Furthermore, this petition and its arguments are a strong answer to those who argue that the law was unnecessary and in fact designed to alienate the minorities, since no one really objected to the fact and the legitimacy of Jewish self-determination as an element of Israel's vision. These petitions and arguments clearly show that there is indeed within Israel an articulated and open challenge to such legitimacy. The court itself is now put in a serious bind against the background of previous decisions but also with regard to the conceded need for self-restraint.[8]

Second, I hope that the intensity of the critique of the law will not blur the real features of the Israeli debate over Israel's vision. The

---

some radical Jews and that of the Jewish opposition and the Druze, who insist on combining Jewish self-determination with democracy and human rights.

7 Member of Knesset Begin reflected this major difference when he abstained in the vote rather than vote against the law as he did in the first reading, before the last amendments. A political player cannot ask for amendments to some especially offensive sections and when the law is changed to accommodate his demands, still say that law is unacceptable in principle. If the law is unacceptable **in principle**, and the declaratory stakes are too high, one does not seek to make it slightly better. This was indeed the bind of the Jewish opposition while debating the law and it is strengthened now, after the law was passed.

8 The question of the power to review Basic Laws is not as trivial as the minister of justice suggests, and I do not think it would be right or wise to reject these petitions summarily. However, affirmation of this particular judicial power by the courts, and especially exercising it in this instance, seem extremely radical. It appears as if the state lawyers will defend the constitutionality of the law. Under these circumstances, for the court to abolish it as an unconstitutional constitutional amendment, even before anything practical is done or justified by invoking it, seems an extremely unfortunate move, again justifying the complaints of the most outspoken critics of the court.

debate among Zionist Jews is very different in kind and in scope from the debate between all Zionist Jews and the political leadership of the Arab minority. Thus, we should make sure that these moves and the rhetoric of some of the criticism of the law and the understandable wish of many Zionist Jews to express solidarity with the anger felt by many Arabs may not inhibit the ability of the majority in Israel to still reaffirm its complex and combined vision as built on Jewish self-determination, democracy, and human rights.

Whatever happens to this law, the claim that the law by its mere enactment resolves the debate about the compatibility of the three components of Israel's vision – Jewish self-determination, democracy, and human rights – in either direction is simply false. In fact, comparing the final version of the law to its previous versions strengthens the conclusion that the issue is not at all resolved. The final version is indeed a law dealing almost exclusively, and declaratively, with the meaning and manifestations of just one element of the vision – Jewish self-determination. Much more so than previous versions that included short references to democracy, a general promise to protect the right of each person to promote their culture, and a proposed entrenchment of a specific interpretation of the principle of return. It therefore lends some support to the claim of the advocates of the law (and legal advisors who stated the law was not unconstitutional) that it does not even seek to contain the internal balance between elements of the vision. The defense of democracy and human rights, they say, continues to rest on the Declaration and on other Basic Laws as well as on regular laws.

Yes, the nation-state law is a major act of legislation. It is indeed the culmination of a process and not a stand-alone action. I disagree with those who think that Arab members of Knesset should not be allowed or expected to seek international intervention against the law (though I have my doubts whether this is a very wise move on their part).

However, my preferred mode of action at this stage is different. I do not want to spend too much of my energy on fights **against** the law.[9] I want to spend my energy in fighting **for** the conditions and

---

9 There is a huge difference between not enacting and abolishing. Amendment of a

arrangements that will allow Israel to strive towards being the state inspired by the vision I have identified: Jewish self-determination as well as a commitment to democracy and human rights and respecting the dignity and humanity of all who live in this country.

I agree that the symbolic and declarative level of the complex vision has suffered a blow. We have become used to the complexity of the Declaration and to the "Jewish and Democratic" formulation of previous legislation. Adding the nation-state law which deals exclusively with the implications of Jewish self-determination based solely on coalitionary discipline and against the unanimous vocal dissent of the whole opposition, does indicate a willingness to communicate bluntly the exclusive and particular element of the vision without balancing it in the same law with other components. But Israel's constitution-in-the-making does include other parts and an impressive history of negotiating the complex vision. I am not willing to assume that the creativity which has been put into this structure cannot integrate the new Basic Law into the complex vision. This is how constitutional, legal, and cultural advances are made everywhere.

The struggle should at least in part be directed towards strengthening aspects of the reality of Israel rather than just the text of its laws, and there are many that support and reinforce Israel as a state committed to democracy and human rights as well as to Jewish self-determination. In fact, I would seek to have both the government and civil society come to see this law as an opportunity to work harder on translating the desired vision of Israel into a reality. The energies

---

Basic Law, which means a legislation of a different Basic Law, is also not a trivial matter. I do not see a political possibility in the foreseeable future of abolishing this law. More important, I do not think Israel as a state and as a society will benefit from such a move if it is grounded on a narrow majority to abolish it. Possibly, the enactment of a comprehensive constitution or even a comprehensive Vision Law might replace it and that would indeed be an improvement. However, I do not see a political possibility for this either. I also fear the rhetorical, political and ideological implications of a continued political struggle to abolish the law by legislation. It will make the polarization and the divisiveness more prolonged and much deeper than they are at present. It may distort the important need to clarify differences in attitude and vision between parties towards the new elections and the need to stress and exclude possible alliances. This emphasis on important differences may later make it much more difficult to work together as all parties must on issues that are critical to the survival and flourishing of the state.

created by the legislation in all sectors, and the understanding that matters need to also be healed, may be an important trigger for such actions.[10]

One's conclusion on both constitutional entrenchment and on how to react to the passage of the law thus depends on what one wants and how one assesses the realities of the present situation. Against this background, my recommendations are clear. I want Israel to be a state with a vision. The vision is Jewish self-determination, democracy, and human rights. All components are critical for the welfare and justice of the state and for its very survival. Negotiating the components should be done within the social, cultural, religious, political, and legal frameworks established in the state. There are, and always will be, tensions within the components as well as among them. This is why a shared democratic political framework is so critical for the success of all pluralistic societies. It allows them to negotiate differences without bloodshed and violence. While the components of the vision are themselves not eternal, they do provide a context for differences that will not undermine society itself. The difference between the vision itself, narrowly interpreted, and the detailed arrangements, is thus critical for a stable, healthy state and society. Any attempt to challenge the very possibility to maintain the complex vision in an all-or-nothing broad interpretation of this or that component is likely to be destructive and counter-productive.

This was the insight of the founders at the time of the Declaration. This is why they refused to give the Declaration a legal binding force. The Declaration served us well. If we could have maintained its spirit without further constitutional legislation that would have been preferable. Refraining from legislation might have defused some superfluous debates about issues that cannot be legally deter-

---

10 People who are concerned about the status of Arabic in Israel may start working on expanding the teaching of Arabic as a language and a culture in Jewish schools. The law may also enhance the learning of Hebrew in Arabic schools, which has been somewhat neglected in the last decades. This in fact could generate effective cooperation between supporters of the nation-state law who expressed such sentiments throughout the legislative process, and those who object to the law among other things because of their concern with the status of Arabic in Israel.

mined and enforced anyway. At the same time, I refuse to accept that the Basic Law: Israel – The Nation-State of the Jewish People is a game-changer; that it succeeds in replacing the vision of Israel as a state that is also committed to democracy and human rights. I would like to see a symbolic and declarative move that might amend this impression created by the law. After its legislation, a constitutional entrenchment of the full vision may now be indeed necessary.

In the meantime, however, we should reaffirm the complex vision in other ways. This is an urgent task, and its urgency is made clearer by the various challenges against its possibility, coherence, and desirability – challenges coming from all political and ideological camps. We can be proud of what we have achieved as we watch out for what is missing and fragile. Against the hopes of the law's advocates, entrenching in 2018 only the elements of the vision relating to Jewish self-determination will not resolve the debates, and has indeed already led to the acute re-emergence of deep disagreements. It will not move Israel closer to negotiating the tension between the particularism of the Jewish component, the civic equality of the Israeli *demos*, and the universality of human rights. This never ending and dynamic negotiation, however, is where progress can and must be made. Ironically, the government that passed this legislation is in fact doing quite a lot to strengthen a more inclusive perception of Israel's citizens – just as the Declaration of Independence did seventy years ago. It is intriguing, possibly even tragic, that the government behaves on this subject like Dr. Jekyll and Mr. Hyde.

However, there are substantial political reasons for this Janus-faced performance of the government. There are many in both coalition and opposition who see the passage of the law as a move that went too far. This is why there may be better chances for my present recommendation: now, after legislation, we need to think creatively about real and immediate declarations and actions by all players, and seek to integrate the new Basic Law into the fabric of Israel's constitutional structure, re-affirming the complex vision with all its elements – Jewish self-determination, democracy and human rights – so as to permit the continued work towards the negotiation between them which is critical to the flourishing of Israel.

Selected Suggestions
for Further Reading

The following websites, books, and articles are a selection of resources, many written by the volume's contributors, helpful for further legal and historical context on Israel's proposed nation-state law. The list was compiled primarily (but not exclusively) from the most directly relevant references in this volume's essays.

Proposed Constitutions

"A Constitution for Israel (Eitan-Koppel Proposal)," proposed by Michael Eitan and Moshe Koppel (2011). http://hukaeitankoppel.blogspot.co.il /2011/06/.

"A Constitution for the State of Israel," proposed by the Institute for Zionist Strategies (2006). Abstract: http://izs.org.il/research/constitution/; full-text: https://u.cs.biu.ac.il/~koppel/constitution-english-04%5B1%5D .07.06-published.pdf.

"Constitution by Consensus," proposed by the Israel Democracy Institute (2005). https://en.idi.org.il/media/6361/constitutionbyconsensus_draft .pdf.

"The Democratic Constitution," proposed by Adalah: The Legal Center for Arab Minority Rights in Israel (2007). https://www.adalah.org/en /content/view/7483.

Reports

"Foundation for a New Covenant among Jews in Matters of Religion and State in Israel," abridged English edition published as *The Gavison-Medan Covenant: Main Points and Principles*, by Yoav Artsieli, Ruth Gavison, and Yaacov Medan. Jerusalem: Israel Democracy Institute and Avi Chai Foundation, 2004. https://en.idi.org.il/publications/6597. Hebrew full-text of the Gavison-Medan Covenant: https://gavison-medan.co.il.

"The Future of the Nation-State of the Jewish People: Consolidation or Rupture?" published by The Reut Institute (2017). http:// reutgroup.org/wp-content/uploads/sites/17/2017/04/20170331-Reut- Nation-State-English-FINAL.pdf; see also http://www.reut-institute.org.

"The Future Vision of the Palestinian Arabs in Israel," compiled by The National Committee for the Heads of the Arab Local Authorities in Israel, Gaida Rinawi-Zoabi, ed. (2006). https://www.adalah.org/uploads /oldfiles/newsletter/eng/dec06/tasawor-mostaqbali.pdf.

"Jewish and Democratic: Perspectives from World Jewry," compiled by the Jewish People Policy Institute (2014). http://jppi.org.il/uploads/jewish _and_democratic-eng.pdf.

Gavison, Ruth. *'Igun khukati la-khazon ha-medina?* Jerusalem: Metzilah Center, 2015. http://www.metzilah.org.il/webfiles/files/Const%20Anchor %20Heb%202nd%20(1).pdf.

"Towards Inclusive Israeli Citizenship: A New Conceptual Framework for Jewish-Arab Relations in Israel. Points for Public Discussion," produced by The Jerusalem Institute for Israel Studies (2011). http:// jerusaleminstitute.org.il/.upload/citizenship[1]en.pdf.

Other Relevant Websites

Adalah: The Legal Center for Arab Minority Rights in Israel: https://www .adalah.org/.

The Association for Civil Rights in Israel: http://www.acri.org.il/en/.

Dirasat, Arab Center for Law and Policy: http://www.dirasat-aclp.org.

Hiddush for Religious Freedom and Equality: http://hiddush.org/.

The Institute for Zionist Strategies: http://izs.org.il/.

The Kohelet Policy Forum: http://en.kohelet.org.il.

The Metzilah Center for Zionist, Jewish, Liberal and Humanist Thought: http://www.metzilah.org.il.

Books and Articles

Azoulay, Ariella and Adi Ophir. *The One-State Condition: Occupation and Democracy in Israel/Palestine.* Translated by Tal Haran. Stanford, CA: Stanford University Press, 2012.

Bâli, Asli Ü. and Hannah Lerner, eds. *Constitution Writing, Religion and Democracy.* Cambridge: Cambridge University Press, 2017.

Barak, Aharon. "A Constitutional Revolution: Israel's Basic Laws." Yale Law School Faculty Scholarship Series, Paper 3697 (1993). http:// digitalcommons.law.yale.edu/cgi/viewcontent.cgi?article=4700&context =fss_papers.

Bartal, Yisrael. *Kozak ve-Bedvi: "'Am" ve-"erets" ba-le'umiyut ha-Yehudit.* Tel Aviv: Am Oved, 2007.

Barzilai, Gad. *Communities and Law: Politics and Cultures of Legal Identities.* Ann Arbor: University of Michigan Press, 2003.

Ben-Porat, Guy and Bryan S. Turner, eds. *The Contradictions of Israeli Citizenship: Land, Religion, and State.* New York: Routledge, 2011.

David, Yossi, ed. *The State of Israel: Between Judaism and Democracy: A Compendium of Interviews and Articles.* Jerusalem: The Israel Democracy Institute, 2003.

Friedman, Menachem. "The State of Israel as a Theological Dilemma," in *The Israeli State and Society: Foundations and Frontiers,* edited by Baruch Kimmerling. Albany: State University of New York Press, 1989, 165–215.

Gavison, Ruth. *The Law of Return at Sixty Years: History, Ideology, Justification.* Jerusalem: Metzilah Center, 2010.

———— and Alan Baker, eds. *Zekhuyoteha shel Yisrael ki-medinat ha-le'om shel ha-'am ha-Yehudi.* Jerusalem: Merkaz ha-Yerushalmi le-'inyene tsibur u-medina, 2012.

Hazony, Yoram. *The Jewish State: The Struggle for Israel's Soul.* New York: Basic Books, 2000.

Jabareen, Yousef T. "The Arab-Palestinian Community in Israel: A Test Case for Collective Rights under International Law," The George Washington International Law Review 47, no. 3 (2015): 449–80.

————. "Constitution Building and Equality in Deeply-Divided Societies: The Case of the Arab Minority in Israel." *Wisconsin International Law Journal* 26, no. 2, (2008): 345–402.

————. "Toward Participatory Equality: Protecting Minority Rights under International Law." Israel Law Review 41, no. 3 (2008): 635–76.

Jamal, Amal. *Arab Minority Nationalism in Israel: The Politics of Indigeneity.* London; New York: Routledge, 2011.

————. "Constitutionalizing Sophisticated Racism: Israel's Proposed Nationality Law." *Journal of Palestine Studies* 45, no. 3 (Spring 2016): 40–51.

————. "The Political Ethos of Palestinian Citizens of Israel: Critical Reading in the Future Vision Documents." *Israel Studies Forum* 23, no. 2 (2008): 3–28.

Kedar, Nir. *Ha'im nakhon le'agen et ha-zehut ha-Yehudit be-mishpat ha-Yisraeli?* Policy Paper 107. Jerusalem: Israel Democracy Institute, 2015. https://en.idi.org.il/media/3412/should-jewish-identity-be-anchored-in-israeli-law.pdf.

————. *Mamlakhtiyut: Ha-tefisa ha-ezrakhit shel David Ben-Guryon*. Jerusalem: Ben-Gurion University/Yad Yitskhak Ben-Tsvi, 2009.

————. *Mishpat kakhol-lavan: Zehut u-mishpat be-Yisrael, me'a shanim shel pulmus*. Sde Boker: Ben-Gurion University/The Open University/Tel Aviv University, 2017.

Kimmerling, Baruch. *The Invention and Decline of Israeliness: State, Society, and the Military*. Berkeley: University of California Press, 2001.

Kymlicka, Will. *Multicultural Citizenship: A Liberal Theory of Minority Rights*. Oxford: Clarendon Press, 1995.

Leibowitz, Yeshayahu. "The Religious Significance of the State of Israel," in *Judaism, Human Values and the Jewish State*, edited by Eliezer Goldman. Cambridge, MA: Harvard University Press, 1992, 214–20.

Liebman, Charles S. and Eliezer Don-Yehiya. *Civil Religion in Israel: Traditional Judaism and Political Culture in the Jewish State*. Berkeley: University of California Press, 1983.

Mautner, Menachem. *Law and the Culture of Israel*. Oxford; New York: Oxford University Press, 2011.

————. *Mishpat ve-tarbut*. Ramat Gan: Bar-Ilan University Press, 2008.

————. *Mishpat ve-tarbut be-Yisrael be-fetakh ha-me'a ha-'esrim ve-akhat*. Tel Aviv: Am Oved, 2008.

Memmi, Albert. *The Colonizer and the Colonized*. Boston: Beacon Press, 1965.

Migdal, Joel S. *State in Society: Studying How States and Societies Transform and Constitute One Another*. Cambridge; New York: Cambridge University Press, 2001.

————. *Through the Lens of Israel: Explorations in State and Society*. Albany: State University of New York Press, 2001.

Miller, David. *On Nationality*. Oxford; New York: Clarendon Press; Oxford University Press, 1995.

Peleg, Ilan and Dov Waxman. *Israel's Palestinians: The Conflict Within*. Cambridge; New York: Cambridge University Press, 2011.

Ravitzky, Aviezer. *Messianism, Zionism, and Jewish Religious Radicalism*. Translated by Michael Swirsky and Jonathan Chipman. Chicago: University of Chicago Press, 1996.

Rozin, Orit. *A Home for All Jews: Citizenship, Rights, and National Identity in the New Israeli State*. Translated by Haim Watzman. Waltham, MA: Brandeis University Press, 2016.

Sapir, Gidon. *Ha-Mahpekha ha-khukatit: Avar, hove ve-'atid*. Tel Aviv: Bar-Ilan University/Yedi'ot Sefarim, 2010.

————— et al., eds. *Israeli Constitutional Law in the Making*. Hart Studies in Comparative Public Law, vol. 2. Oxford: Hart Publishing, 2013.

————— [Gideon]. "Religion and State in Israel." *Oxford Bibliographies in Jewish Studies*, edited by Naomi Seidman (www.oxfordbibliographies.com). New York: Oxford University Press, 2015.

Schweid, Eliezer. *Ra'ayon ha-'am ha-nivkhar ve-ha-liberaliut ha-khadasha*. Jerusalem: Hakibbutz Hameuchad, 2016.

Shelef, Nadav G. *Evolving Nationalism: Homeland, Identity, and Religion in Israel, 1925–2005*. Ithaca, NY: Cornell University Press, 2010.

Smooha, Sammy. *Arabs and Jews in Israel*. Boulder, CO: Westview Press, 1989.

—————. "The Model of Ethnic Democracy: Israel as a Jewish and Democratic State." *Nations and Nationalism* 8, no. 4 (2002): 475–503.

Stern, Yedidia, et al. *Ke-she-Yahadut pogeshet medina*. Tel Aviv: Yedioth Ahronoth and the Israel Democracy Institute, 2015. See in particular Benyamin Brown, "Ha-Yahadut ha-Kharedit ve-ha-medina," (79–270) and Kalman Neuman, "Ha-Tsiyonut ha-datit ve-ha-medina," (271–422).

Yakobson, Alexander. "Jewish Peoplehood and the Jewish State, How Unique? – A Comparative Survey." *Israel Studies* 13, no. 2 (2008): 1–27.

—————, and Amnon Rubinstein. *Israel and the Family of Nations: The Jewish Nation-State and Human Rights*. Translated by Ruth Morris and Ruchie Avital. London; New York: Routledge, 2009.

Yiftachel, Oren. *Ethnocracy: Land and Identity Politics in Israel/Palestine*. Philadelphia: University of Pennsylvania Press, 2006.

Contributor Biographies

Israel Bartal is Avraham Harman Professor Emeritus of Jewish History, and former Dean of the Faculty of Humanities, at the Hebrew University of Jerusalem (2006-2010). He is a member of the Israel Academy of Sciences, and is one of the founders of *Cathedra*, a leading scholarly journal on the history of the land of Israel. In addition, since 2006 he has been chair of the Historical Society of Israel. His books include *To Redeem a People: Enlightenment and Nationalism in Eastern Europe* (Hebrew, 2013), *Cossack and Bedouin: Land and People in Jewish Nationalism* (Hebrew, 2007), and *The Jews of Eastern Europe, 1772–1881* (2005, 2006, published also in Russian and German).

Ze'ev Binyamin Begin, a geologist, served as a Member of the Israeli Knesset during the years 1988–1999 and 2009–2013, and has been an MK on behalf of the Likud Party since 2015. He served as the Minister of Science and as Minister without Portfolio. He published a collection of his articles on the Oslo agreements (*A Sad Story*), as well as a book on the last years of the Kingdom of Judah (*As We Do Not See Azekah*).

Ruth Calderon served as a member of the 19th Knesset for the party Yesh Atid between 2013 and 2015. A scholar of Talmud, Calderon founded Elul Beit Midrash in Jerusalem and Alma: Home for Hebrew Culture in Tel Aviv. Calderon is the author of *A Bride for One Night: Talmud Tales* (2014).

Ruth Gavison is Haim H. Cohn Professor Emerita of Human Rights at the Hebrew University of Jerusalem, winner of the Israel Prize in Law 2011, and the founding president of Metzilah, a Center for Zionist, Jewish, Liberal and Humanist Thought. She has taught at Yale University and the University of Southern California, and was a fellow at Princeton's Center for Human Values and at the Strauss center at NYU. She has been a member of numerous Israeli Public Inquiry Committees, including the Winograd Commission to investigate the 2006 Lebanon War. She was a founding member of the Association for Civil Rights in Israel, served for many years as its chairperson, and, from 1996–1999, as its president.

Yoram Hazony is President of the Herzl Institute in Jerusalem. His books include *The Jewish State: The Struggle for Israel's Soul* (2000), *The Virtue of Nationalism* (2018), and *The Philosophy of Hebrew Scripture* (2012). He has contributed numerous articles to the *Wall Street Journal, The New York Times, Commentary, The New Republic,* and *Azure*. Hazony publishes a series of occasional essays entitled Jerusalem Letters.

Yousef Jabareen is a member of Israel's 20th Knesset for the Joint (Arab) List. He is the Head of the List's International Relations Committee. He is also Researcher and Lecturer at Tel-Hai College, where he heads the program for social education, and publishes on human rights and minority rights protection. He is founding director of Dirasat, the Arab Center for Law and Policy, based in Nazareth, and was previously Legal Director at the northern branch of the Association for Civil Rights in Israel. His writings include "Constitution Building and Equality in Deeply-Divided Societies: The Case of the Arab Minority in Israel," in the *Wisconsin International Law Journal* (2008).

Amal Jamal is Professor and former chair of the Department of Political Science at Tel Aviv University and head of the Walter Leibach Institute. He has published extensively on state structure and civil society, democratization, social movements, minority nationalism, and other topics. His books include *Arab Minority Nationalism in Israel: The Politics of Indigeneity* (2011) and *The Arab Public Sphere in Israel: Media, Space and Cultural Resistance* (2009).

Moshe Koppel is a Professor in the Department of Computer Science at Bar-Ilan University. He has published academic papers in leading journals in computer science, mathematics, linguistics, economics, law, political science and other disciplines and has written two books on the Talmud. Koppel is the founder and chairman of the Kohelet Policy Forum, a Jerusalem-based libertarian-conservative policy center. He has co-drafted two proposed constitutions for Israel, as well as several laws that have been passed by the Knesset.

Nahum Karlinsky teaches modern Jewish history and Israel Studies at the Ben-Gurion Research Institute, Ben-Gurion University of the Negev. Since 2008 he also has been a Visiting Associate Professor at the Massachusetts Institute of Technology, and also, since 2014, at Boston University. His books include *California Dreaming: Ideology, Society, and Technology in the Citrus Industry in Palestine, 1890–1930* (2005), and he is currently writing, together with Mustafa Kabha from the Open University of Israel, a new book on the Palestinian-Arab citrus industry before 1948.

Nir Kedar is a Professor of Law and History at Bar-Ilan University and the former Dean of Sapir College School of Law. His main fields of scholarship are Israeli history, modern legal history, legal and political theory, and comparative law. The English version of his recent book *Blue and White Law: Identity and Law in Israel, A Century-Long Polemic* (2017) will be published by Brill in 2018.

Amnon Lord is a journalist with *Israel Hayom*. He was previously a columnist with *Makor Rishon*, and was for five years the paper's editor. He has also written for *The Jerusalem Post, Mida, Azure, Nativ, and Achshav,* and is the author of *The Israeli Left: From Socialism to Nihilism* (Hebrew, 2000) and *The Lost Generation: The Story of the Yom Kippur War* (Hebrew, 2013).

Tzipi Livni was first elected to the Knesset in 1999 and is currently a member of Israel's 20th Knesset for the Zionist Union Party. Livni has served as minister of justice, foreign minister, vice prime minister and as leader of the opposition, as well as in other roles in government.

Michael Marmur served as the Jack, Joseph and Morton Mandel Provost at Hebrew Union College-Jewish Institute of Religion (2009–2018), and is associate professor of Jewish theology at Hebrew Union College-Jewish Institute of Religion in Jerusalem. He is the author of many articles and the recent book *Abraham Joshua Heschel and the Sources of Wonder* (2016).

Yehudah Mirsky teaches in the Department of Near Eastern and Judaic Studies and the Schusterman Center for Israel Studies of Brandeis University. He served in the US State Department's Human Rights Bureau during the Clinton Administration, was a grass-roots activist in Jerusalem and helped found the Yerushalmit Movement for a Viable and Pluralistic Jerusalem. Mirsky has written widely on politics, theology and culture and is the author of *Rav Kook: Mystic in a Time of Revolution* (2014).

David N. Myers is the Sady and Ludwig Kahn Chair in Jewish History at the University of California, Los Angeles, and served in 2017–18 as President and Chief Executive Officer of the Center for Jewish History in New York. He is an editor of the *Jewish Quarterly Review* and the author of numerous books, including *Between Jew and Arab: The Lost Voice of Simon Rawidowicz* (2008), and most recently, *The Stakes of History: On the Use and Abuse of Jewish History for Life* (2018).

Kalman Neuman teaches history at Herzog College. He has published in Hebrew and English on politics and religion in Israel and has written for *The Jewish Review of Books*, *Shma*, and *The New York Jewish Week*, among other publications.

Simon Rabinovitch teaches modern Jewish and European history at Boston University. He served as Senior Editor at *The Marginalia Review of Books* and is a contributor to *Haaretz*. He is the author of *Jewish Rights, National Rites: Nationalism and Autonomy in Late Imperial and Revolutionary Russia* (2014) and the editor of *Jews and Diaspora Nationalism: Writings on Jewish Peoplehood in Europe and the United States* (2012).

Gideon Sapir is Professor of Law at Bar-Ilan University, a Senior Fellow at the Center for the Study of Law and Religion at Emory University, and is a member of the Kohelet Policy Forum. He is the author and editor of several books and many articles on constitutional law and theory. His latest book (with Daniel Statman) is *Religion & State: Legal & Philosophic Inquiry* (Hebrew, 2014).

Tanya Zion-Waldoks is currently Israel Institute Post-Doctoral Fellow at the Ben-Gurion Research Institute for the Study of Israel and Zionism, Ben-Gurion University of the Negev. She has published on the intersection of religion, gender, and politics with a focus on women's social movements in Israel. Her upcoming book (with Ronit Irshai and Banna Shoughry) is titled *Rethinking Multiculturalism and Gender: How Jewish and Muslim Women Transform Culture and Law*. She is also a feminist activist who has initiated and led a series of Israeli projects on Orthodox LGBT, *aguna* rights, human trafficking, Jewish rituals, community building, and social justice.

INDEX

A

Academia, targeting of, 289

Academic discourse, as veiling mechanism, 160

Academic freedom, de-legitimation of the state, 65

Academics
as attacking Israeli identity, 35
consultation, 44
Israeli: shift in political values, 150
radicalism and, 247–48

Academy
criticism of Israeli government, 278
public role of, xvi
trampled by ultra-nationalists, 161

Acceptance of Communities bill, 278

Accountability, of Rabbinic courts, 200

Activism
Jewishness and, 132
Judicial. *See* Judicial activism
religious, 282

Adalah: The Legal Center for Arab Minority Rights in Israel, 179, 263
draft constitution, 4–5

Adjudication, conflicting rights and values, 296

Africa, postwar nation-states, 310

Agranat, Shimon
on Jewish nation-state, 108
ruling on Declaration, 223
Yerador case, 244

Agudat Yisrael party, 269

Aguna plight, 199

Ahad Ha'am, 138
Jewish identity, 235
Zionist criticism of, 236

AJC. *See* American Jewish Committee

Akiva (Rabbi), ideals of, 137

Al Ard party
blocked from Knesset, 243, 247

Al-Aqsa Mosque, threatened, 281

Alawites, in Syria, 155

Aliya. See Law of Return; Right of Return; Immigration

Allied Powers, 183
political promises of, 307

Alma, educational center, 323, 329–30

Almog, Oz, 271

Aloni, Shulamit, criticism of Jewish state, 151

Altneuland (Herzl), 226

Amalek, Palestinians and, 280–81

Ambiguity
Gavison on, 309
importance of, 48
in law, 34, 46, 58, 122n2, 237, 296
in values, 48
legal exploitation of, 177
in Declaration of Independence, 211
in social life, 67
in state vision, 55, 60–61

America, liberal order and, 307

American exceptionalism, 308

American Jewish Committee (AJC), on nation-state law, 20n30

American Jewry, 320
response to nation-state law, 19

American jurisprudence, judicial activism and, 305

American liberalism, influence on Basic Law, 137

Amir, Yigal, halted Oslo process, 287

Amona settlement, evacuation of, 290

Amos (Prophet), law in, 230

Anderson, Benedict, 209